Week 2:
CH. 7-9

# WHY CHRIST MATTERS

# WHY CHRIST MATTERS

*Toward a New Testament Christology*

Leander E. Keck

BAYLOR UNIVERSITY PRESS

Scripture quotations, where not the author's own translation, are from the New Revised Standard Version Bible, copyright 1989, Division of Christian Education of the National Council of the Churches of Christ in the United States of America. Used by permission. All rights reserved.

*Cover Design* by Hannah Feldmeier

Library of Congress Cataloging-in-Publication Data

Keck, Leander E.
   [Works. Selections]
   Why Christ matters : toward a New Testament Christology / Leander E. Keck.
      pages cm
   Includes bibliographical references and index.
   ISBN 978-1-4813-0297-5 (hardback : alk. paper)
1. Jesus Christ—Person and offices. I. Title.
   BT203.K43 2015
   232--dc23
                        2014039119

Printed in the United States of America on acid-free paper with a minimum of 30 percent post-consumer waste recycled content.

In honor of

Robert Morgan

four decades
an esteemed colleague
and a cherished friend

# Contents

# Preface

Why Christ matters is the subject of New Testament Christology. The pursuit of this theme has energized much of my work, resulting in various publications, including *Who Is Jesus?* (2000). The diverse studies selected for the present volume not only illumine how the New Testament accounts for its claims about Jesus' significance, but also advocate a particular view of how New Testament Christology should be studied—by all its interpreters.

This view is outlined in the first piece, and is complemented by the second. The next three concern a major dimension of New Testament Christology, Jesus' relation to the religion he inherited and never abandoned. The discussion of two differing New Testament writings, Romans and John, show how close attention to the texts can disclose aspects of Christ's stated significance that should not be passed over. The last, and longest, study looks at the New Testament's Christologies in light of fourth-century issues, and so provides the kind of retrospective overview not usually found in treatments of New Testament Christology.

Except for minor editorial adjustments, the studies have not been revised, nor have their footnotes been updated. These pieces remain what they were: precipitates of my efforts to hear what the New Testament says about Christ and to understand what that means theologically.

Assuming that the assembled whole is greater than the scattered parts, I am grateful to Baylor University Press and its director, Dr. Carey C. Newman, for making these explorations available to a wider public. In dedicating the book to Robert Morgan (Linacre College, Oxford), I am making public my deep gratitude for the many benefits of our on-going conversation.

# The Renewal of
# New Testament Christology

The study of New Testament Christology will be renewed if it recovers its proper subject matter—Christology—and its proper scope, the New Testament.

The scholarly literature shows that what is called NT Christology is, by and large, really the history of christological materials and motifs in early Christianity, and their ancestry. This massive preoccupation with history has, to be sure, produced impressive results. In fact, it is difficult today to imagine a study of NT Christology which is not influenced by this historical analysis of early Christian conceptions of Christ and their antecedents. Nevertheless, the time is at hand to take up again what was set aside—an explicitly theological approach to NT Christology, one which will be informed by the history of ideas but which will deliberately pursue Christology as a theological discipline. It is doubtful whether the study of NT Christology can be renewed in any other way. This essay intends to illumine and substantiate this claim by considering briefly the nature of Christology, then by reviewing the turn to history and its consequences for the study of NT Christology, and finally by sketching elements of an alternative.

## I

Because this essay discusses the renewal of a discipline by recovering its true subject matter, what will be said here about the nature of Christology should be more a reminder than something wholly new. What might be new is *that* it is being said in just this way, and that it is *being applied* to the study of Christology in the NT.[1]

---

[1] The fact that "NT Christology" is used here in the sense of "Christology in the NT" is a

"Christology" is a comprehensive term for the statement of the identity and significance of Jesus. Although the vast preponderance of such statements occur in Christian contexts, this phenomenological definition recognizes that christological statements are implied also whenever Jesus' identity and significance is expressed, be it "religious genius" or avatar.[2] It is, however, with Christian discourse that this essay is concerned. Among Christians, the scope of Christology has, from the start, been wider than "the man Jesus" because neither his identity nor his significance could be stated by speaking of him alone, as an isolate. "Jesus" is really an abbreviation for the person who is the center of an event whose boundaries are not self-evident—unless one is prepared to deny that to a person belongs one's appropriation of a heritage on the one hand and one's relationships on the other. What needs clarification in this context is the rationale of christological statements about this event, the "rules of the game." In view here is the formal structure of Christology, its "grammar"—or perhaps better, the syntax of the signification of Jesus for Christian theology.

"Significance" is intelligible only in relation to something or someone. Accordingly, the subject matter of Christology is really the syntax of relationships or correlations. In developed Christology this structure of signification is expressed in relation to God (the *theo*logical correlation proper), the created order (the cosmological correlation), and humanity (the anthropological correlation);[3] each of these impinges on the others

---

matter of style and nuance; it refers to Christology as the subject matter of a particular body of material. In no way does this usage imply that there is a single Christology in the NT.

[2] The identity and significance of Jesus can, of course, be expressed in nonchristological ways, as in an attempt to identify and assess his impact on Western culture, and through it on the modern world. That would be an historical judgment, comparable to judgments about Moses or Muhammed. A statement of Jesus' identity and significance becomes christological when that significance explicates his religious meaning. Whoever affirms the religious significance of Jesus (a first-order statement) implies a christological statement (a second-order statement). Schillebeeckx introduces the distinction between first- and second-order statements in order to account for the inevitability of Christology. On this basis, "living contact" with Jesus "was experienced as God-given salvation," which in turn produced reflection on the experience, which yielded "the creedal affirmation: God himself . . . has acted decisively in Jesus" (a first-order statement); this produces a second-order statement designed to explicate the first by focusing on his identity. This whole discussion, however, occurs in a context in which Schillebeeckx wants to explain the movement from a " 'Theology' of Jesus of Nazareth" to Christology. By the former he means "reflection upon what Jesus himself had to say." However, these are two quite different moves, because reflection on Jesus' message is not the same as reflection on a first-order statement grounded in the experience of salvation. Edward Schillebeeckx, *Jesus* (New York: Seabury, 1979), 545–50.

[3] Current sensibility having outlawed the use of "man" in English theological discourse,

whether or not this impingement is made explicit. Consequently, from statements about God or world or humanity one can infer the appropriate christological correlates, and vice versa.

Of these correlations, two have not received their due—the cosmological and the theological. Nils A. Dahl has rightly observed that the understanding of God has been the neglected factor in the study of NT theology as a whole.[4] This is particularly true of the study of NT Christology, even though every statement about Christ implicates God, beginning with the designation of Jesus as the Anointed. This neglect of the theological correlate has constricted Christology and skewed Christianity as a whole, for it is not enough to say with Melanchthon that "to know Christ is to know his benefits."[5] The neglect of the cosmological correlate is even more striking, despite the current interest in the use of Wisdom traditions and themes in the NT—an interest which thus far has generally remained on the historical plane.

The correlation which receives most attention concerns anthropology—the human condition and the salvific alternative brought (or brought about) by (or through) Jesus. In this connection three observations are called for.

(1) There would be no Christology if there were no soteriology because it is what Christians claim about Jesus as the bringer or effecter of salvation that generates the question of his identity. To oversimplify: soteriology makes Christology necessary; Christology makes soteriology possible. To paraphrase: Jesus' significance must be grounded adequately in his identity. At the same time, Christology is not reducible to soteriology because, at least in the classical Christian tradition, Christ is always more than Savior.[6] Even the Gospel according to John, in which the work of Christ is to manifest his

---

"humanity" must serve as a surrogate, despite its intrinsic inability to function as a real equivalent.

[4] Nils A. Dahl, "The Neglected Factor in New Testament Theology," *Reflection* 73 (1975): 5–8.

[5] In this connection, one should ponder Jean Milet's *God or Christ? The Excesses of Christo-centricity* (New York: Crossroad, 1981). He contends that although Christianity is constitutively bipolar (God *and* Christ), the modern difficulty of thinking cogently about God has produced such a one-sided preoccupation with Christ that virtually one religion has been substituted for another—a religion with a one-sided emphasis on redemption.

[6] It should not be overlooked that the formula, "Creator, Redeemer, and Sustainer," which is now being substituted, in some Anglo-Saxon quarters, for "Father, Son, and Holy Spirit," not only replaces a trinity of persons with a triadic functionalism but also constricts the role of the second person to redemption—a move which lacks clear warrant in the NT.

identity, knows this, for its Christ is the incarnate Logos "through whom all things were made."

(2) Just as a grammar allows all sorts of things to be thought, said or written, so the grammar of Christology permits a variety of things to be expressed concerning Jesus' identity and significance. The formal structure is constant,[7] but the material content can vary. Further, each of these material contents has its own integrity within its linguistic field. Thus, if the human condition is viewed as bondage, Christ is the liberator and soteriology will be expressed in the idiom of liberation. Christology will then show what there is about Christ that makes it possible for liberation to occur through him. Or, if Christ is hailed as the great teacher, the human condition will be construed as ignorance or illusion, so that salvation will be a matter of learning the truth. Moreover, one of the ways that Christology develops nuance and subtlety is by asserting new mutations of categories. Thus one can speak of ignorance as bondage, and so construe Christ as the liberator from unknowing. What must not be overlooked is this: because Christology and anthropology are always correlates, one cannot agree with Herbert Braun's claim that anthropology is the constant but Christology is the variable.[8] A changed Christology entails a changed anthropology as well.

Being aware of the correlational aspect of Christology allows one to see the high degree of theological sophistication of many NT passages, as in Paul's "If anyone is in Christ, one is a new creation." Understanding this christologically entails delineating the soteriology/anthropology of "new creation" (including what is implied about "old creation") as well as of being "in Christ" (including being "outside Christ"); then one can analyze the effect of juxtaposing these two expressions. Naturally, one cannot recover the steps in Paul's reasoning by which he produced this remarkable statement. That would be only of historical or psychological interest anyway. What one can do is to expose the logic, the grammar, of what his text says, and thereby make its tacit meaning explicit.

(3) Christological correlations tend to obey the law of parsimony. That is, generally speaking, Christology and soteriology/anthropology are not

[7] To speak of the constancy of grammar vis-à-vis variable formulations is not to imply that grammar is static; to the contrary, that grammars have histories also suggests that the "grammar" of christological discourse also undergoes change (not the same as the history of Christology, the history of formulations). The matter deserves exploration, which cannot be undertaken here, however.

[8] Herbert Braun, "The Meaning of New Testament Christology," *Journal for Theology and Church* 5 (1968), 89–127; German original: "Der Sinn der neutestamentlichen Christologie," *ZTK* 54 (1957): 341–77.

wasted on each other, because the understanding of Jesus' identity and significance should not exceed what is required to resolve the human dilemma. A superficial view of sin requires only a superficial view of salvation, just as a superficial view of Jesus cannot deal with a profound view of sin. This implies, further, that unless a tragic view of sin is correlated with a radical view of salvation grounded in a strong Christology, the human dilemma will be too deep to be dealt with decisively by Christ.

This principle can be applied fruitfully to three quite different Christologies in the NT. Over against the fear of the Colossian Christians that the *stoicheia* must be placated even by Christians, the author of the Epistle to the Colossians insists that there is no dimension of the human condition which has not already been dealt with decisively in the event of Christ. Consequently, he explicates a christological hymn in such a way as to show that believers do not live in a world whose hostility outruns Christ's capacity to deliver them. When, however, one reads Matthew in light of this principle, a basic question emerges: Is Matthew an exception to the rule, or does it actually lack an integrated Christology, since its view of the human dilemma does not really require all the Christology which the text contains? The virgin birth, for instance, really adds nothing to the identity and significance of Jesus which is required if the human dilemma is centered on the need to acquire the rectitude necessary to enter the kingdom. Again, important light is cast on the vexing problem of Paul's apparent nonuse of Jesus' teachings, save in paraenesis, or of his deeds. Given Paul's view of the human predicament as bondage to powers like sin and death, what could be gained by quoting Jesus or by appealing to his precedent, even if thematically appropriate logia and stories had come to the apostle's attention? Where the human condition is bondage, there one needs emancipation, not a teacher or a theologian to explain it or the example of a free man (especially one whose deeds of freedom were followed by his execution!). Furthermore, one may also ask whether the Matthean construal of Jesus would be able to deal salvifically with the Pauline construal of the human condition—especially if the Matthean Jesus is the bringer but not the effecter of salvation. In short, had the syntax of Christology been kept in mind, NT study would have been spared a great deal of misplaced worry about Paul's disinterest in Jesus' words and deeds which is not at all to be confused with an alleged disinterest in Jesus.[9]

---

[9] These terse, and perhaps cryptic, formulations beg for elaboration and substantiation, which cannot be provided here.

Having reminded ourselves, in a rather terse and formal way, of the nature of Christology, of its syntax, the significance of turning away from Christology to history can come into view more perceptively.

## II

If the study of NT Christology is to become explicitly christological, it must come to terms with a legacy which, apart from the Bultmannian tradition, has been dominated by historical questions. Then it can be free to find its own way. To understand this preoccupation with history, no one is more useful than William Wrede, who insisted that the study of NT theology (and hence of Christology as well) must become a purely descriptive, historical enterprise, "totally indifferent to all dogmatic and systematic theology."[10]

Wrede called for a turn away from presenting NT theology as a compendium of doctrines. The real subject matter was to be *"what was believed, thought, taught, hoped, required and striven for in the earliest period of Christianity, not what certain writings say about faith, doctrine, hope, etc."* (84–85; emphasis in original). The texts were not to be analyzed theologically but used as sources of information in order to describe major types of piety. These, in turn, were to be seen in organic relation to their antecedents in antiquity, on the one hand, and to their subsequent developments in Christianity on the other. "How the systematic theologian gets on with the results—that is his own affair."[11] What Wrede called for at the end of the nineteenth century did, to a remarkable degree, come about in the twentieth.

Wrede saw that for the task of reconstructing early Christian religion the NT alone was inadequate; all early Christian literature must be consulted. Moreover, the NT had to be disassembled and its parts rearranged into a sequence that was historical. Subsequently, certain texts themselves were disassembled so that their component parts or sources, such as Q, also could be assigned their proper place in a comprehensive, chronologically ordered history of early Christian sources. Only then could the history of early Christianity, including its theology, be written properly. Non-Christian materials were used intensively not only to illumine the context

[10] William Wrede's essay, published in 1897, is available in English as "The Task and Methods of New Testament Theology," in *The Nature of New Testament Theology: The Contribution of William Wrede and Adolf Schlatter* (trans. and ed. Robert Morgan; SBT 2/25; Naperville, Ill.: Alec R. Allenson, 1973), 68–116, 69. Morgan's own extensive introduction, which deals as well with Schlatter's essay on the same theme (also included), merits careful reading.

[11] Wrede, *Nature of New Testament Theology*, 69.

of early Christianity (and its Christology), but to explain it. With regard to Christology, Wrede's program was carried out by Bousset's magisterial *Kyrios Christos*,[12] whose subtitle shows the relation to Wrede's program: "A History of the Belief in Christ from the Beginning of Christianity to Irenaeus." Neither the legitimacy nor the importance of this enterprise is in question here, whatever one must say about Bousset's conclusions. It is as valid, and as important, to reconstruct the history of early Christian Christology as it is to reconstruct the history of early Christianity or the social structure of early Christian communities.[13] The point, rather, is that the history of early Christian Christology should not be called NT Christology because (a) in such a move the NT has in fact disappeared into early Christian literature, (b) the problem for Christology created by the pursuit of the historical task cannot be solved by continued historical inquiry, and (c) Christology has been abandoned for something else—the history of titles. Each of these results merits further comment.

(a) Replacing the NT with "early Christian literature" has consequences—precisely for historiography—which are as serious as they are subtle. No one will deny that all texts must be treated alike, that there is no privileged status for canonical texts, when one is looking for information, or "facts," about the past; nor will anyone argue that noncanonical texts are of inferior value for historical inquiry because they are not part of Scripture. However, problems arise when this stance becomes more than a procedural principle for carrying out a particular task. Not only is the category "early Christian literature" an anachronism which has become historically significant only in the scholarly guild, but relying on it alone obscures precisely the phenomenon being studied—namely, that some of

---

[12] Wilhelm Bousset, *Kyrios Christos: A History of the Belief in Christ from the Beginnings of Christianity to Irenaeus* (Nashville: Abingdon, 1970; repr., Waco, Tex.: Baylor University Press, 2013; German original, 1913).

[13] This essay's contention that the study of NT Christology should become avowedly theological in no way entails a repudiation of historical reconstruction or of sociological reconstruction and analysis, which I have defended elsewhere. To the contrary, my "On the Ethos of the Early Christians," *JAAR* 42 (1974): 435–52 (also published as "Das Ethos der frühen Christen," in *Zur Soziologie des Urchristentums* [ed. Wayne A. Meeks; Munich: Chr. Kaiser, 1979], 13–36) is a programmatic call for NT scholarship to attend to the social realities which shaped early Christianity and which were affected by it. Likewise, over against a tendency on the part of some literary criticism to be ahistorical if not plainly antihistorical, I defended the necessity of historical work in "Will the Historical-Critical Method Survive? Some Observations," in *Orientation by Disorientation* (ed. R. A. Spencer; Beardslee Festschrift; Pittsburgh: Pickwick, 1980), 115–27. In *The Bible in the Pulpit* (Nashville: Abingdon, 1978), I sought to show how the historical-critical method can become fruitful for preaching.

this literature was regularly and increasingly shaping early Christianity, and its Christology, by being used repeatedly as Scripture on the way to becoming canon. In fact, were it not for this emerging canon and the results of its complex interaction with the developing church, the rest of the literary products of early Christianity would be of but marginal interest and of even less significance as footnotes to the religious history of antiquity.[14]

Moreover, to excavate the Christology of Q or of the Johannine signs source is surely historically valid and useful, but to treat these as if they were more than momentary efforts which were absorbed into texts which *did* have a future is to skew historical understanding at the outset. Wrede himself insisted that the historian must distinguish what was influential from what was of passing importance. In other words, sound historiography itself requires that due attention be given to the Christology of texts which were on the way toward becoming canonical. Otherwise, what will be reconstructed is not the history of Christology that was something else—the history that might have been.

(b) The turn to history has, unexpectedly for the most part, called into question the legitimacy of Christology itself because the key historical question became ever more difficult to answer historically—namely, why did these christological materials come to be used of Jesus, a Jesus who was reconstructed historically by separating him from just this early Christology? When Hendrikus Boers reviewed the English translation of Bousset, he formulated the issue so well that he deserves to be quoted fully:

> The fundamental problem of a Christology of the New Testament as posed by *Kyrios Christos* . . . was that the view of Jesus found in the New Testament was not historically true of Jesus himself. This undercuts the basic assumption on which the Christology of the New Testament depends, namely, that it is an expression of the truth about the historical Jesus. Thus New Testament Christology is confronted by an irresolvable dilemma: to recognize that Christology is a composite product of the early Christian communities and not the truth about the historical Jesus is the dissolution of Christology itself, but to justify a Christology by attempting to confirm that its claims about Jesus are somehow valid is possible only at the expense of not recognizing the early Christian communities as their true authors. New Testament Christology since *Kyrios Christos* has been

---

[14] For a more extended discussion of this point, see my "Is the New Testament a Field of Study? or, From Outler to Overbeck and Back," *Second Century* 1 (1981): 19–35.

a constant struggle with, and clarification of, this dilemma, whether in conscious recognition of Bousset or not.[15]

C. F. D. Moule, however, takes note of Boers and argues exactly the opposite, contending that "Jesus was, *from the beginning*, such a one as appropriately to be described in the ways in which, sooner or later, he did come to be described in the New Testament period."[16] For Moule, the later Christologies represent "various stages in the development of perception," not the accretion of "any alien factors that were not there from the beginning." Such an accretion would have been an evolution of Christology. Development, on the other hand, is an organic unfolding, like the transition from bud to flower. The development of Christology, therefore, did not take the church further from the fact of Jesus but into it more deeply. Just as Boers' historically couched contention requires critical assessment from the standpoint of Christology, so Moule's theological assertion requires historical confirmation. Neither can be undertaken in this context, however.

It suffices to point out that the unwanted outcome of concentrating on origins is that the historical link between Jesus and Christology has grown weaker rather than stronger. The clearer this result became, or threatened to become, the more vigorously the historical question was pursued, either by attempting to show that Jesus did use certain christological titles of himself, or that what they express agrees with his Christology, which was implicit in his sense of identity and authority expressed in his use of "Abba" and "Amen," respectively. The more relentlessly such efforts were pursued, the more difficult it actually became to show that Jesus had used *any* title for himself, or why the early church acknowledged his sense of authority by developing precisely *these* Christologies. Indeed, the one title with which Jesus might have been comfortable—prophet—had no future except in certain strands of Jewish Christianity, but they are not represented in the NT.[17] In a word, if the legitimacy of Christology depends on establishing

---

[15] Hendrikus Boers, "Jesus and the Christian Faith: New Testament Christology since Bousset's *Kyrios Christos," JBL* 89 (1970): 452.

[16] C. F. D. Moule, *The Origin of Christology* (Cambridge: Cambridge University Press, 1977), 2–3; emphasis in original.

[17] According to John Knox, early Christian nonuse of "prophet" for Jesus reflects the fact that this title had been appropriated by the disciples of John the Baptist. " 'The Prophet' in the New Testament Christology," in *Lux in Lumine* (ed. R. A. Norris; Pittenger Festschrift; New York: Seabury, 1966), 22–34. It is more likely, however, that the major strands of early Christianity found "prophet" incapable of embracing the soteriological correlates which they wanted to express.

historically the continuity between the historically reconstructed Jesus and the Christology of the church, then the turn to history alone has not only made suspect all Christology which goes beyond that which was in the mind of Jesus but continued historical work is unable to resolve the dilemma.

(c) The consequences of turning to history are most evident in the pre-occupation with christological titles. Indeed, it is often assumed that NT Christology *is* a matter of the history of titles. Probably no other factor has contributed more to the current aridity of the discipline than this fascination with the palaeontology of christological titles. To reconstruct the history of titles as if this were the study of Christology is like trying to understand the windows of Chartres cathedral by studying the history of colored glass. In fact, concentration on titles finally makes the Christologies of the NT unintelligible as Christologies, and insignificant theologically. Renewing the discipline of NT Christology requires, therefore, liberating it from the tyranny of titles—though obviously they cannot be ignored. Three considerations, at least, warrant this claim.

To begin with, title-dominated study of NT Christology reflects an inadequate view of language, because it assumes that meaning resides in words like "Lord." Just as this assumption misled Vincent Taylor when he wrote, "the question, who Jesus is, is approached best by considering how men named Him, for it is by His names that He is revealed and known,"[18] so an alternative pointed James Barr in the right direction when he declared that "it is in sentences that real theological thinking is done."[19] Furthermore, where titles dominate the scene, the difference between a word and a concept is blurred. A word is identical with a concept only if it is a technical term which has no synonyms. Barr is essentially correct, as Gerhard Friedrich more or less concedes,[20] when he complains that because Gerhard Kittel's dictionary has not thought out this difference, its writers sometimes talk about concepts when they should be discussing words.[21] This confusion

---

[18] Vincent Taylor, *The Names of Jesus* (London: Macmillan, 1953), 1.

[19] James Barr, *The Semantics of Biblical Language* (Oxford: Oxford University Press, 1961), 234.

[20] Gerhard Friedrich, "'Begriffsgeschichtliche' Untersuchungen im Theologisches Wörterbuch zum Neuen Testament," *Archiv für Begriffsgeschichte* 20 (1976): 151–77. Friedrich, under whose leadership Kittel's project was completed, also defends the dictionary against Barr's criticism by noting that Kittel followed L. Weisgerber (1927), who contended that word and concept are interrelated. Friedrich's views on the need for a NT concept lexicon are found in "Das bisher noch fehlende Begriffslexikon zum Neuen Testament," *NTS* 19 (1972/1973): 127–52.

[21] Barr, *Semantics,* 209.

can be found also in Ferdinand Hahn's influential monograph which gave a new legitimacy to this approach, despite the searching criticism pressed by Philipp Vielhauer.[22]

Next, concentrating on titles actually hampers the effort to understand Christology in the NT texts. This can be seen in the following five considerations.

(1) Concentration on titles cannot deal adequately with christologically important passages in which no title appears, whether they be narratives or sayings in the Gospels or discursive arguments in the Epistles. The Gospels often refer simply to "Jesus" just as the Epistles use "Christ" as a proper name; in Matthew the Jesus-Moses theme never gets expressed in a title. So strong has been the influence of titles, however, that frequently scholars have supplied them as if the creators of the text had forgotten to include them. For instance, the concluding scene in Matthew, highly important for the Christology of this book, does not mention any title but is content to mention only "Jesus"; yet some scholars have provided the "missing" title in order to read the story in terms of the Danielic Son of Man,[23] others in terms of "Son of God."[24] In the case of miracle stories, a "title" has been introduced which never appears in the NT at all—*theios anēr*.[25]

(2) The title-dominated approach does not, and perhaps cannot, deal adequately with the plurality of titles in a given text. Just as the Christology of no major NT book coincides with a single title, so it is not the aggregate of titles either. Moreover, the texts show neither embarrassment over the many titles,[26] nor concern to do what their

---

[22] Ferdinand Hahn, *The Titles of Jesus in Christology* (Cleveland: World Publishing, 1969), esp. the chapter on "Christ." See also Philipp Vielhauer, "Ein Weg zur neutestamentliche Christologie?" *EvT* 25 (1965): 24–72; idem, "Zur Frage der christologischen Hoheitstitel," *TLZ* 90 (1965): 569–88.

[23] See, e.g., John P. Meier, "Salvation History in Matthew: In Search of a Starting Point," *CBQ* 37 (1975): 210–12.

[24] So Jack Dean Kingsbury, "The Composition and Christology of Mt 28:16-20," *JBL* 93 (1974): 573–84.

[25] Although the phrase *theios anēr* is absent from the NT, its use in recent scholarship is unclear; sometimes it is used virtually as a title, at other times as a category (like "hero"), a motif, an image, or a concept. For an assessment of its role, see Jack Dean Kingsbury, "The 'Divine Man' as the Key to Mark's Christology—The End of an Era?" *Interpretation* 35 (1981): 243–57. Kingsbury calls it a concept.

[26] Martin Hengel observed, "The multiplicity of christological titles does not mean a multiplicity of exclusive 'Christologies' but an accumulative glorification of Jesus"; "Christology and New Testament Chronology," in *Between Jesus and Paul* (Philadelphia: Fortress, 1983; repr., Waco, Tex.: Baylor University Press, 2013; German original, 1972), 41.

modern interpreters find necessary—instruct the reader about the relation of one title to another.[27]

(3) More important, concentrating on titles can lead one to miss the Christology which is in the text. For example, because Paul uses "Christ" virtually as a proper name (except for Rom 9:5), neither the etymology of *Christos* nor the history of pre-Christian messianic hopes and messianic claimants is relevant for his construal of Jesus. Nothing the apostle says about the identity and significance of Jesus for the revelation of God's righteousness depends on a christological title. In fact, concentrating on titles does not lead one into Paul's Christology but right past it.

(4) Titular Christology tends to see but half of the christological hermeneutic—that half in which titles are supposed to do the interpreting, namely, of the person and event called "Jesus." This is rather odd, since the pre-Christian history of the titles shows that none of them (except prophet) really fit Jesus. It is not surprising that scholarship has been unable to show that he applied them to himself. Consequently, the other half of the christological hermeneutic needs to be brought into view—that the Jesus-event interprets the titles. This is obvious in John (e.g., 7:40-43), but it is no less true elsewhere as well (e.g., Mark 9:30-32), but the customary focus on titles will not disclose it. Interestingly enough, the point of this paragraph is tacitly acknowledged by all those treatments of the matter which contend that Jesus, in applying titles to himself, simultaneously reinterpreted, "spiritualized," or transformed them.

(5) In title-dominated study of NT Christology, the identity and significance of Jesus in relation to the OT is objectified and concentrated in a way that shortchanges the truly significant christological issues. Title-dominated Christology has nothing to contribute, for example, to understanding Paul's dictum that "Christ is the *telos* of the law" (Rom 10:4), however telos be understood. The author of Hebrews understands this point intuitively, for he not only allows the Jesus-event to reinterpret the title "priest," but his understanding of why the earthly cultus is now obsolete does not turn on the titles used (Heb 10:1-10). In fact, it is hard to see what the title approach to NT Christology can contribute to the clarification of the complex and important, though widely neglected, issues epitomized by the rubric "Christ and the OT."

The third reason why the study of NT Christology must be liberated from the tyranny of titles should by now be clear: it bypasses Christology

---

[27] See, e.g., Jack Dean Kingsbury, *Matthew: Structure, Christology, Kingdom* (Philadelphia: Fortress, 1975), chap. 2.

itself, because it does not respect either its formal grammar or its material contents (the correlations). Instead, it deals with matters pertaining to Christology in a piecemeal way. In light of the nature of Christology, as outlined above, concentrating on titles tells us little that we need to know in order to understand the Christologies in the NT, and helps us even less to think christologically. An alternative is needed, and to that we now turn.

## III

First of all, a more adequate approach will concentrate on its proper subject matter by respecting the grammar of christological discourse. To do so is not to introduce the old loci system because what will be sought is not a set of doctrines but a systemic grasp of the way the correlates of Christ and God, world and the human condition are expressed or implied. Nor does an explicitly christological approach require that historical and philological questions be abandoned; what is required is that Christology not be confused with historical reconstruction of the history of ideas but be free to be what it claims to be—Christology. Otherwise the study of NT Christology will continue under the illusion that the history of ideas pertaining to Christology *is* Christology.[28] Attending to the correlates of Christology is, moreover, particularly appropriate to the NT because this literature consistently expresses the identity and significance of Jesus in relation to something else—doxology, paraenesis, cult narrative, and so on. There are no sections of the NT devoted to Christology as a discrete topic in its own right. Attending to the syntax of the signification of Jesus is therefore not an attempt to impose an alien structure on the texts but a way of ordering the relational character of Christology as it appears in the NT.

In the second place, the study of Christology in the NT should be just that—Christology as it appears, or is implied, in the NT. It is the Christology of this particular corpus of texts that must remain central. This deliberate concentration on these texts has a number of consequences, three of which deserve to be noted here. (1) A focus on texts, or in the case of Paul (and to some extent of John as well) a corpus of texts, keeps in view the fragmentary character of Christology in the NT.[29] Because the Christology of a text, or corpus of texts, cannot be equated with the Christology of the writer, one should speak of the Christology of persons only in carefully circumscribed

---

[28] See also Erhardt Güttgemanns, *Der leidende Apostel und sein Herr* (FRLANT 90; Göttingen: Vandenhoeck & Ruprecht, 1966), 46, 196, for similar observations.

[29] Ernst Käsemann called attention to the fragmented nature of the material in "The Problem of a New Testament Theology," *NTS* 19 (1973): 242–43.

contexts. Given the occasional character of the NT texts, as well as their several genres and functions, a text's Christology is but a partial expression of
what the writer thought about Jesus' identity and significance. Just as there
is no reason to think that any Evangelist wrote into his gospel everything
he knew about Jesus, so there is no reason to think that he expressed completely his construal of Jesus' identity and significance in the particular
narrative that now bears his name. So too, there is no adequate reason to
equate the Christology of a text or of its sources with the Christology of a
particular group. To assume that the Christology of Q or John or the Pastoral
Epistles is a profile of the Christology of distinct communities, and then to
assume that each community had but this one Christology so that one can
use discrete Christologies to reconstruct diverse groups is surely an unwarranted procedure. What is characteristic of communities is their capacity to
affirm multiple and diverse Christologies simultaneously. It is more likely
that various Christian communities had different configurations of Christologies. In any case, the point is that the Christology of individual authors
and of communities is largely hidden because what we have is but a set of
fragments which cannot be assumed to be representative cross-sections of
how the identity and significance of Jesus were construed. Concentrating on
the Christology of NT texts is an essential way of remembering how much is
unknown and remains unknowable.

(2) A focus on texts will deal with the text or corpus of texts as they
actually exist and, so far as possible, with what they were designed to do.
Historical questions customarily treated in introductions, including those
of genre, are indeed important because the form and function for which
the text was created affected what the writer emphasized and neglected.
The current use of literary, discourse, and rhetorical analyses accords with
this insistence that what must remain in focus is the thought-structure and
argument of the text as we have it. Respect for genre entails exploring, for
instance, the ways in which narrative creates both possibilities and con-
straints which are different from argumentative discourses or the vision-
reports of apocalypses.[30] For example, the fact that in John the protagonist
of the story articulates in first-person singular elements of the author's
Christology (the "I am . . ." form) which a discourse would express in third-
person singular ("he is . . .") poses an interesting question for Johannine
Christology: What is the significance of the fact that the disciples do not

[30] For a suggestive exploration of narrative Christology, see M. Eugene Boring, "The
Christology of Mark: Hermeneutical Issues for Systematic Theology," *Semeia* 30 (1984): 125–
53, esp. 136–45.

confess that Jesus is the Light, the Door, and so on, but that instead Jesus proclaims himself in these terms? That is, what is the difference for Christology between Christian predication and Christ's own self-proclamation? That is probably a more fruitful question for understanding John's Christology than asking where the *Ego eimi* sayings came from. In a word, the central questions to be pursued and answered are: What is the overall construal of Jesus' identity and significance in the text? What is the structure of this Christology and to what extent are the logical correlates expressed? What degree of coherence and completeness does this Christology have? It is the structure and dynamic of a given Christology that should become clear. What is in view here comports with E. P. Sanders' call for a systemic grasp of Paul's theology.[31] A systemic approach will make it clear that a text's Christology is not simply the sum of its parts but a construal of Jesus which must be seen as a whole.

(3) Concentrating on the Christology of existing texts in a systemic way makes it manifest that the decisive questions are not the origin of Christology or of particular Christologies. Concretely, it keeps in focus the true subject matter—the construal of Jesus' identity and significance—precisely because inquiry is not deflected onto the historical question of whether Jesus' self-interpretation is its origin. Jesus' own construal of his identity and significance is indeed a valid historical question in its own right. Christology, however, brings to expression the Christian construal of Jesus as the focal point of a network of theological correlations. Because the religious and theological significance of Jesus emerges only when one reflects on this event in relation to God, world, and the human condition and its resolution, it is of but secondary importance whether this understanding was derived from Jesus himself (derivation must not be confused with consonance). Neither the effort to understand a Christology, nor to discern its capacity, nor to assess its validity depends on an historian's success in tracing it to the mind of Jesus. Nor, conversely, may a Christology be disallowed because it did not occur to Jesus to avow it. In other words, the Christology of the critically reconstructed historical Jesus is not part of the Christology of the NT.[32] The historical relation between Jesus' self-interpretation and the early Christian interpretations of Jesus is another matter.

---

[31] See E. P. Sanders, "Patterns of Religion in Paul and Rabbinic Judaism: A Holistic Method of Comparison," *HTR* 66 (1973): 455–78; idem, *Paul and Palestinian Judaism* (London: SCM Press, 1977), 12–18.

[32] A clear instance of a well-known work based on exactly the opposite point of view is Joachim Jeremias, *New Testament Theology* (New York: Scribners, 1971); vol. 1 of this work

The NT texts have their own ways of making the Jesus-event central to their Christologies, and studying these texts should identify and illumine those ways. Here too, one must guard against introducing modern categories which obscure one's vision and skew the agenda. In this regard, "earthly Jesus" is almost as alien to the texts as "historical Jesus." Paul has been falsely accused of having no interest in Jesus, allegedly being preoccupied with the exalted Christ, because his modern interpreters assumed that they already knew what an interest in Jesus would, and should, look like, and so they did not ask sufficiently how Paul himself viewed the matter. What a text includes in the word "Jesus" (or in the phrase "Jesus Christ") is exactly what the study of NT Christology should reveal, just as it should clarify why the text does not draw our kind of line between an "earthly Jesus" and some other. (To insist on this is not to imply that the texts made no distinctions within the Jesus-event at all; Romans 1:3-4 is but one way in which distinctions were made.) Even the current emphasis on the identity of the earthly Jesus and the exalted Christ is not really appropriate for texts which never separated them to begin with. In other words, the subject matter of NT Christology can be said to have two poles; the one is "Jesus," and the other concerns how the various correlations between Jesus and God, world, and the human condition affect the content of this "Jesus." The study of NT Christology should expose why this polarity exists and how it works itself out in the texts.

Renewing the study of NT Christology entails not only attending to the grammar of Christology and a deliberate focus on the NT texts, but also, in the third place, a somewhat different approach to the plurality and diversity of the Christologies in the canon. What is in view here does not "solve" the problem of diversity by shifting into the historical mode which, as in the creation of trajectories, for example, turns generic similarities into genetic relationships; nor does it proceed theologically in order to unify the several Christologies by integrating them into a common conceptual structure as in Cullmann's *Heilsgeschichte* scheme, or in Herbert Braun's reduction of all Christologies to a single anthropology. Rather, what is envisioned keeps the various Christologies in a focus that is itself christological, and does so in several respects.

A systemic analysis indicates that there are two basic types of Christologies in the NT; the one works with preexistence and the other

---

bears the title "The Proclamation of Jesus." Even if one were to grant that Jeremias has reconstructed accurately the teachings of Jesus as well as Jesus' understanding of his mission, that reconstruction is precisely *not* part of the theology (and hence the Christology) of the NT.

does not.[33] The possibilities and limitations of each deserve to be analyzed by asking christological questions of each. For example, what sort of anthropology does each entail? What is the range and depth of the human condition which each allows to become visible? What are the dangers of each type? Which type is more amenable to an adequate view of the relation between Jesus and the OT? Is there any correlation between a type of Christology and the social identity and location of the people who espouse it? Here too, inquiring who first spoke of Christ's preexistence is no substitute for trying to understand what doing so entails.

A christological approach to the diversity of NT Christologies will pursue the consequences of the canon's juxtaposing precisely these Christologies. The incompleteness of these Christologies is not such that each simply complements the other, as in a jigsaw puzzle. Even if the virgin birth can be harmonized with the incarnation, at many other points the tensions are simply too great. What needs attention is the ways in which the diverse Christologies interact with each other. It is ironic that although historical criticism was developed largely to overcome the church's integrative interpretation by emphasizing the particularity of each text in its own historical context, the result of historical work shows in detail how NT texts embody a continuum of interpretation, and an interaction of traditions and texts with the communities that used them. Unless one thinks early Christians lived in isolated groups where only one Christology prevailed, one must assume that diverse Christologies interacted with each other almost from the start, even though they do not refer to each other explicitly. The point is that the juxtaposition of diverse Christologies in the canon is not an arbitrary, unfortunate imposition by ecclesiastics but a rather natural outgrowth of what had been occurring for some time. After all, the vexing problem of "John and the Synoptics" was not created by the canon.[34] To put the matter differently, what is true of each gospel, where elements of diverse Christologies, logically incommensurate with each other, now interact in the overall construal of Jesus' identity and significance, is true also of the NT as a whole. This interaction of existing

---

[33] The common distinction between two-stage and three-stage Christologies also relies on preexistence as the key. There are of course, other ways of classifying NT Christologies. For example, one can group them according to the genre in which they are found (doxological materials, terse formulae, narratives, etc.), or according to what they emphasize in the Christ-event (e.g., the character of Jesus' public mission, herald of the kingdom, death). The advantage of using preexistence is that it keeps in focus the shape of the event as a whole.

[34] See the four essays on the subject in D. Moody Smith, *Johannine Christianity* (Columbia: University of South Carolina Press, 1984), pt. 2.

texts deserves to be explored.[35] Meaning, after all, is not limited to the moment of a text's creation or to the aims of the author. It is generated also by the contexts in which the text exists and functions, including the context of the canon.

A major christological issue posed by the plurality of NT Christologies concerns the identity of Jesus: How do we know that it is the same Jesus who is being construed?[36] Paul's accusation that his opponents in Corinth preach "another Jesus" (2 Cor 11:4) shows that this question is continuous with the NT itself. To ask whether the diverse Christologies construe the same Jesus is to seek criteria for discerning what is constitutive about his identity. At this point, the limits of christological exegesis become evident because the criteria of Jesus' identity cannot be found by exegeting one more NT text. Here a sustained conversation with fundamental and systematic theology is required. Without it, NT study ceases to be vital and significant.

The renewal of the study of NT Christology will be the work of many minds, just as it will require the raising of explicitly christological issues, some of which this essay has identified and formulated, albeit in an abbreviated way.

---

[35] Concern for this question is one of the themes in Brevard S. Childs, *The New Testament as Canon: An Introduction* (Philadelphia: Fortress, 1984).

[36] In formulating this issue I was stimulated by the programmatic article by Rolf Knierim, "The Task of an Old Testament Theology," *HBT* 6 (1984): 25–57.

2

# What, Then, Is New Testament Christology?

The editors of this book[1] provided the title of this chapter. The table of contents for the book shows that, on the one hand, each of the first eleven contributions discusses the Christology of a specific text or cluster of texts, thereby implying that each has a distinct Christology that should be seen on its own terms; accordingly, one might use "New Testament Christologies," because the singular noun skews the subject matter. This view, in fact, has become the accepted wisdom of the scholars' guild. On the other hand, the last four chapters listed in this volume's Contents retain the singular, implying that when one turns to the "significance" of the subject matter for systematic theology, ethics, ministry, or preaching, it suddenly become legitimate (necessary?) to revert to "New Testament Christology" after all. Putting this chapter between the two parts of the anthology implies that the subject matter needs to be redefined if the discipline is to be clear about its task and if its work is to be available for the church—both results being wholly in accord with the distinguished career of the honoree.

Redefining the subject matter implies dissatisfaction with the ways in which historical scholarship has already dealt with it, for it is this legacy that makes the question inevitable and the answer essential. First, however, it is useful to remind ourselves briefly of the ways in which Christology appears in the New Testament.

[1] *Who Do You Say That I Am?: Essays on Christology*, festschrift for Jack Dean Kingsbury, edited by Mark Allan Powell and David R. Bauer (Louisville, Ky.: Westminster John Knox, 1999). I want to record my appreciation of Professor Jack Dean Kingsbury's multifaceted contribution to the study of the New Testament's Christology. Our interests overlap at many points, despite our long-standing disagreement over the significance of christological titles; indeed, our disagreements have prompted me to reconsider many matters and have deepened our collegiality and friendship.

## I

Since Christology expresses the identity and significance of Jesus Christ, it permeates the whole NT, though not in equal measure throughout. One first observes that explicit christological statements are embedded in passages concerned with moral and pastoral matters, for which they provide warrants for the author's counsel. For instance, the extended christological passage in Philippians 2:6-11 is adduced as a warrant for a mode of behavior, and even Hebrews, while dominated by a particular Christology, is essentially a paraenetic book. This feature has three significant consequences: (1) At no point do we have the author's full Christology, only those aspects of it that he deemed pertinent to the issue at hand. The rest is assumed; (2) It is precarious to convert this silence into evidence of the author's ignorance or disinterest, as the discussions of Paul's knowledge of the Jesus traditions show; and (3) These diverse, incomplete christological passages cannot be assembled into a single "Christology of the NT," as if they were scattered pieces of a jigsaw puzzle that various authors used as they saw fit.

Second, the Christology is expressed in quite diverse literary forms: titles, assertions, arguments, parables, poetry, vision reports, kerygmatic appeals, allegories, and narratives ranging from brief accounts to entire Gospels. The Gospels themselves are complex bearers of Christology, for not only do they contain many of the aforementioned forms but they also build Christology into their narrative structures, thereby creating a "show and tell" Christology. Moreover, the Gospels contain both the narrator's christological assertions and Jesus' self-interpretations.

Third, the NT's christological materials are derived from diverse religious/cultural concepts and modes of thought, each with its own complex history. One finds Jewish apocalyptic and midrash, as well as Gentile (Stoic) formulas (1 Cor 8:6 refers to Christ "through whom are all things and through whom we exist"), as well as concepts and motifs used in hellenized Judaism. Especially important is the role of the synagogue's Scripture, cited in Greek (LXX).

Fourth, not to be overlooked is the persistent polemical character of many passages. According to Matthew 24:4-5, Jesus himself warns against deceivers ("false Christs" in 24:24) who will come in his name saying "I am the Christ." Paul mentions those who "proclaim another Jesus" (2 Cor 11:4), and 1 John does not hesitate to label those with the wrong view of Jesus as "antichrists" (1 John 2:18-25)—to cite but the best known of such passages. In other words, the NT comes with a warning: "The wrong Christology can be dangerous to your health!"

Finally, Jesus is related to the same topic in quite different ways. For example, Paul, John, and Hebrews clearly understand Jesus to be the incarnation of the preexistent Son of God,[2] but in Matthew and Luke he is Son of God from conception onward. The former offer a three-stage Christology (preexistence, existence, postexistence), the latter a two-stage one (existence, postexistence). Another difference pertains to Jesus' relation to the law. According to Matthew 5:17-21, Jesus came to fulfill it completely, but according to Hebrews, as the priest like Melchizedek (i.e., Christ did not become a priest through lineage but "through the power of an indestructible life") he set aside the "earlier commandment" because it "made nothing perfect" (Heb 7:15-19). A third difference concerns the relation of the believer to Christ: whereas the Synoptics emphasize discipleship, following Jesus and taking up one's own cross, Paul writes of being "in Christ" and of being baptized "into [Christ's] death" (Rom 6:3); *disciple* is not part of Paul's vocabulary, and participation in Christ is absent from the Synoptics. To be sure, these are not flat contradictions (mutually exclusive assertions) but perspectives that often can be correlated by taking them up into a more comprehensive conceptuality (such as "the Christian life"), thereby making each view, adequate in its own context, a contributor to something not found in, or necessarily required by, the texts themselves. But is this what one means by "NT Christology"? That is precisely the view that historical criticism rejected. But is its own treatment of the subject matter any better?

## II

Historical criticism, determined to overcome the habit of quarrying Scripture for passages adduced to support the loci of Christian doctrine, undertook to reconstruct the history of early Christian thought so that each author, text, or idea could be explained in situ. Thereby the texts became sources of information about "Christian origins," whose shaping factor was said to be the hellenization of the originally Jewish–Christian faith, the adjustments made to accommodate the unfulfilled apocalyptic hope of the Parousia, the rise of institutional "early catholicism," or some combination of such trends. To reconstruct this history, the NT alone does not suffice; all early Christian literature, and pertinent non-Christian texts as well, must be taken into account.

[2] This is to be maintained despite Dunn's attempt to show that Paul's Christology does not include preexistence. See James D. G. Dunn, *Christology in the Making* (Philadelphia: Westminster, 1980).

With the rise of the "history of religion" approach in the closing decades of the nineteenth century, the scope and task were broadened to place early Christianity more precisely in the context of the history of religious belief and practice, especially cultic, in antiquity. Inevitably, historical-critical study of early Christian belief and practice concentrated more and more on non-Christian parallels that could be regarded as antecedents to, and influences on, early Christianity, which in turn was regarded as a particular instance of ancient religiosity. Thus, the formative factor was no longer located in the church's Scripture but in the beliefs, myths, and rituals of the ancient Near Eastern and Greek religions.

Among NT scholars, no one grasped more fully the import of this paradigm for the study of NT theology or advocated its consequences more vigorously than William Wrede (1859–1906), whose famous "The Task and Methods of 'New Testament Theology'" clearly pertains to Christology as well.[3] Noting that many of the Epistles are too brief to provide "doctrinal positions," and that most of the NT is "practical advice" in which creedal statements "are touched on in passing or presupposed, rather than consciously developed," he accuses NT theology of making "doctrine out of what in itself is not doctrine."[4] Moreover, since rigorous historical study cannot be limited to canonical texts, "the name New Testament theology is wrong in both its terms," for the subject matter is "the history of early Christian religion and theology,"[5] understood as "what was believed, thought, taught, hoped, required and striven for . . . not what certain writings say about faith, doctrine, hope, etc."[6]

Wrede would have little patience with my perspective on Christology, for he contended that the thoughts of individual writings and authors (apart from Paul and John) are secondary; what matters are "connections and effects. Where does this come from? How did this happen? What conditioned it? . . . Every historical datum is only made comprehensible so far as we are able to set it in the context out of which it has grown."[7] To find

---

[3] The quotation marks around "New Testament theology" replace the German *sogenannte* (so-called). This essay, "The Task and Methods of 'New Testament Theology,'" expanding a series of lectures to pastors in 1897, is available in Robert Morgan, *The Nature of New Testament Theology* (SBT 2/25; Naperville, Ill.: Alec R. Allenson, 1973), 68–116. The book also includes Adolf Schlatter's "The Theology of the New Testament and Dogmatics," as well as Morgan's valuable introduction (1–67).

[4] Wrede, "Task and Methods," 75.

[5] Wrede, "Task and Methods," 116.

[6] Wrede, "Task and Methods," 85–85.

[7] Wrede, "Task and Methods," 96.

what was historically decisive, "we must go for the dominant features."[8] Because "Paul signifies the very wide distance from Jesus," it is necessary to "measure the distance between them and, so far as one can, to explain it" and to detect the "after-effects of Paul" as well.[9] Given the focus of his essay, Wrede said little about the relation of the emerging Christian religion to other religions of the time; he did, however, point out that "Judaism, not the Old Testament, is the basis of Christianity in the history of religion," and that "Greco-Roman paganism" must be considered as well, meaning "the typical outlook of the man in the street," not the philosophers.[10]

What Wrede "prophesied" was largely "fulfilled" in Wilhelm Bousset's (1865–1920) magisterial *Kyrios Christos*, in which hellenization is the decisive factor.[11] Like Wrede and other champions of this approach, he insisted that early Christianity "has nothing, nothing at all, to do with the truly philosophical literature of the educated circles";[12] hellenization came through the influence of the mystery religions and Gnosticism, the latter understood as a pre-Christian phenomenon, not merely a Christian heresy. Bousset located the pivotal turn to Hellenism in the Gentile Christian worship of Jesus the Lord (*Kyrios*) who was present in the enthusiastic cult. It was Paul who turned Christianity into "a 'redemption' religion in the supernatural sense," in which Jesus is the redeemed redeemer, similar to the myth of the dying and rising gods. Thereby "the Jewish primitive Christian eschatology is finally overcome."[13] Christ mysticism was developed differently in John, where Jesus appears as "the mystagogue who with his marvelous words leads his people to the goal"; he is the Son of God, or God, "sojourning on

---

[8] Wrede, "Task and Methods," 101.

[9] Wrede, "Task and Methods," 108. Wrede's subsequent *Paulus* (Tübingen: J. C. B. Mohr, 1904; ET: *Paul* [Boston: American Unitarian Association, 1907]) would call the apostle "the second founder of Christianity." Although many considerations have made this view of Paul untenable, it has been reasserted with ill-concealed animus by Hyam Maccoby, *The Myth-Maker: Paul and the Invention of Christianity* (San Francisco: Harper & Row, 1986). For a convenient summary and perceptive critique, see the review by J. Louis Martyn, in his collected essays *Theological Issues in the Letters of Paul* (Nashville: Abingdon, 1997), 70–75.

[10] Wrede, "Task and Methods," 114–15.

[11] *Kyrios Christos* was first published in 1913; a revised edition, containing the author's rewritten first four chapters and incorporating his notes in the margins of his personal copy, was published in 1921. Not until 1970 was this important work available in English, when Abingdon Press published John Steely's translation of the fifth edition, for which Rudolf Bultmann provided an appreciative "Introductory Word." This work was reprinted in 2013 by Baylor University Press with a new introduction by Larry W. Hurtado.

[12] Wrede, "Task and Methods," 15.

[13] Wrede, "Task and Methods," 182, 258, 198.

the earth," though still retaining "the little bit of humanity."[14] Bousset writes so vividly and empathetically of the religious experience of Paul that one scarcely notices that he makes almost no mention of the law in relation to God's righteousness and human justification. In the postapostolic era, we hear only echoes of Paul's language, as the office replaced the Spirit; what endured was Christianity as a "cultic society" in which the frequent references to Christ's death, atonement, and person are "thankful confessions of a believing community to the Kyrios who has done so much for his own," but these are "no real theology"—and hence, no real Christology either.[15]

The Wrede-Bousset legacy turned out to be especially influential for one dimension of the study of early Christian Christology—its relation to Jesus. After the Great War, Rudolf Bultmann used Bousset's grand portrayal of hellenization to distinguish earlier Palestinian items in the Jesus tradition from later Hellenistic accretions. Wrede had already shown that Mark's Jesus story, basic to both Matthew and Luke, was not history but a narrative in which the dogma of Jesus' secret messiahship was imposed on the tradition of a nonmessianic Jesus,[16] thus severing the link between Jesus' self-interpretation and that of Christian faith in him. Bultmann's detailed form-critical analysis of each item in the Jesus tradition reinforced this by claiming to show how little of the tradition actually went back to Jesus.[17] Like Mark, the other Synoptists were neither historians nor theologians but compilers and editors of the hellenized Jesus traditions.[18]

Were it not for the impact of redaction criticism, which flourished for several decades after the Second World War, it is doubtful whether this book would include essays devoted to the Christology of each of the Synoptics, for it is by analyzing in great detail exactly how the Synoptic evangelists structured and modified their materials that redaction critics exposed

---

[14] Wrede, "Task and Methods," 228, 217, 220.

[15] Wrede, "Task and Methods," 318.

[16] William Wrede's *The Messianic Secret* was published in 1901; not until seventy years later did an English translation appear, published by James Clarke in Cambridge and London in 1971.

[17] Rudolf Bultmann's *History of the Synoptic Tradition* appeared in 1921. The English version, published in 1963 by Harper & Row and by Basil Blackwell in Oxford, translates the third edition of 1958 and includes Bultmann's notes that he had added to the second edition of 1931.

[18] According to Bultmann, Mark combined the Hellenistic kerygma (like that in Paul, except for preexistence) with the Jesus traditions, but he was "not sufficiently master of his material to be able to venture on a systematic construction himself" (*History of the Synoptic Tradition,* 347, 350). This assessment of Mark's ability has been contested vigorously, especially by redaction critics.

each Gospel's distinctive theological views. However, redaction criticism was not limited to the Gospels, for virtually every NT text was subjected to this type of analysis. Furthermore, scholars did not hesitate to locate the excavated traditions, and the inferred communities that allegedly formed and used them, on the map of early Christianity. Steadily it became evident that early Christianity was a highly diverse phenomenon. In other words, while redaction criticism made it possible to speak of the theology of each Gospel, it also had the effect of fragmenting the picture of early Christianity and its thought. The method itself made this result inevitable, for in order to locate and delineate a piece of tradition thought to be used in an existing text, one emphasized as much as possible the difference between tradition and redaction. Indeed, it was not unusual to read that the author's own view differed so much from the tradition that he cited the latter only to correct it.

Three important factors have made the results of this intensive work ever more hypothetical: (1) Frequently, scholars have been unable to achieve a consensus about the traditions' actual scope and wording; the same is true of alleged aggregates of traditions (e.g., Q, the signs source used in John, the antecedents of the Sermon on the Mount). In some cases, even the existence of such antecedent materials has been vigorously contested. (2) The explicit christological traditions that have been recovered usually consist of a few lines, a formulaic phrase or two, or a motif—hardly enough evidence from which to infer discrete communities and their Christologies. (3) The task of assembling the disparate pieces into a coherent, convincing history of early Christianity has had to proceed with no controls other than the historical reasoning—and often the lively imagination—of the critic, who inevitably produced an account of what might have been if communities had adhered to a single Christology and if their historical development had been in a straight line. Early Christianity indeed was far more diverse and conflicted than had generally been surmised,[19] but the sources simply do not permit one to tell the whole story accurately. Understandably, in recent years many NT students have turned to nonhistorical literary ways of reading the texts, to rhetorical analyses, or to synchronic sociological/ anthropological modes of inquiry.

But by no means all; to the contrary, many have intensified precisely their diachronic—that is, historical—study of earliest Christology in the

---

[19] The picture of early Christianity becomes even more complex when one adds the various opponents of Paul, the so-called Colossian heresy, those opposed by the Johannine Epistles, and the various groups denounced in the Apocalypse.

quest of the origins of various christological ideas, motifs, and titles. Once the keystone of Bousset's grand history disintegrated, namely, his claim that it was the Hellenistic (i.e., predominantly Gentile) Christians who first hailed Jesus as Lord (*Kyrios*), it became natural to look to Palestinian Judaism and to Jewish literature of the Second Temple era generally for the roots of earliest Christology, especially after the Dead Sea Scrolls (and scraps) began to be known. Above all, there were renewed efforts to trace the earliest Christology to the self-interpretation of Jesus in order to overcome the alleged historical hiatus between Jesus and the earliest church.[20] However one evaluates the results, the overall outcome supports the wise word of Marinus de Jonge, who views NT Christology as responses to Jesus: "Jesus is at the center of all early (and later) Christology. This presupposes some degree of continuity between what he said and did and people's reactions. It also presupposes some continuity between the situation of his followers before Jesus' cross and resurrection and their situation after these events." Difficult as it is to get back to Jesus, "we *have* to speak of Jesus' own teaching, including his teaching about himself, if we want to do justice to the early Christian message about him."[21]

Despite the vast and undeniably significant increase in our knowledge of both Jesus and early Christianity, and their roots in the religious and cultural environment of the time, for the study of Christology in the NT the record of scholarship hardly constitutes a grand success story. This is largely because the preoccupation with historical questions—especially the quest for the origins of christological concepts and titles—has obscured the subject matter itself. One has the suspicion that George Berkeley's quip, doubtless made in a quite different context, is appropriate here: We "first raised a dust and then complained that we cannot see."[22] Perhaps a new start is possible, one that neither ignores nor repudiates historical inquiry but that understands the subject matter differently, one that does not simply use the NT as source material for the first chapter in the history of Christian thought. Such a new beginning entails going back to the point where the

---

[20] See the broad-based study *The Christology of Jesus,* by Ben Witherington III (Minneapolis: Fortress, 1990). N. T. Wright prefers to speak of Jesus' "vocation," which he sees as symbolizing and enacting both Israel's vocation and God's coming. See Wright, *Jesus and the Victory of God* (Minneapolis: Fortress, 1996), esp. chap. 13.

[21] Marinus de Jonge, *Christology in Context: The Earliest Christian Response to Jesus* (Philadelphia: Westminster, 1988), 26, 205; emphasis in original.

[22] I found the quip in Colin E. Gunton, *Yesterday and Today: A Study of Continuities in Christology* (London: Darton, Longman & Todd, 1983), 63.

study of Christology in the NT was absorbed into the study of early Christian religion.

## III

Wrede's programmatic piece rested on three basic convictions, which he stated at the outset:[23] (1) Analyzing the NT writings for their theology (read: Christology) "does considerable violence" to their occasioned, practical character, whereas (he implied) using them as evidence for the history of early Christian religion does not. (2) There is no demonstrable reason for treating these writings as a special group because "where the doctrine of inspiration has been discarded, it is impossible to maintain the dogmatic conception of the canon." Consequently, since "no New Testament writing was born with the predicate 'canonical' attached," these texts are to be seen "simply as early Christian writings." (3) A strictly historical account of early Christian religion is "guided by a pure disinterested concern for knowledge," and the result will be "totally indifferent to all dogma and systematic theology. What could dogmatics offer it?"

Appropriate as Wrede's convictions may be for an unprejudiced study of early Christian history, they cannot inhibit a fresh approach to the study of Christology in the NT, because they pertain to another mode of inquiry. To begin with, his call for an unbridgeable gulf between the reconstruction of early Christian religion and theology simply cannot be transferred to the study of Christology (in the latter sense), because by definition Christology is part of systematic theology. Isolating Christology from the study of NT Christology would be like insulating the study of Plato from philosophy. To the contrary, just as a grasp of the rhetoric and logic of philosophy alerts one to what to look for in Plato, so a grasp of the rhetoric and inner logic of Christology identifies what is to be looked for in the NT's Christology. Likewise, Wrede's first point also does not preclude studying the NT for its Christology because if one knows what to look for, one need not do "considerable violence" to the NT's character. Because Christology is a distinct mode of discourse with its own "grammar" (to be sketched shortly), there is no need to replace NT Christology with the history of early Christian religion in order to respect the nature of the NT writings; for history and Christology are two distinct, though related, undertakings that look for different things in the same material. The one is as legitimate as the other. Indeed, an overall view of early Christian history is necessary if one is not to portray the NT's Christology in an ahistorical way for ahistorical readers. Finally, Wrede's second

---

[23] Wrede, "Task and Methods," 69–73.

conviction—that without a doctrine of inspiration one has no warrant for limiting the inquiry to the NT—is also valid for the study of Christian origins but not for the study of Christology in the NT. It is no more arbitrary to deal only with the NT than it is to restrict one's study to any other intelligible body of materials. In fact, one can say that for precisely historical reasons it is less arbitrary, because the NT canon is an historical fact, and its writings have been influential precisely because they were canonized. By contrast, "early Christian writings" as such never existed, for this is but a convenient, necessary, modern label for distinguishing one body of texts from another, and its boundaries are both elastic and porous.[24] These writings can, of course, be studied for Christology—if one knows what to look for.

## IV

Christology is a coherent statement of Christ's identity and significance—in traditional language, the person and work of Christ. ("Christ" is used to indicate that the subject matter exceeds Jesus of Nazareth, though he remains its historical center.) Were it not for his significance there would be no need to speak of his identity. Thus, we may say that Christology is the discourse by means of which Christians account for what they believe they have experienced, and will experience, through Jesus Christ (liberation, new life, forgiveness), customarily understood as "salvation" (Gk., *sōtēria*). Consequently, one can also say that in a coherent Christology the understanding of salvation (soteriology, the work of Christ) implies the identity (the person of Christ) as its ground, and that his person, or identity, implies soteriology as its significance or work. Because each implies the other, one may enter the discourse at either point, for a full-orbed Christology embraces both.

This initial consideration has two important consequences. First, Christology, even when it focuses attention on the person of Christ, never concerns Christ alone, like a Kantian *Ding an sich*, but always understands him in specific relationships or correlations. Second, the coherence of Christology refers to the requirement that the correlations be appropriate, that they make sense conceptually. Since the cure must fit the disease, the salvation effected by Jesus Christ must be correlated appropriately with the understanding of the human condition. In other words, the soteriological correlate implies an anthropology, and vice versa. Thus, if the human condition is essentially ignorance and folly, what is needed is instruction

---

[24] For a fuller discussion of these observations, see my "Is the New Testament a Field of Study? or, From Outler to Overbeck and Back," *Second Century* 1 (1981): 19–35.

and wisdom. There is then no need of forgiveness—unless, of course, ignorance and folly are understood as sin against God. But then more is required than instruction and wisdom.

It is precisely at this point that the construal of Christ's significance or work becomes decisive, because if it is to have an adequate ground, there must be a basis in Christ for what he does to remedy the human condition. Since "the human condition" refers at its deepest level to the relation to God, the coherence of christological discourse requires that the person of Christ be related rightly to God and that the question "Who, then, is he really?" be answered properly. Thus, if Jesus is really a sage who deals effectively and sufficiently with the human condition by imparting wisdom to those who will receive it, his relation to God is adequately accounted for by saying that he was inspired or endowed by God with divine wisdom. If his work is to free us from the tyranny of death and mortality, he must be related to God quite differently, for an inspired sage might liberate us from misconceptions of death and mortality but could not free us from death itself. In short, the deeper the problem, the "higher" the Christology needed to deal with it definitively. Accordingly, for instance, were it not for the prologue of John, the claims of the Johannine Jesus would be preposterous, arrogant assertions without a grounding in reality. It is the identification of Jesus as the Logos enfleshed that makes the Johannine Jesus intelligible and credible if one believes the prologue.

This formal correlation between the person and the work of Christ would leave Christology totally vulnerable to the human propensity to make of Christ whatever legitimates a congenial view of salvation or "religious experience," were it not for the fact that the person in view was a particular historical individual who was executed on the cross. The historicity of Jesus, when taken with full seriousness, resists making him into a construct completely deduced from Christian experience. At this point, therefore, another element in the grammar of Christology comes into play—the solution discloses the plight. The Christ-event is a given that exposes dimensions of the human condition that otherwise would be overlooked or suppressed. In this light, one may paraphrase de Jong's observation (that Christology is response to Jesus): Christology is ex post facto reasoning about Christ.

This formal understanding of the grammar of Christology (how it "works") communicates the long history of reflection and debate about the subject matter, whose beginnings are in the NT. None of its writings or authors studied the rules or followed this script deliberately. Rather, in construing the identity and significance of Christ for their communities, they intuitively created the grammar of christological discourse, because the logic of the situation required them to do so. Nonetheless, it is as legitimate to use the developed rationale of Christology to analyze the Christology in their writings as it is to use musicology to study folk music created by persons with no inkling of music theory or composition.

V

The definition itself is quite simple and straightforward; the implications are more subtle. First of all, NT Christology is Christology as it appears in the NT texts. They are the only thing that exists; all else is inference. Not even a correct inference is evidence. Reconstructing, insofar as possible, the Christology of groups (Hellenistic Jewish Christians in Antioch) or of traditions and sources used in the texts (e.g., Q or the signs source allegedly used by John) is essential for tracing the history of early Christology as the context of the Christology of NT texts. But the Christology of inferred sources and traditions exists only as an element in the Christology of existing texts. What concerns the student of the Christology of the present text is the role of the received material in the Christology that results from using it. For example, it is quite likely that John 1:1-18 is the result of incorporating and modifying several earlier traditions. Identifying these as precisely as possible can contribute to the history of Christology; but even if the resulting reconstruction were beyond reasonable question, it would not be the Christology of the existing prologue, for here, too, the whole is greater than the sum of the parts. Even if the prologue were added relatively late to an earlier version of the Fourth Gospel, as is sometimes argued, the fact that it is a prologue and not an epilogue requires one to treat it as the key signature for the whole Gospel and not as an afterthought.

Given the occasional character of the writings, it is not surprising that the Christology of a text will be focused and logically incomplete, or that the anthropological correlate will appear separately from what is said elsewhere about Christ. Thus, for Paul's Christology in Romans, for example, it does not matter that the construal of the human condition in chapters 1–3 and chapter 7 lacks references to Christ, or that the straightforward references to Christ do not always refer explicitly to the anthropological passages. For being alert to the nature of Christology enables one to correlate the material according to the grammar of Christology. To do so is not to impose an alien Christology on the text but to make explicit what is logically implicit.

The fact that the NT contains seven—and some would say more than seven—letters from one author, Paul, is no reason to be deflected from this understanding of the subject matter; the effect of having this corpus is rather to provide a much richer context in which to read the Christology of each writing. For one thing, using the whole corpus to get a more complete picture of Paul's views of Christ and his significance enables one to see the Christology of 1 Thessalonians, for example, in light of the whole, to position his thinking more precisely in emerging Christianity, and so forth—but the results belong more to the history of Paul and of early Christology than to the Christology of the letter itself. The focus or emphasis of that particular Christology is, in turn, illumined by what can be inferred about Paul's reading of the situation in the Thessalonian church. Moreover, seeing as best as one can Paul's understanding of Christ as a whole can illumine the Christology of a particular passage or letter because it helps one see how Paul thinks,[25] not only about Christ but also about the connections he makes with his view of Christ. Still, by not letting the study of the Christology of Paul's letters simply lapse into the study of the Christology of Paul, one guards against trying to understand the subject by recourse to the psychology of his "conversion."

The Christology of the text cannot be grasped by concentrating on christological titles used in it. Most texts use several titles, with no evident concern to show how they are related to one another. More important, "Christ" largely lost its original "messianic" meaning and became virtually a proper name, no longer capable of expressing both the *theo*logical and the soteriological/anthropological correlate implied in its (Hebrew) etymology-shaped meaning (God's Anointed, through whom God's reign was made effective in the people of God); consequently, like Son or Son of God, it derives its actual meaning from its usage. This is hardly surprising, since in general "meaning" is conveyed not by single words but by sentences and paragraphs and by the tissue of the whole text. It is in these larger linguistic constructions that the relationship of persons, things, and concepts is expressed. This is especially true of extended narratives like the Gospels and of discourses. Accordingly, in Romans the significance of Jesus for the disclosure of God's righteousness is neither expressed nor implied in any christological title but requires Paul's argument; similarly, in John the whole narrative interprets the "Son." Further, because titles that accent Jesus' identity in terms of his relation to God (for instance, Logos, Son, Son of Man) can be used in connection with various views of his significance,

---

[25] For two attempts to grasp the character of Paul's thinking, see my "Paul and Apocalyptic Theology," *Interpretation* 38 (1984): 229–41; and "Paul as Thinker," *Interpretation* 47 (1993): 27–38. Both articles are reprinted in *Christ's First Theologian: The Shape of Paul's Thought* (Waco, Tex.: Baylor University Press, 2015), 75–87 and 89–101 respectively.

concentrating on the titles tends to rupture the inherent nature Christology as bipolar discourse, in which person and work must be thought together.[26]

Above all, one would grossly misread the NT were one to assume that the historical figure of Jesus was merely the passive recipient of sundry christological titles; for not only do the titles identify him but he also redefines them. Otherwise, they do not really "fit" Jesus, especially in light of his decision to go to Jerusalem, where he would end up on a cross. This is precisely the point of the Markan story of Jesus' response to Peter's "confession" at Caesarea Philippi. Indeed, it underlies the whole Markan insistence that the disciples, having heard Peter use the "right" title for Jesus, nonetheless fail to grasp who he really is.

Since the NT indeed presents numerous Christologies, the continued use of the customary singular noun requires justification. At the most rudimentary level, it simply identifies the texts in view, without necessarily implying anything significant about the NT's content or its canonical standing. The phrase becomes problematic when it is construed to mean that the NT contains a single, coherent Christology, sufficiently unified conceptually that it can be treated as a single voice; at that point, like a lightning rod, it attracts all the energies generated by the stormy debates over the unity of the NT. But *unity* is too ambiguous a term, and it readily seduces one to look for the wrong things.

More promising is the effort to identify the persistent features, the common traits, that mark Christology in the NT, even if they are not found exclusively in the canonical texts. In fact, it would be quite unfortunate if these traits were found only in the NT; were that the case, its Christology not only would be sundered from its roots in early Christianity but would also have forfeited its influence. It is the canonical status of the NT that gives special standing to the shared features of these Christologies. Whereas the contents of the Christologies in NT canon are understandings that can be repudiated only by rupturing the continuity of the church's teaching, their persistent traits serve as guidelines or as channel markers that help safeguard the integrity of continuing christological thought.

Since channel markers indicate where the dangerous water begins, it is useful to formulate the traits of these Christologies negatively. Five are especially crucial: (1) Consistently, the NT canon does not integrate Jesus

---

[26] For a more extended critique of the preoccupation with titles, see chap. 1, "The Renewal of New Testament Christology," pp. 10–13.

into an open-ended series; rather, Jesus the Christ is the event in which God acted decisively and definitively to overcome what had gone awry. Because the consummation of what was begun in Christ is not contingent on the arrival of another, none of the NT Christologies abandons completely the "return" of Christ himself. (2) No matter how "high" the Christology, Christ never competes with or replaces God; to the contrary, the high exaltation of Christ is precisely "to the glory of God the Father," as Philippians 2:11 puts it. Christian monotheism may be Christomorphic, but it is not Christocentric. (3) Christ never becomes a Christ-figure, a symbol of something else, such as an idea or a process, but retains his particularity as a being who once, as a human, bore a personal name in a particular place and time. (4) Although Christ's relation to Israel and the Old Testament is portrayed in quite different ways, the relation is stubbornly positive. By no means is this a matter of integrating Christ into an alleged salvation history (*Heilsgeschichte*)—a modern invention—nor is the synagogue's Scripture (LXX) to be absorbed into "Second Temple literature" (the Jewish equivalent to "early Christian literature") in order expand the range of material to be scoured for the "background" of christological concepts, motifs, and titles, essential as such sources may be for the history of early Christology and its vocabulary. It is rather a matter of taking seriously the actual NT exegesis of LXX as an essential part of the Christology of the text. (5) The Spirit (the immediate presence of the divine) never displaces Jesus Christ; consequently, no religious experience, however "meaningful," makes Christology irrelevant. To the contrary, [The] Spirit is the mode in which Christ is present to the believer in the community.

Taken together, these characteristics of the NT's several Christologies provide a profile of Christology sufficient for measuring the faithfulness and the adequacy of subsequent Christologies, including those of our own day. The NT's Christologies do not simply provide "answers" made obligatory by its canonical status; they also pose questions that summon its interpreters to think as theologians.

The essential thing, therefore, is to see that the study of Christology in the NT will find its vitality and relevance renewed if it is reconceived as a theological discipline with historical horizons. Wrede's question "What can dogmatics offer it?," albeit posed with reference to the study of history, can be asked appropriately here also. The answer is not arcane: it can define and focus the subject matter so that the Christologies of the NT can be studied as Christology, not as something else.

# 3

# The Second Coming of the Liberal Jesus?

"The historical Jesus" is back. For the third time, we are told. The resurgence of interest in the Jesus of history is evidenced not only by the books from Marcus Borg, John Dominic Crossan, and Géza Vermès but also by the publication of *The Five Gospels*, reflecting the conclusions of R. W. Funk's Jesus Seminar in which Borg and Crossan are active participants. Whether or not these works represent a "third quest of the historical Jesus," it is instructive to view them in light of earlier efforts to recover Jesus "as he really was," and to ask whether the second coming of the liberal Jesus is at hand.

On the whole, nineteenth-century (German) Protestant scholarship, no longer able to affirm inherited christological doctrines such as atonement and parousia, preferred "the Jesus of history" before he became "the Christ of faith" (to use the title of D. F. Strauss' book-length review of Schleiermacher's *Life of Jesus*). To show, nonetheless, that Jesus was both a credible founder of Christianity and the continuing object of devotion, critical historiography had to show his truly heroic quality, usually contrasting him with his Jewish heritage and environment. The first quest of the historical Jesus foundered, however, when it became apparent that the Synoptic Gospels and their sources were so thoroughly permeated by Christian theology that an uninterpreted Jesus could be glimpsed only here and there. Furthermore, the historical Jesus that could be recovered turned out to be an apocalyptic preacher of the kingdom of God—as alien to liberal Protestantism as the Christ of dogma.

In the wake of Barthian theology, Bultmann declared the whole quest impossible on critical grounds and illegitimate on theological ones. He deemed it simply another attempt to base faith on works (this time, certified facts) rather than on the word of God. What sort of continuity, if any, could be discerned between the message of Jesus and the kerygma of the church? If there were only discontinuity between Jesus himself and the proclaimed Jesus Christ, the gospel would be a myth imposed on history, and Jesus would not be the church's sovereign but its hapless victim.

In response to such questions, Ernst Käsemann launched within the Bultmannian circle a fresh search, later dubbed "a New Quest" by James Robinson. This venture found continuity between the existential understanding of the self before God, expressed in one way by Jesus and in another by the kerygma. This second quest, like "the new hermeneutic" with which it was linked, was short-lived, especially on the American scene. The questions that it generated were simply ignored as interest in social and sociological matters took center stage.

The alleged third quest, while no more uniform than its predecessors, rejects Bultmann's double verdict about quests, and is determined to know as precisely as possible what Jesus did and did not say, and to understand the critically certified Jesus as an historical phenomenon in the social landscape of his time. Moreover, some of its practitioners, especially Crossan, insist that the noncanonical evidence has as much right to be taken seriously as the New Testament Gospels.

Especially important is the Coptic Gospel of Thomas found in 1947, which consists of 114 sayings of Jesus but has no Passion story. It appears as the fifth gospel in the color-coded *Five Gospels*, showing at a glance what the Jesus Seminar decided was truly from Jesus (red), what probably represents his thought but not his words (pink), what he surely did not say (black), and what he probably neither said nor thought (gray). According to this wisdom, there is but one genuine saying of Jesus in the entire Gospel of Mark, while three are preserved in Thomas. Overall, only 18 percent of what the sources attribute to Jesus is deemed to have been actually said by him. The difference between the Jesus of history and the Christ of faith (any form of early Christian faith will do) has seldom been greater. And because the Jesus of history is again portrayed in heroic terms which protect him from becoming a *skandalon*, one must ask whether we are witnessing the Parousia of the liberal Jesus.

Borg, Crossan, and Vermès present quite different portrayals of Jesus. *The Religion of Jesus the Jew* by Vermès, a renowned Oxford expert on the Dead Sea Scrolls, is the most focused because it completes a trilogy (*Jesus the Jew*, 1973; *Jesus and the World of Judaism*, 1983). Crossan's *Jesus: A Revolutionary Biography* is essentially a condensation of his *The Historical Jesus* (1991); Borg's *Meeting Jesus again for the First Time* (1995), while drawing on his *Jesus: A New Vision* (1987), not only records the author's personal pilgrimage of faith and understanding but is the only one that reflects on the import of the critics' Jesus for contemporary Christian faith.

Only in part do the different portrayals reflect the fact that Borg is a Lutheran, Crossan a Roman Catholic, and Vermès a Jew. Much more significant is their divergent stance toward the Gospels. Not only does Vermès ignore Thomas, but in contrast with the Jesus Seminar's passion for methodological rigor, admits that "methodology . . . makes me see red, perhaps because more than once I have been rebuked by trans-Atlantic dogmatists for illegitimately arriving at the right conclusion following a path not sanctioned by my critics' sacred rule book."[1] Vermès sees the Gospels (and the whole NT) as "one particular sector on the general map of Jewish cultural history," not as an independent corpus. Whereas Vermès first stakes out a topic and then works his way to particulars by adducing historical considerations, Crossan isolates a cluster of sayings on a topic, considers only the earliest and doubly attested, and then compares the treatment of the themes with Greek as well as Jewish materials in order to develop an interpretation based on anthropological studies of Mediterranean peasants. Vermès finds this approach quite inappropriate.

For Vermès, Jesus was a "charismatic prophetic preacher and miracle worker" who "represents the charismatic Judaism of wonder-working holy men."[2] Vermès examines the nature, style, and content of Jesus' preaching, discusses the idea of God as King and Father in relation to Jesus' "eschatological enthusiasm"; and portrays "Jesus the Religious Man" before reaching the epilogue "intended to bring into sharp relief the difference between this religion and historic, ecclesiastical Christianity."[3]

Borg explicitly accepts Vermès' classification of Jesus and goes beyond it: "The most crucial fact about Jesus was that he was a 'spirit person' . . . one . . . to whom the Spirit was an experiential reality." To this he adds three other categories: a teacher of wisdom, social prophet, and founder of a "Jewish renewal or revitalization movement that challenged and shattered the social boundaries of his day."[4]

For Crossan, in contrast with Vermès and Borg, the religious dimension of Jesus' word and deed is almost totally absorbed into his social role as a

---

[1] Géza Vermès, *The Religion of Jesus the Jew* (Minneapolis: Augsburg Fortress, 1993), 7.

[2] Vermès, *Religion of Jesus*, 5.

[3] Vermès, *Religion of Jesus*, 10.

[4] Marcus Borg, *Meeting Jesus again for the First Time: The Historical Jesus and the Heart of Contemporary Faith* (New York: HarperCollins, 1995), 31-32, 30.

countercultural itinerant on the border of revolt. Relying heavily on studies of ancient peasantry in order to extract from Josephus and the Gospels a picture of Galilean antipathies and unrest, Crossan regards Jesus as a Jewish edition of the Greco-Roman cynic. "Jesus and his first followers . . . were hippies in a world of Augustan yuppies"[5]—a remarkably succinct summary. Jesus had a social program which "sought to rebuild a society upwards from its grass roots, but on principles of religious and economic egalitarianism"[6] made concrete in "the combination of *free healing and common eating*," which "negated alike and at once the hierarchical and patronal normalcies of Jewish religion and Roman power."[7] Whereas Borg's Jesus mediated the sacred, Crossan's Jesus refused to be the broker or mediator of God and God's kingdom; he was "the announcer that neither should exist between humanity and divinity, or between humanity and itself."[8]

In anchoring Jesus firmly in the religion of first-century Judaism, Vermès is part of a growing circle of Jewish scholars whose work makes it possible for modern Judaism to reclaim Jesus as one of its own. His Jesus is not unlike the prodigal son who was welcomed home after years among the Gentile Christians. Once back home, there is nothing about the religion of Jesus the Jew that is particularly offensive to Judaism; at the same time, Vermès is spared the temptation to portray the Jesus of history as the center of a fleeting, brilliant moment that stands sharply against the oppressive darkness that surrounded him.

However, for Crossan (and to some extent Borg) the Jesus of history was the center of a Galilean Camelot, the halcyon days when Jesus and his band roamed the countryside, disregarding societal structures, defying hierarchical patterns, irritating elites, and confounding the powerful, creating a grassroots movement with nobodies while at the same time refusing to be its leader or mediator of the new because that would be brokering the kingdom. Ironically, the brokerless Jesus is himself thoroughly brokered by his biographer.

The marked differences among the three quests should not obscure the continuity that results from shared reliance on key aspects of the historical-critical method and its judgments about the Gospels and early Christianity. Basic for all three quests is the view that Matthew and Luke used both Mark

---

[5] John Dominic Crossan, *Jesus: A Revolutionary Biography* (New York: HarperCollins, 1995), 222.

[6] Crossan, *Jesus*, 220.

[7] Crossan, *Jesus*, 222; emphasis in original.

[8] Crossan, *Jesus*, 222.

and Q, and that between Jesus and all written sources stands the oral tradition which shaped and expanded the Jesus materials, so that recovering
the Jesus of history entails differentiating what the texts report from what
Jesus really said and did. As a result, the volume of "hard data" on which
the historical reconstruction of Jesus can rely is markedly smaller than that
of the sources. After subtracting sayings in which Jesus speaks of himself
in suspiciously Christian terms, as well as those in which he uses Jewish
commonplaces, the figure who remains was baptized by John, preached the
kingdom of God, healed the sick, relied on striking aphorisms and parables,
indiscriminately consorted with those deemed "sinners," and was executed
by Roman authorities for reasons difficult to ascertain. Having given up
the Gospels' reports that Jesus deliberately sought death, criticism has
been unable to determine whether he was executed because he was rightly
perceived to threaten the existing order, or was misunderstood, or simply
found himself at the wrong place at the wrong time.

Whether the relentless use of methodological skepticism which marks
this strand of historical criticism has yielded credible history is precisely
what is contested. Peter Stuhlmacher, for instance, says flatly that "without
. . . acknowledging that the human Jesus already laid claim to being the
messianic Son of Man whom God sent to Israel, one cannot make sense
historically of Jesus' ministry or even of the passion narrative."[9] Crossan
says virtually the opposite.

What links Borg's and Crossan's Jesus with the liberal Jesus of the
first quest is the absence of the futurist (apocalyptic) horizon of Jesus'
message and mission, including the widely accepted view that he believed
the coming kingdom was making itself effective proleptically in his work.
According to Borg, Jesus was "noneschatological": he did not expect "the
supernatural coming of the kingdom of God as a world-ending event in his
own generation."[10] With the highly problematic modifier of "a world-ending
event" the statement is quite misleading, since there is no evidence that the
coming of the kingdom meant "the end of the world." Without this modifier,
the statement becomes highly questionable. For Borg, of course, futurity is
obviated by a Jesus who mediates the divine.

Crossan, on the other hand, retains the term "eschatological" but
reduces it to meaning world-negation—"a radical criticism of culture and

---

[9] Peter Stuhlmacher, *Jesus of Nazareth, Christ of Faith* (trans. Siegfried Schatzmann;
Peabody, Mass.: Hendrickson, 1993), 6. Cf. Crossan, *Jesus*, 93.

[10] Borg, *Meeting Jesus again*, 29.

civilization."[11] Whereas Borg has little to say about Jesus' message of the kingdom, Crossan emphasizes it as the theme of Jesus' egalitarian activity as well as of his teaching. Crossan too disabuses Jesus of expecting divine intervention to bring the kingdom, and claims not only that Jesus became "almost the exact opposite of the Baptist"[12] but also that Jesus taught a present sapiential kingdom, though as understood not by elites (like Wisdom of Solomon or Philo) but by peasants, whose dream of an egalitarian world was a matter of social protest.

It may surprise readers to learn that the result of Jesus' enacting the kingdom ("what the world would be if God were directly and immediately in charge" or "a community of radical and unbrokered equality in which individuals are in direct contact with each other and with God"[13]) was a band of hippies among yuppies. In fact, it is by no means clear why "kingdom of God" should be retained at all for world-negation—unless one is willing to think of God and world in Marcionite terms. Crossan in fact attributes to Jesus "a very different message from a very different God."[14] Nor is it clear why such a Jesus would have been executed. The idea that this Jewish cynic (and his dozen hippies), with his demeanor and aphorisms, was a serious threat to society sounds more like a conceit of alienated academics than sound historical judgment.

Vermès' Jesus is much more plausible. While regarding the Parousia as a Christian idea, he not only relates Jesus to first-century Jewish religion but emphasizes his eschatological awareness: "the religion of Jesus the Jew is a rare, possibly unique, manifestation of undiluted eschatological enthusiasm."[15] It is Vermès who sees the correlation between the keen sense that God's imminent kingdom is breaking in and repentance (*teshuvah*, turning), faithful surrender to God (*'emunah*), and "an untiring effort to follow God as a model, a constant *imitatio Dei*"[16]—motifs absent from Borg and Crossan, for whom Jesus is only externally a Jew. Though Crossan says that "Jesus' Jewishness is particularly important in terms of the body/society interaction" (body as microcosm), there is virtually nothing particularly Jewish left in Crossan's portrait of this Mediterranean peasant. Jesus' social location is far more important for Crossan than his religious

---

[11] Crossan, *Jesus*, 52.

[12] Crossan, *Jesus*, 47.

[13] Crossan, *Jesus*, 101.

[14] Crossan, *Jesus*, 119.

[15] Vermès, *Religion of Jesus*, 190.

[16] Vermès, *Religion of Jesus*, 200.

location. Indeed, whereas first-century Jewish religion was the wellspring of Jesus' life and mission, for both Borg and Crossan that religion was in effect the oppressive structure that he negated. They neither discuss the role of Torah in Jewish life nor have anything good to say about the Judaism that shaped Jesus and his matrix.

To be sure, Borg insists that Jesus was and remained Jewish, just as he asserts that it was not "the Jews" but the "elite" Jewish collaborators with Roman power who rejected him. He too finds the *imitatio Dei* motif in Judaism—two motifs, in fact: be compassionate (i.e., merciful) as God is compassionate, and be holy as God is holy. Although compassion and holiness were in conflict, the latter was dominant, producing a "purity system" (with sharp social boundaries). Jesus' mission was really an "attack upon the purity system"; in other words, on the allegedly prevailing form of Jewish religion maintained by priests and the elite, while construed somewhat differently by Pharisees and Qumranians.

Interestingly, Borg apparently has fewer doubts about the Gospels' portrait of Judaism (which reflect the evangelists' time more than that of Jesus) than about their portrayal of Jesus. Understandably so, for seeing Jesus against the background of later first-century Judaism makes it easier to portray him as the hero of moderns alienated from religious traditions and structures. Vermès is surely on the more solid ground here in contending that there is no evidence that Jesus was "hostile to the Torah in principle or refused to abide by it in practice"; to the contrary, "he acknowledged the Law of Moses as the foundation stone of his Judaism."[17]

What must not be overlooked is that the authors' separation of Jesus from futurist eschatology, the secularized reduction of his message and mission to (peasant) class protest and social reconstruction, and the refusal to acknowledge the positive and formative influence of Jewish piety on Jesus are all of a piece. Whereas the second quest demythologized the apocalyptic eschatology that informed Jesus' message of the kingdom in such a way that the kingdom remained God's initiative and gift eliciting a new ethos, thereby respecting the biblical-Jewish roots of Jesus' word and deed, the Borg-Crossan construal tacitly posits an inert deity who at best provides a formal warrant for a class-based cultural criticism and who apparently has allowed the covenant-commitment to Israel to lapse, for there remains neither promise nor fulfillment. In this interpretation of the kingdom, Jesus may refer to God but not defer to God's action. It is by

[17] Vermès, *Religion of Jesus*, 188–89.

no means clear why this egalitarian Eden, which relies wholly on human willpower, is less illusory—especially in the blood-soaked century when human capacity is unmasked—than the Jewish apocalyptic hope for the coming of God's kingdom.

The value of these books is not in what they say about Jesus so much as in what their saying these things prompts one to think about. The quest itself continues—as it must.

# 4

# Jesus the Jew

Not since the first century has it been as possible as today for Jews and Christians to talk together about Jesus without anxiety or bitterness. Since World War II there has emerged a remarkable interest in Jesus on the part of Jews, particularly in Israel. It is not for me, a Gentile Christian, to tell Jews how to integrate Jesus into their history or to say what the consequences of doing so might be for Judaism. I can, however, try to understand why the Jewishness of Jesus has been a problem for any historian who sets out to discern and interpret the Jesus of history in historical terms. I can also suggest what is at stake for Gentile Christians in the fact that Jesus was not a Christian but a Jew.

I will first show how the quest for the Jesus of history made the Jewishness of Jesus a central theme, and the problems this raised first for liberal Protestant questers and then also for Jews. Next, I will look briefly at three unavoidable historical questions that emerge from seeing Jesus in his Jewish context, and then conclude with a few brief observations.

## I

Whoever wants to learn about the Jesus of history must derive the information from Christian texts. Roman historians do not describe his lifework, and the one passage about him in the writings of the Jewish historian, Josephus, has the marks of Christian editing. The few scattered references to Jesus in the Talmud are not only late but also reflect a polemic against the Christ of the Byzantine church more than independent memory. The Christian texts are primarily the Gospels, including some not in the New Testament, as well as fragments of Jewish–Christian gospels quoted by various Christian writers from the second to the fifth centuries. In effect, this means that all the sources assume and reflect Christian bias toward Jesus. On the whole, the historian of ancient Israel faces the same phenomenon in the Hebrew Bible.

Beginning with the seventeenth century, and especially with the deists, doubts arose among those who no longer believed what the church had been teaching. The more they doubted the inherited beliefs, the more they believed their doubts about the Gospels, and so began the whole effort to get behind the Christian Gospels to Jesus as he really was. They assumed from the start that the Jesus of history differed from the Christ of faith for the historical Jesus was not a Christian but a Jew. This unprecedented quest for the Jesus of history was controversial, and has continued to be until today; consequently, the controversies over the quest and its results inevitably involve the Jewishness of Jesus.

Since the real, factual Jesus cannot be verified by checking neutral sources, the Jesus of history can never be more than a Jesus with differing degrees of probability. To avoid the impossible and minimize the improbable, most of the quest therefore eliminated from consideration the Easter stories and all miracle stories except those that might report psychosomatic healings, and concentrated on Jesus' teachings. How does one decide what Jesus probably said, especially since the Gospels were written in Greek whereas he probably spoke Aramaic? Basically, scholars relied on subtraction, beginning with words and phrases that had no Aramaic equivalent. Most important, however, have been efforts to subtract sayings whose ideas appeared unlikely to have come from Jesus the Jew. And that meant relying on what is called either the criterion of dissimilarity or the negative criterion. I want to explain what it is and how it works.

The whole effort to recover the real Jesus of history assumes that the Gospels present a Christianized Jesus because Christians attributed to him what they themselves believed about him. The more the Jesus of the Gospels teaches what the church taught, the less likely that the real Jesus had said it. So the critics subtracted all the sayings of Jesus in which he predicted his crucifixion and resurrection, interpreted his death as a sacrifice for sin, implied he would return from heaven, and so on. The result was clear: the more the Jesus of the Gospels was de-Christianized, the more Jewish became the Jesus of history.

That is only half of the story. The first Christians were Jews, and so the critics also assumed that Christian Jews were just as likely to have added Jewish elements to the Jesus tradition as distinctly Christian ones. Therefore, the negative criterion was applied also to what was left of the Jesus tradition after the Christian elements were removed. As a result, only those teachings came to be regarded as genuinely from Jesus himself which do not express typically Jewish ideas either, such as "till heaven and earth pass away, not an iota, not a dot, will pass away from the law until all is accomplished" (Matt 5:18). In short, the consistent use of the negative criterion produced a Jesus who differed from his Christian followers on the one hand and from his Jewish forebears on the other. Only that is probably from Jesus which is original, distinctive, and unexpected. Clearly, with this method, not many sayings survive the scrutiny of the skeptics. Moreover, critics also deleted those sayings of Jesus that express hostility to Judaism, because they reflect the polemic of the church to the later synagogue, not Jesus himself. As a result, the historical Jesus has been purged of both Christian theology and negative attitudes toward Judaism. The result is rather ironic, for now Jesus is related negatively to Christianity and positively to the Judaism of his time.

With few exceptions, most of the questers of Jesus were Protestants. None of their efforts to recover the real Jesus was motivated by a desire to make him more credible to Jews. Rather, the driving impulses were oriented to Christianity, and were of two kinds.

(1) Those critics who were alienated from traditional Christianity used the search for the real Jesus to undermine the credibility of orthodox Christian teaching. The greater the difference between the Christ of faith and the real Jesus, the more obvious it would be that the Christ of faith would have no future because it did not have enough hard facts. These critics shared a rather widespread repudiation of Christianity among the intelligentsia in late eighteenth- and nineteenth-century Germany. Some writers produced biographies of Jesus that were as incredible as the Gospels. For instance, two of them (Bahrdt and Venturini) claimed that Jesus had secretly been one of the Essenes who stage-managed the crucifixion and a fake resurrection.

(2) Much more important were those critics who were convinced that although many of the classical doctrines of Christianity were no longer credible, the real meaning of the faith could be salvaged if it were placed on a more solid factual foundation, namely the Jesus of history. If the efforts were successful, one could be loyal to Jesus himself without having to believe all the Christian theology that had been added to the tradition. It was assumed, in other words, that the facts of history, the facts about the real Jesus, will show that faith in him is neither irrational nor unwarranted, but adequately grounded in facts. What looked promising proved to be disastrous, however. On the one hand, liberal Protestantism delivered religious faith into the hands of the historical critics, who now had the right

to tell believers what they could and could not believe. But were believers supposed to wait until the critics agreed? On the other hand, this agenda demanded too much from history. Wherever critics located Jesus on the map of Second Temple Judaism, there one had to show historically that he was not just another instance of it but superior to it. Thus history, the history of Jesus, was expected to provide an adequate basis for a religious commitment to Jesus.

In trying to meet the religious need of liberal Protestantism, critics drew on two outlooks of the day, the one rarely acknowledged—antipathy toward Judaism often reflecting ignorance and stereotypes—and the other commonly advocated, namely German idealist thought with its lofty, somewhat ethereal, view of pure religion as a spiritual state of the soul, an inner kinship with the divine. This viewpoint valued what it regarded as the essence of religion and it disdained the outward trappings in creeds, liturgies, clergy, and the like. These externals change, because they are historical but the essence itself does not change. The combination of these two outlooks, the worst and the best of German thought, determined how liberal critics would view Jesus' Jewishness. Three examples must do, though one is French.

One was Adolf Harnack, the greatest historian of Christianity in the late nineteenth and early twentieth centuries. In the winter semester of 1899 he gave a series of public lectures at the University of Berlin in which he said, "The Christian religion is something simple and sublime; it means one thing and one thing only: Eternal life in the midst of time, by the strength and under the eyes of God."[1] Given this view of pure religion, Harnack excoriated Eastern Orthodoxy, Roman Catholicism, and even aspects of Protestantism for obscuring the essence. For him the key metaphor was the kernel (the essence) and the husk (historical externals).[2] It is not surprising then that Harnack would say rather harsh things about the relation of Jesus to Judaism, which he once referred to as "the wreck of the Jewish religion."[3] As a man of his time, Jesus of course shared some ideas with his contemporaries, but they were not the essence, the kernel; they were only the husk. "Husks were the whole of the Jewish limitations attaching to Jesus' message; husks were also such definite statements as 'I am not sent but unto the lost

[1] Adolf von Harnack, *What Is Christianity?* (trans. Thomas Bailey Sanders; Philadelphia: Fortress, 1986), 8.

[2] Harnack, *What Is Christianity?* 12.

[3] Harnack, *What Is Christianity?* 191.

sheep of the house of Israel.'"[4] Although Jesus and the early church broke through these barriers and overcame these limitations, others took their place when Christianity entered the Greek world.[5]

Another famous scholar, Wilhelm Bousset, claimed that while externally Jesus remained entirely within the framework of Judaism, inwardly he was free of it, much freer, in fact, than Paul for whom humanity remained divided between Jew and Gentile, whereas Jesus had a truly universal outlook.[6] Although Bousset asserted that knowledge of Judaism is essential if one is to understand Jesus (he wrote an important book on it himself), he also insisted that Judaism does not account for Jesus because there are "complete contradictions" (vollständige Gegensätze) between them."[7]

Even more extreme views were expressed by the French biblical scholar, Ernest Renan, whose Life of Jesus was read very widely. According to Renan, Jesus was surrounded by Judaism but was never really part of it for "he was ignorant of the strange scholasticism which was taught in Jerusalem and which was soon to constitute the Talmud. If some Pharisees had already brought it into Galilee, he did not associate with them . . . and when later he encountered this silly casuistry, it only inspired him with disgust."[8] After a visit to Jerusalem, Jesus saw "that there was no union possible between him and the ancient Jewish religion. The abrogation of the sacrifices which had caused him so much disgust, the suppression of an impious and haughty priesthood, and, in a general sense, the abrogation of the law, appeared to him as absolute necessity. From this time he appears no more as a Jewish reformer but as a destroyer of Judaism. . . . In other words, Jesus was no longer a Jew. . . . He proclaimed the rights of man, not the rights of the Jew; the religion of man, not the religion of the Jew; the deliverance of man, not the deliverance of the Jew."[9]

One can detect a pattern: even when recent scholars grant that in many ways Jesus really shared much with Pharisaism, they still feel compelled to distance him from it in whatever matters most, for only in that way can one claim to provide historical evidence that Jesus was manifestly superior, and therefore worthy of what some nineteenth-century liberal Protestants called our positive value judgments about him.

---

[4] Harnack, What Is Christianity? 180.

[5] Harnack, What Is Christianity? 180, 187.

[6] Wilhelm Bousset, Jesu Predigt in ihrem Gegensatz zum Judentum: Ein religionsgeschichtlicher Vergleich (Göttingen: Vandenhoeck & Ruprecht, 1892), 82–87.

[7] Bousset, Jesu Predigt in ihrem Gegensatz, 130.

[8] Ernest Renan, Life of Jesus (Amherst, N.Y.: Prometheus, 1991), 92.

[9] Renan, Life of Jesus, 224–26.

Beginning with the middle of the last century, liberal Protestant scholars saw that the central theme of Jesus' preaching was the kingdom of God, which they understood as the reign of God in the human soul and as a moral task. It came as a shock, therefore, when Albert Schweitzer and others pointed out that this is not at all what Jesus meant by "kingdom of God." What he had in mind was a state of affairs that God would bring about at the end of history. In other words, Jesus understood the kingdom of God in apocalyptic terms. If that was the case, then Jesus was an apocalyptic Jew. And since apocalyptists were commonly regarded as other-worldly fanatics given to speculations about the imminent end of the world, there began a scramble to show that Jesus was not such a fantasizing futurist at all, for if he had been, he was wrong. Usually scholars argued that for Jesus the kingdom of God was both future and present, and that his mission was to make that evident by what he did and said.

Currently, some scholars are contending that virtually all of Jesus' sayings that refer to a future apocalyptic kingdom actually come from the later Jewish church and not from Jesus himself. And so once again, Jesus is relieved of Jewish error. According to the Jesus Seminar, and some associated with it, Jesus was a sage, a wandering wise man like the Greek Cynics who were famous for puncturing pretensions and mocking customs by confronting people with memorable one-liners. As one scholar put it, Jesus and his band of followers were hippies among yuppies, deliberately flaunting their disdain for Jewish customs pertaining to ritual purity. Like Bousset's Jesus, theirs is a Jew only outwardly, if that, for scarcely any trace of the Jewish religion remains.

I have lingered so long with these various and persistent attempts to distance Jesus from some form of Judaism in order to show that repeatedly, scholars—sometimes alienated from their own church tradition—have made Jesus great by demeaning Judaism. Thereby the alleged Jesus of history has been isolated from both the Christian religion that the critics inherited and from the unacceptable features of the Jewish religion that Jesus inherited. The result is a Jesus who is always theologically correct, a Jesus who coincides rather well with the sensibilities and values of the critics.

It is not surprising that the landscape looks rather different when one enters the field of Jewish studies of Jesus. Jewish scholarship has had a double aim: on the one hand, it intended to show Jewish readers that Jesus can, and must, be integrated into Judaism as one of its own and not as a renegade, while on the other hand, it intended to show Gentile Christian readers that the Judaism of which he was a part was not a legalistic, sterile religion.

Those who first undertook this dual task were the emancipated and partly assimilated Jews in Germany, as well as liberal or Reform Jews in Britain and America. Today, Orthodox, Conservative, and Reform Jews as well as Israeli scholars are engaged in the quest, and they do not speak with one voice either. Their divergent views cannot be summarized or adjudicated here. Three observations must suffice.

First, as we have seen, the quest of the historical Jesus is predicated on the assumption that the Jesus of history differs from the Christ of faith, the Jesus Christ portrayed in the Gospels. Consequently, many Christian historians of Jesus have worried how the two can be related, for in classical Christianity Jesus Christ is held to be both truly human and truly divine. No Jew, and certainly no Jewish historian of Jesus, has had to worry about that question, for doing so would lead to or reflect conversion. All Jewish historians have therefore assumed that Jesus was a human being, period. Frequently, Jews have regarded the notion that Jesus was divine as a blasphemous result of the pagan deification of a man. Given this conviction, it was easy for Jewish scholars to apply the negative criterion to the Gospels in order to subtract from them as unhistorical all manifestly Christian traits, but Jewish scholars have generally refrained from applying the negative criterion to the Jewish-sounding materials that remained after the Christian elements were deleted.[10] This more conservative treatment of the de-Christianized Jesus tradition was inevitable, for they could hardly integrate Jesus into Judaism if they disallowed the sayings in which he sounded thoroughly Jewish, just as they could not integrate him into Judaism if they had accepted as genuine those sayings that made him unacceptable to Judaism.

Second, since classical Judaism is shaped by the Talmud and the Midrashim produced by the rabbis, it was natural for Jewish students to claim Jesus for Judaism by relating him positively to the rabbis' predecessors in Jesus' day, the Pharisees. Moreover, since the Jewish study of Jesus was pioneered by liberal or Reform Jews for whom the moral principles of the prophets were more important than the ritual laws of the Pentateuch, it was also natural that these Jewish scholars regarded the Pharisees, especially liberal-minded ones like Hillel, as teachers who combined piety and ethics the way they themselves did. Since much of the Jesus tradition is also concerned with piety and ethics, it was relatively easy for liberal Jewish scholars to integrate Jesus into first-century Pharisaism, for his criticism of

[10] N.B., Kaufmann Kohler is an exception.

the Pharisees was aimed at abuses and abberations, not at Pharisaism itself. Here, too, a few notable examples will have to do.

Joseph Klausner, who in 1922 published the first scholarly life of Jesus in Hebrew, spoke for many of his colleagues when he wrote, "throughout the Gospels there is not one item of ethical teaching which cannot be paralleled either in the Old Testament, the Apocrypha, or in the Talmudic and Midrashic literature of the period near to the time of Jesus."[11] Indeed, "he is wholly explainable by the scriptural and Pharisaic Judaism of his time"—exactly the opposite of what Bousset had said.[12] What is different about Jesus is that he "condensed and concentrated" his ethical teachings, whereas in the rabbinic collections "they are interspersed among more commonplace and worthless matter."[13] Klausner went on to say that "Jesus surpassed Hillel in his ethical ideals," but then adds that "his teaching has not proved possible in practice."[14] In the end Klausner faulted Jesus for not being sufficiently concerned for culture and the national state, and for ignoring "anything concerned with material civilization."[15]

A quarter century later, another Jewish scholar, this time writing in England while supporting himself by working in the post office by day, declared flatly, "in historical reality Jesus was a Pharisee. . . . In the whole of the NT we are unable to find a single historically reliable instance of a religious difference between Jesus and the Pharisaic guild."[16] No one went further in integrating Jesus into liberal Judaism's understanding of Pharisaism than Kaufmann Kohler, the eminent leader of Reform Judaism in America. He cited Jesus' use of the Shema and then observed, "Jesus was a perfect Jew."[17]

The ease with which Jesus was integrated into the Pharisaism of his day begins to be diminished, however, as soon as one admits that Jewish life as a whole became decisively different after the first war against Rome in 66–70 and even more so after the second revolt in 132–135. Since the rabbis began to compile the oldest part of the Talmud, the Mishnah, only after the

---

[11] Joseph Klausner, *Jesus of Nazareth: His Life, Times, and Teaching* (trans. Herbert Danby; London: Allen & Unwin, 1925),384.

[12] Klausner, *Jesus of Nazareth*, 363.

[13] Klausner, *Jesus of Nazareth*, 389.

[14] Klausner, *Jesus of Nazareth*, 397.

[15] Klausner, *Jesus of Nazareth*, 375—matters important for Klausner, who had moved to Jerusalem as a Zionist.

[16] Joseph Winters, *On the Trial of Jesus* (SJ; Berlin: de Gruyter, 1961), 132–33.

[17] Kaufmann Kohler, *Jewish Theology Systematically and Historically Considered* (New York: Macmillan, 1918).

second revolt and then did so with a particular view of Judaism in mind, it is risky to use this material to portray the Pharisaism that Jesus had known. That would be like quoting today's Presbyterians in order to explain a seventeenth-century English Puritan. Jacob Neusner insists that in spite of the role of memory and tradition, scholarship must reckon much more seriously with the effects of the two wars on the way the tradition was codified.

Neusner contends for something else as well. As he sees it, Pharisaism's "central metaphor is the cult"—namely the original temple concern for what is clean and unclean ritually; this implies a distinct ontology, one that emphasizes "regularity, permanence, recurrence." But for the Gospels, the central ontological affirmation is "very disruptive and disintegrative, profoundly historical and even world-denying."[18] Although Neusner refers to the Gospels and not to Jesus himself, his observation is suggestive nonetheless. If Jesus understood the kingdom of God as a God-given irruption into history, then Jesus too would have operated with a disruptive ontology close to that of the Gospels, and then it would be hard to integrate him into Pharisaism—unless the Pharisees too had an apocalyptic, disruptive ontology (which Neusner seems loathe to admit.)

This is, however, precisely one of the disputed points about Pharisaism. Put in more traditional terms, there is a long-standing debate over whether the Pharisees were indeed as nonpolitical as Neusner insists, or whether at least a significant number of them were also intensely political, as deeply committed to the expulsion of the Romans as those later called Zealots. If so, then integrating Jesus into Judaism by calling him a Pharisee might have quite different consequences. And this brings us to the third observation.

The third thing to be observed is that during the past thirty years, some Jewish scholars have changed markedly the way they integrate Jesus into Jewish history. What Klausner missed in Jesus—concern for culture and the nation—these scholars claim to find: a passionate commitment to the liberation of both people and land from Roman tyranny so that Israel could actualize its God-given destiny. If there were two strands of Pharisaism, a quietistic and an activist one, then Jesus belonged to the latter, for he was indeed a religious Zionist. Israeli scholars are not the only ones thinking along these lines for a few Christian students also have insisted from time to time that Jesus was a revolutionary freedom fighter whose quixotic, failed insurrection (the so-called cleansing of the temple) led to his arrest and

---

[18] Jacob Neusner, "The Use of the Later Rabbinic Evidence for the Study of First-Century Pharisaism," in *Approaches to Ancient Judaism: Theory and Practice* (BJS 1; Missoula, Mont.: Scholars Press, 1978), 224–25.

execution; on the whole, however, such a revisionist view of Jesus remained marginal at best. But Israeli scholars take it seriously. What should not be overlooked is this: just as nineteenth-century Protestant liberals found their concern for pure and true religion to have been epitomized in Jesus, so also the twentieth-century folks, who see and value everything in terms of political power, be they Jew or Christian, now see Jesus as a forerunner of themselves. As already noted, in their own ways, the Gospel writers did the same sort of thing when they attributed words to Jesus that actually expressed their own tensions with the synagogue.

To represent this shift toward a Zionist Jesus, I will translate some lines from a book about Jesus by Pinchas Lapide, a rabbi in Frankfurt, Germany, who frequently participates in Christian-Jewish dialogues.

> If Jesus was really the pious, Torah-faithful Jew that the Synoptic Gospels unanimously portray, he can neither have been indifferent politically nor have collaborated treasonably. Only an active anti-Roman attitude is harmonizable with his intense love for Israel. Also his fiery temperament, that often flashes in his controversy speeches, and his dynamism contradict every passivity in the face of the brutal pagan hegemony of Roman power and its intrusive blasphemous idolatry.
>
> For most of today's authors, this patriotic militancy does not preclude a hyper-Jewish deepening of the biblical ethic. To the contrary! If the impatient assailant of heaven, following the footsteps of the Maccabees, wanted to liberate Israel from the heathen yoke, he nonetheless knew that only a national return to the basic values of the Torah could bring the "kingdom of heaven" to a liberated Israel.
>
> Struggle against Rome and return to God were, from the modern Jewish standpoint, the two reciprocally enhancing demands of Jesus.[19]

Like Kaufmann Kohler's Jesus, Pinchas Lapide's too might be called "a perfect Jew"—but of an entirely different sort. Even if, with Israeli writers, one were to see the Jewish rehabilitation of Jesus as the return of the prodigal son from nineteen centuries among Christians, it is not easy to describe the home to which he returned, because the historical problems resist easy solutions. That comment brings us to the next part of this presentation.

## II

Any historian who wants to study and interpret the Jesus of Jewish history faces three interlocking questions (we have already noted the first): (1) given

---

[19] Rabbi Pinchas Lapide, *Der Rabbi von Nazaret: Wandlungen des jüdischen Jesusbildes* (Trier: Spee-Verlag, 1974), 132.

the nature of the sources, Jewish and Christian, what counts as reliable evidence for Jesus?; (2) What got Jesus executed by Rome?; and (3) How does one account for the character of earliest Christianity?

The shift to a Zionist Jesus makes it necessary to say a bit more about the answer to the first question: "What counts for evidence?" As we observed, the negative criterion has been used first of all to identity the manifestly Christian elements in the Jesus traditions so that they can be set aside, thereby leaving a Jewish Jesus. Most of these deleted elements express an early Christian belief about Jesus, whether as Messiah or Son of God, for instance, or as the one whose death was a sacrifice that brought salvation from sin. The shift to a Zionist Jesus has pointed to another sorting out that is required, because the remaining sayings of Jesus point in quite different directions. On the one hand, there are sayings like "Love your enemy," or "Turn the other cheek," or "Blessed are the peacemakers for they shall be called the children of God." All such sayings come under the rubric of "the peaceable Jesus." On the other hand, there are sayings like, "I did not come to bring peace but a sword," and the famous reply to the question whether Jews should pay the tribute tax to Rome, "Give back to Caesar what is Caesar's and give to God what is God's"—which Lapide insists means an uncompromising rupture to the existing political order since every Jew belongs to God, not to Caesar.[20] And then there is the report that during Jesus' last night of freedom he said, "Let him who has no sword sell his mantle and buy one" (Luke 22:36), which if genuine, must have been said previously, when it would have been possible to do so. In any case, when Jesus was arrested that night, one of the disciples did have a sword, and used it to cut off the ear of the high priest's slave.

The issue can be put this way: Did the Christianization of Jesus make him a teacher of nonresistance, thus concealing his political and revolutionary character so that Christians would not endanger themselves? Or, were the militant sayings included by Christianized Jews who themselves were more caught up in anti-Roman passions than he had been? It would be easier to decide which kind of saying counts as evidence for the real Jesus if we knew the extent to which the Book of Revelation, more or less contemporary with the Gospels and full of hatred of Rome, reflects the mind-set of the early Christians who transmitted the Jesus traditions.

The second historical problem concerns Jesus' execution: "What got him killed?" The usual question is: "Who killed Jesus?" This "Who?" question has a fairly clear answer to which puzzles are attached. The answer is:

[20] Lapide, *Der Rabbi von Nazaret*, 47.

the Romans crucified him. The puzzles concern the roles of other people, primarily the priests and the Sanhedrin, that fatal week, including the possible role of Jesus himself. That turns out to be the heart of the "What?" question, which I want to ponder as a historian. I will not try to answer it but to think about what is entailed in trying to answer it. Three brief observations must do.

First, the negative criterion sets aside the straightforward answer in the Gospels: what got Jesus killed was his own sense of vocation to offer his life as a ransom for sin. When that and similar sayings have been set aside from consideration, there is that other saying in which Jesus was determined to go to Jerusalem because that is where prophets met their fate (Luke 13:33). Here, perhaps most of all, is where the negative criterion must be used with great care. As we noted repeatedly, it generally accepts as genuinely from Jesus those sayings that sound neither typically Jewish nor characteristically Christian, and so are therefore distinct, unique, unexpected. Now if it is the case, as often argued, that in Judaism there is no precedent for a messianic figure deliberately offering himself as a ransom or sacrifice for sin, then the problematic sayings appear to have passed the test of the negative criterion with respect to the Jewish tradition, for Jesus would be as original and as unexpected in saying these things as he was in his parables, probably more so. The question of genuineness then shifts to the Christian tradition, some of which did see Jesus as a sacrifice for sin (e.g., Rom 3:24-25). What is by no means clear, however, is whether the gospel sayings were created by Christians and attributed to Jesus in light of Christian convictions, or whether the Gospels put into more specifically Christian language what Jesus might have said or implied in other terms. A Christian paraphrase is not the same as a Christian creation (as can be seen in the summary of Jesus' preaching in Mark 1:14-15). There are many questions whose answers never reach more than a low grade of probability, and this is surely one of them. In any case, once one sets aside the sayings in which Jesus speaks of his impending death in ways that sound suspiciously Christian, one soon begins to speculate about his motives and state of mind and so ends up replacing one unlikelihood with another.

Second, the answer to the question, "What got Jesus killed?" cannot be separated from the answer to the question about the kind of Judaism into which he is to be integrated. Here the Zionist reading of Jesus appears to have the clearest answer: like many other patriots from the time of the Maccabees onward, Jesus was quite willing to do something provocative to trigger an anti-Roman uprising, convinced that God would turn it into victory.

Lapide observes that for this nationalist reading of Jesus, the complete failure of his action, ending with crucifixion between two other insurrectionists usually mislabeled "thieves," no more discredits him than the Roman executions of all other patriots dishonor them. To the contrary, his failure seals his solidarity with all other Jewish martyrs, and thereby enhances his assimilation into what is alleged was the mainline, not a lunatic fringe as Josephus wants his Roman readers to think. However, attractive as this may be, this way of answering the question, "What got Jesus killed?" requires one to rewrite the Gospels, as well as other parts of the NT, and to claim that virtually the entire Jesus tradition transformed a pacific Jesus into a reckless militant one.

On the other hand, those who assimilate Jesus into any nonviolent, quietistic form of Judaism, be it Pharisaism or an alleged Cynic-Stoic dropout, face a quite different puzzle: What was there about Jesus' teaching, represented by the Sermon on the Mount or the parables, that would have been seen by Rome or by the priestly collaborators in Jerusalem to be such a threat that he must be done away with? Was Jesus arrested and executed because the implications of his teaching were understood, or because they were misunderstood? Here too, demonstrating the desired probability eludes us.

The third observation makes explicit what has been implied already, namely, every explanation of what got Jesus killed entails explaining also the character of the earliest Christian community in Jerusalem. Here those who integrate Jesus into a noninsurrectionist form of Judaism appear to have the easier task, because what evidence we have shows that the original church and its leaders, who had been Jesus' followers, were left unmolested and were free to go to the temple and continue to be observant Jews in other ways as well. It is hard to think that a group of insurrection-minded followers was transformed into a peaceful temple-attending community by believing that Jesus had been raised from the dead. It is even harder to believe that Rome, hearing that the Jesus-people now believed he was raised from the dead, would have hesitated to arrest and execute all of them while they were still in the city.

III

I have simplified rather drastically many complex historical questions that have tantalized and frustrated all who have sought to understand Jesus as a Jew of his time, place, and circumstance. I have done so because I am ever more convinced that how one recovers and portrays the past can have consequences that historians themselves might not anticipate. I am equally convinced that what one brings to the study of the sources of the past controls what one finds there more subtly and more surely than we are usually prepared to acknowledge, and that the historical study of Jesus the Jew—whether by Jew or Christian—illustrates this amply. Such comments lead me to the following reflections:

(1) Given the brutal history that unites Jews and Christians, the figure of Jesus will continue to divide all Jews from all those Christians who are unwilling to substitute the Jesus of history for the Christ of their faith.

(1) Even those Christians who abandon the traditional Christ of faith for the Jesus of history will not necessarily find themselves viewing Jesus in the same way as Jews do, because another fault line cuts across both communities. As a result, some Christians and some Jews will be on one side, and some Christians and some Jews will be on the other. This fault line separates those who find the Jesus of history to have been a nonviolent preacher of God's kingdom from those who hold that the kingdom's coming somehow made him an insurrectionist freedom fighter. This fault line raises issues that are so basic to both Christians and Jews that we will have enough to work on together for a long time.

(3) The kind of Jew Jesus probably was matters more to Christians than it does to Jews. For Jews, what is at stake in a historically accurate profile of Jesus is fairness to a man whose role in Christianity made him persona non grata among his own people. Since Judaism does not pivot on Jesus, or on any historical individual, it can locate him in whatever kind of Judaism the evidence calls for and not be affected by the result. Judaism has nothing at all at stake in the kind of Jew he was. Not so for Christians. Because he remains the heart of Christianity, they need to know what kind of Jew he really was. The more they see that, the more they find that he does not become smaller but greater.

# 5

# Jesus and Judaism in the New Testament

The topic "Jesus and Judaism" turns out to be far more complex than we expect. For one thing, getting a fair and accurate picture of Judaism as Jesus knew it has proven to be difficult, partly because historians now have considerably more data with which to work and partly because the growing sophistication in the use of the data has made untenable the simpler generalizations of previous generations. Moreover, the historical task of recovering an unbiased picture of Jesus from the Gospels has also grown more difficult because in recent years scholars have become more alert to the complex and subtle factors that influenced the ways in which the New Testament writers dealt with Jesus' relation to Judaism.

Four preliminary remarks about the title of this essay will expose important dimensions of the subject matter. Then I will look briefly at three NT writers. Some general observations will conclude the discussion.

The first preliminary remark has to do with the word "Judaism." The word *Ioudaismos* was coined by Greek-speaking Jews to identify the Jewish religion and culture as a whole, as a discrete and distinctive phenomenon in the Greco-Roman world. In 2 and 4 Maccabees, it is used to speak of a religious culture as a whole, as if from the point of view of the outsider. This usage is also found in the letters of Bishop Ignatius, who, writing around 115 of our era, uses it as the opposite of *Christianismos*. In the NT only Paul uses it, and only in Galatians (1:13-14), to speak of his pre-Christian life.[1] Never does the NT use the word "Judaism" in relation to Jesus. "Jesus and Judaism" is our own modern formulation. We use it, nonetheless, because it is

---

[1] See Hans Dieter Betz, *Galatians: A Commentary on Paul's Letter to the Churches in Galatia* (Hermeneia; Philadelphia: Fortress, 1979), 79 n. 105, for references.

a customary and convenient way of identifying a field of inquiry within which one can differentiate various kinds of "Judaisms" in the NT era.

Next and second, it is important to distinguish what is entailed in "Jesus and Judaism in the New Testament" from what is involved in "Jesus in Judaism." Because almost everything we can learn about Jesus is derived from the NT, it is easy to assume that the two topics are virtually interchangeable. In fact, it is just this assumption that has caused considerable mischief. So it is essential to see, albeit briefly, why the difference between the two topics should not be blurred, even if they overlap.

What comes into focus here is the difference between historical exegesis and historical reconstruction. "Jesus and Judaism in the New Testament" attempts to explain, understand, and interpret the relation of Jesus to Judaism as it appears in the NT texts. It is an historical enterprise insofar as one attempts to account for what these texts say (or imply) about the subject matter by placing them in their respective historical contexts. Whether their treatments of the subject matter are consistent with each other, complete, or correct (consonant with all the evidence) is another matter. In contrast, "Jesus in Judaism" attempts to explain, understand, and interpret the figure of Jesus by placing him as accurately as possible within the historical phenomenon of "Judaism." To do so, one must reconstruct both "Jesus" and "Judaism" by assembling as much reliable data, usually derived from a variety of sources, as possible.

To simplify: the former, "Jesus and Judaism in the New Testament," asks, "What does the NT say happened?," the latter, "Jesus in Judaism," asks, "What really happened?"; or "What, if any, is the difference between the report and the event (to the extent that we can reconstruct it)?" In principle, all sources (texts, inscriptions, coins, archaeological evidence, etc.) should be interpreted before one derives historically reliable evidence from them; their purposes, limitations, and biases need to be taken into account lest one simply repeat what they say.

Third, having distinguished the two topics, it is essential to note briefly that the relation between them has a particular history, one that we inherit. Ever since the beginnings of modern critical historiography in the Enlightenment, historians have been "professional skeptics"—they have refused to accept as "fact" any report until it has been tested. Consequently, historians pursuing the theme of "Jesus and Judaism" doubted, as a matter of principle, that what the NT said was historically accurate until it could be shown to be probably true. Inevitably, considerable doubt arose whether the NT portrait was historically correct. Moreover, one motive driving the historical study of Jesus has been the conviction that the truth of Christianity would have a firmer foundation if it rested on solid facts rather than on reports from the texts. This suggested, at least to some, that "the real Jesus"[2] was to be found in Judaism rather than in Christianity, which allegedly made a god out of a Jew.[3] In other words, the older liberal historical-critical study of Jesus drove a wedge between the Christian interpretation of Jesus in the NT and Jesus himself; the "historical Jesus" was the Jesus in Judaism.

Those who promoted the "historical Jesus" as the surer foundation for Christian faith in him did not suspect the dilemma they were creating. The more Jesus was painted into the Jewish landscape the less he stood out, and the less he stood out the less reason there was to single him out as the one who was decisive. So the pressure was on to show historically that at every point that mattered, Jesus transcended Judaism. He could be in Judaism but not really of it. In other words, in order to show historically that Jesus merits our faith, scholars were driven to show that Jesus was superior to the Judaism that surrounded him. To do so, they often created an unhistorical picture of Judaism as a religion of either harsh and barren legalism or of overheated apocalyptic illusions.[4] The reason for this is not simply that Christian scholars were incorrigibly anti-Semitic. The real reason lies in the idea that a more sound Christian religion could be based on facts that were established historically. Once one decides to base faith on facts, then one's

[2] The allusion is to the title of Chester C. McCown's survey of the history of attempts to recover the Jesus of history from the Gospels and other evidence: *The Search for the Real Jesus* (New York: Scribner's, 1940).

[3] E.g., Maurice Casey's study of the development of early Christology declares flatly, "It took some 50 or 60 years to turn a Jewish prophet into a Greek God" (*From Jewish Prophet to Gentile God* [Louisville, Ky.: Westminster John Knox, 1991], 97). See my review in *Interpretation* 47 (1993): 413–14.

[4] Günther Bornkamm's influential *Jesus of Nazareth* (New York: Harper, 1960; German original, 1956) is a convenient example of this misrepresentation. He compares Judaism with "a soil hardened and barren through its age-long history and tradition [i.e., legalism], yet a volcanic, eruptive ground, out of whose cracks and crevices breaks forth again and again the fire of a burning expectation [i.e., apocalypse]." They both have the same origin: "a faith in a God beyond the world and history." Given God as distant in such a Judaism, the decisive, historically demonstrable difference in Jesus is that he makes God present. "There is nothing in contemporary Judaism which corresponds to the immediacy with which he teaches." In fact, "the reality of God and the authority of his will are always directly present, and are fulfilled in him" (55–56, 57). For an extensive critique, see my "Bornkamm's *Jesus of Nazareth* Revisited," *JR* 49 (1969): 1–17. In the 10th, revised edition (not translated), Bornkamm acknowledged the force of my critique (*Jesus von Nazareth* [Urban Taschenbücher; Stuttgart: Kohlhammer, 1975]; Epilogue, esp. 209–10) and observed that his intent was to express Jesus' own critique

allegiance to Jesus must be based on facts about Jesus, and the only way to justify loyalty to Jesus instead of Hillel or some other teacher is to show that Jesus is better, more profound, more spiritual, less parochial, and free of apocalyptic notions about the end of the world.

Fortunately, the prejudicial portrayal of Judaism is no longer credible in contemporary scholarship, though one can still find it. Fortunate also is the discovery that history cannot establish the superiority of Jesus. This means that allegiance to Jesus cannot be based on the results of history, because the Jesus of history is ambiguous.[5] This means that whoever follows Jesus does so because this Jewish figure is interpreted in a particular way. Without this interpretive framework, Jesus in Judaism is just another interesting first-century Palestinian teacher from whom we may learn. In other words, the decisiveness of Jesus for faith becomes visible and plausible only within an interpretive framework that includes and transcends history without canceling it.

This brings us to the fourth preliminary remark. The most important frameworks for understanding Jesus' relation to Judaism are those in the NT. They are not the only ones. There is a Muslim framework that regards Jesus as a prophet, just as there is a Hindu framework that sees him as one of a series of avatars or manifestations of an eternal principle. While it would be useful to compare these interpretive frameworks, I will not do so. My aim is to help us understand and appreciate three interpretive frameworks in the NT. They will invite us to think afresh about Jesus and Judaism.

I

The Gospel according to Matthew has the reputation of being the most Jewish Gospel in the NT while at the same time being an anti-Jewish Gospel like John. I continue to think that Matthew was written about 90 C.E. in the general area around Antioch, where there was a large Jewish community. Twenty years before, Judaism underwent its great shock when the Romans captured Jerusalem. As a result, the temple was burned and the priestly Sadducees disappeared from the scene, as did the Essenes at Qumran who first hid their scrolls in the desert caves. The one group that survived was the Pharisees, who were now consolidating their influence and laying the

---

of Judaism, which admittedly offends Jews. Unfortunately, Bornkamm also claimed to be writing as a historian, and it is precisely the historian's view of Judaism that was made to serve apologetic interests.

[5] This point is emphasized in my *A Future for the Historical Jesus* (2nd rev. ed.; Philadelphia: Fortress, 1981).

foundations for the Rabbinic Judaism that followed. Consequently, Matthew's readers confronted a Judaism that was closing its ranks, forcing Jewish Christians to choose between their Jewish heritage and Christian identity. What Jesus predicts in Matthew 10 actually refers to Matthew's own time: Christians will be flogged in the synagogue, brothers will betray brothers, parents betray children, and children the parents (10:18-21). Matthew no longer expects that the Jewish people will believe that Jesus is the Messiah.

The Gospel of Matthew used traditions about Jesus, who lived forty years before the fall of Jerusalem, but shaped them into an account about Jesus for use in a church that faced a new form of Judaism as a result of that disaster.[6] This means that Matthew used material about Jesus in Judaism in order to write a gospel about Jesus and Judaism. As a result, the Matthean Jesus stands over against Judaism more or less as the Matthean readers do. Matthew's readers know a hostile synagogue but may have never seen a Sadducee; and the Pharisees they know differed from those mentioned in the stories about Jesus. Three questions will bring into focus the effect of Matthew's situation on the way it portrays Jesus and Judaism.

1. *How does Matthew portray the Judaism to which Jesus is related?* To begin with, one would never detect from Matthew that in Jesus' day Judaism had many faces, or, as we would say, was pluralistic. If we had only Matthew we would not surmise that there were Essenes either in the Palestinian villages or west of the Dead Sea. Nor would we guess that much of Palestinian Jewry was deeply Hellenized. Matthew is simply not interested in presenting Jesus in an historically accurate and balanced picture of Judaism. Moreover, apart from Jesus' parents, Jesus himself, and his disciples, Matthew gives us only three names of individual Jews: John the Baptist, Joseph of Arimathea, and Caiaphas the High Priest. With but one exception (8:19), Jewish leaders appear in groups of unspecified size: scribes, Pharisees, Sadducees, priests, and chief priests. Matthew does not explain who they are or what distinguishes one group from another. Either Matthew assumes that the readers know enough about Palestine sixty years before to need no information, or it regards the differences as relatively unimportant because all these groups represent the religious establishment. The latter is the more likely. In other words, the evangelist Matthew is not ignorant of the differences within the Judaism of Jesus' day but generally indifferent to them because his eye is on

---

[6] For an instructive discussion, see J. Andrew Overman, *Matthew's Gospel and Formative Judaism: The Social World of the Matthean Community* (Minneapolis: Fortress, 1990).

the conflict between Jesus and the leaders of Judaism, a conflict that intensifies as the story develops.[7]

Further, Matthew shows Jesus in relation to three institutions of Judaism: the synagogue, the temple, and the Sanhedrin. Several times we read that Jesus preached in the synagogues (9:35; 13:54), but we learn nothing about the synagogue itself or what Jesus said there. What we do learn is that healing a withered hand in the synagogue on the Sabbath triggered a plot against Jesus (12:9-14). About the temple too Matthew tells us nothing. It is, however, the place where Jesus' confrontation with the Jewish leaders reaches its climax. In Matthew, Jesus not only expelled those who sold what was needed to maintain the sacrificial system, but healed people and on the following day silenced the opposition (21:12–22:46). Having made his point Jesus left the temple and pronounced its impending destruction (24:1--2). The Sanhedrin appears only in connection with the trial of Jesus (26:59), though it is twice mentioned in a saying of Jesus (5:22; 10:17).

Of the Jewish festivals, the only one that is mentioned is the Passover, because this figures prominently in the Passion story. About New Year, Day of Atonement, Pentecost, Succoth, we hear nothing at all. Sabbath is mentioned because it is the necessary setting for the conflict over its observance, but about its role in Judaism Matthew is silent.

To sum up, what Matthew says about Judaism is virtually nothing. Of its multifaceted character he mentions only those elements that are necessary for the story of Jesus' conflicts with the religious leaders—a conflict that does not end even with Jesus' death (28:11-15). Matthew is more sympathetic to the Jewish people; for he not only portrays the crowds as responding to Jesus (9:35-38; 15:29-31), but reports that he had compassion for them. Still, before the story is over, the leadership corrupts the crowds, so that they join in the demand for Jesus' death. At the climax of this opposition, Matthew reports they shouted, "Let him be crucified!" (27:23) and that when Pilate pronounced him innocent, "all the people answered, 'His blood be on us and on our children' " (27:25). In other words, in Matthew, Jesus is ever more alienated from Judaism.

2. *Is Matthew interested only in Jesus versus Judaism? Is there only opposition?* That would be too simple, too stark, and without enough subtlety. This judgment rests on two considerations. First is the fact that Matthew

---

[7] See Jack Dean Kingsbury, "The Developing Conflict between Jesus and the Jewish Leaders in Matthew's Gospel: A Literary-Critical Study," *CBQ* 49 (1987): 57–73.

emphasizes more than any other NT book that Jesus fulfills Scripture and Israel's hope. From the "begats" onward, Matthew reminds the reader of this theme. Seven times Matthew actually points out that what we have just read happened as the fulfillment of Scripture (1:22; 2:15, 23; 4:14-16; 8:17; 12:17-21; 13:35; 21:4). This evangelist also shows that Jesus is like Moses, first as a baby who was nearly killed by a king (2:13-18) and then by bringing God's law on a mountain (chaps. 5–7). Moreover, Matthew's Jesus explicitly limits the mission of the disciples to the lost sheep of the house of Israel and tells them to avoid the Gentiles, of whom there were many in the Galilee of the day (10:5). When Jesus rides into Jerusalem on an ass' colt, he comes as the king spoken of by the prophet Zechariah, and over his thorn-crowned head on the cross is nailed the charge: "King of the Jews." Indeed, the language of the Passion story echoes again and again the words of the Old Testament, for Matthew has told the story of Jesus as the one in whom the words of Scripture become event.

That "Jesus versus Judaism" is too simple is clear also from a second consideration: Matthew's Jesus says unambiguously what God's will is. And this will is nothing other than what the Scripture of Judaism has also said. This is especially clear in chapter 15, in which the Pharisees and scribes come from Jerusalem, the center of Judaism, to ask why the disciples transgress the traditions of the elders and do not wash their hands when they eat. This is not a matter of eating with dirty hands but with hands that have not been ritually cleansed. (The Pharisees were taking the rules that applied to the priests in the temple and applying them to themselves, laymen, and to all the people, so that the whole nation would be a kingdom of priests, a holy people, just as the Bible said; Exod 19:6.) Instead of answering the question put to him, Jesus takes the initiative and attacks the Pharisees for emphasizing the traditions of the elders, the oral Torah. The Pharisees believed that the unwritten Torah, the oral tradition, was as much a part of God's revelation at Sinai as what was written. But not Jesus. He accuses them of annulling God's word in order to hold on to the traditions (15:6).

In chapter 23, Matthew has Jesus affirm that the scribes and Pharisees sit on Moses' seat—that is, they interpret the law of Moses. So do what they say but do not do as they do (23:1-3). In the following sevenfold denunciation of the scribes and Pharisees as "hypocrites," Jesus accuses them of missing the point of the Scriptures that they do know. Again and again he makes it clear that he does not bring a new law of God, but states the meaning of the law they already had but obscured by tradition and self-serving interpretation. It is Matthew's Jesus who says that he did not come to destroy the law and the prophets but to fulfill them (5:17-20). In a word, in Matthew Jesus opposes Judaism in the name of God's will in its own Scripture. In so doing, he does not want to displace Judaism but to bring it back to its real center.[8]

3. *What, then, is Jesus' relation to Judaism in Matthew?* Simply this: because Jesus is the one in whom Scripture is fulfilled, the King of Israel, the Wisdom of God, and the Son of God, Judaism's rejection of Jesus is the rejection of its own fulfillment and future. As the conclusion to the parable says, the kingdom will be taken away from them and given to others (21:44). In other words, from Matthew's angle the relation of Jesus to Judaism is tragic. Because Jesus *in* Judaism was rejected, he became the doom of the Judaism that rejected him.

This perspective, combined with the fact that early Christians used those traditions about Jesus that helped them in their own conflicts with Judaism, explains why Matthew emphasizes the points of tension between Jesus and the Judaism of his day. All points of continuity are bypassed, leaving us to guess (probably rightly) that he observed Sabbath and festivals, as well as food laws. One can hardly expect a community that is defining itself over against another group to have emphasized the continuity between its founder and the current opposition. Even so, in Matthew the theme of Jesus and Judaism is played out within Judaism. Matthew's Jesus stands over against Judaism just like the Old Testament prophets stood over against the religion of Israel.

## II

The Gospel according to John, interestingly enough, comes not only from the same time (about 90–95 C.E.) but, I believe, also from the same place: Antioch or its vicinity. Both gospels reflect the growing tension between the church and the synagogue. What is distinctive about John, however, is that the narrator speaks of Jesus' opponents as "the Jews"—as if Jesus himself were not a Jew. Jesus distances himself from Judaism when he refers to the Torah as "your law" (John 8:17; 10:34). Recent study of John, as of Matthew, has explored the history and situation of the community in which this gospel was formed and thereby has come to emphasize its Jewish character and context. It appears that the Christian Jews had experienced increased hostility from the synagogue that at first tolerated them and had recently been excluded from it (reflected in the anachronistic statement in

---

[8] This is why Samuel Sandmel thinks that Matthew is appealing to Jews over the heads of the religious establishment. Sandmel, *Anti-Semitism in the New Testament?* (Philadelphia: Fortress, 1978), 69.

9:22, and in Jesus' prediction in 16:2). Jesus' disputes with "the Jews" therefore reflect this later alienation.[9] At the same time, John retains its Jewish character because many of its traditions are traceable to their Palestinian origins. Some of these traditions contain accurate local information (e.g., the pool in Jerusalem, 5:2-3); others use language that is thoroughly Jewish, such as the epithet "Samaritan" hurled at Jesus in 8:48 or "sons of light" in 12:36, which is common in the Dead Sea Scrolls.[10]

Again, we begin by asking how Judaism is portrayed here. Generally speaking, we learn more about Judaism in John than in Matthew. Also in John we meet Pharisees (one of whom is named Nicodemus) and priests, but we do not hear of Sadducees any more than we do of Essenes. We encounter Samaritans and learn both that they do not regard Jerusalem as the legitimate place of worship and that Jews have no dealings with Samaritans (4:9, 21). As in Matthew, we hear also about synagogue and temple. Although Jesus tells the high priest, "I have always taught in synagogues and in the temple" (18:20), only once does John place Jesus' teaching in the synagogue (almost as an afterthought, 6:59), but he has Jesus teach in the temple several times (7:28-31; 8:20; 10:22-30). What distinguishes John, however, is the fact that he organizes the story around Jewish festivals: three Passovers (2:19-22; 6:4; 12:55), Tabernacles (7:1), Hanukkah (10:22), and an unnamed "feast" (5:1). But again, New Year, Day of Atonement, and Pentecost are missing. We learn also some details about Jewish customs—the water jars at Cana are for ritual purification (2:6); the Passover-Sabbath is a special Sabbath (19:31); Jews were concerned about not being ritually impure for Passover (18:28). We learn that one may circumcise on the Sabbath (7:22) because the oral Torah allows it. Such details, coupled with the many place names, give John's reader a more vivid picture of the setting of Jesus' words and deeds than Matthew provides.

In John, Jesus never uses the word "hypocrite" to denounce the Pharisees. They are portrayed as having great influence, so much that even the unnamed authorities who believed in Jesus would not admit it "for fear of the Pharisees . . . lest they should be put out of the synagogue" (12:42).

---

[9] See the pathbreaking work by J. Louis Martyn, *History and Theology in the Fourth Gospel* (Nashville: Abingdon, 1968; 2nd ed., 1979), followed by Raymond E. Brown, *The Community of the Beloved Disciple* (New York: Paulist Press, 1979), which reconstructs the history of the Johannine community into the second century.

[10] The impact of the Scrolls has been emphasized by James H. Charlesworth, "How the Dead Sea Scrolls Have Revolutionized Our Understanding of the Gospel of John," *BRev* 9 (1993): 27–38.

Throughout, the Pharisees and chief priests together plot against Jesus (7:32; 11:47, 57; 18:3), but it is the Pharisees who oppose him most resolutely. Indeed, they speak for the Jewish religion and the Jews. In fact, a basic feature of this Gospel is that Jews, Judaism, Pharisees, and priests all flow into one another, with little differentiation.

The Johannine Jesus stands over against this relatively undifferentiated entity of Judaism and Jews, and the conclusion of the prologue states the reason: "the law was given through Moses; grace and truth came through Jesus Christ"—as if there were no grace or truth in the law (1:17). Yet Moses is said to have written about Christ (1:45). So the Jews are indicted for not really believing Moses, even if they claim to be his disciples (9:28); if they had been, they would have believed Jesus too (5:45-46). It is not simply that under Pharisaic influence they distorted the law. The resistance to the claims of Jesus and to his word shows that no one keeps the law (7:19).

So in John the issue between Jesus and Judaism is not the right way to obey Moses and achieve righteousness, as in Matthew. In fact, righteousness in this sense is not part of the Johannine vocabulary. The issue between them is Jesus himself. In a word, in John the Jews and Judaism represent the unbelieving world as it refuses to acknowledge Jesus as the Creator, the Logos incarnate, who is the interpreter of God (1:18). Therefore, what in Matthew appears at the end—the self-condemnation of the Jews in calling for Jesus' death—is the thread that runs through the whole story in John. One cannot reject the incarnate Logos without incurring self-condemnation. This is why John shows the Pharisees and the Jews as repeatedly either misunderstanding what Jesus says or flatly rejecting it.

By any ordinary criteria the Jews are right. When Jesus claims to be the bread from heaven, they say that they know very well where he comes from because they know his parents (6:41-42). When he says that whoever eats this bread will live forever, why should not the Jews ask, "How can this man give us his flesh to eat?" (6:52)? When he says that they cannot go where he is going, why should they not wonder whether he is planning a trip to the diaspora (7:32-35) or even whether he is planning suicide (8:21-22)? In other words, the Jews misunderstand because they take Jesus' words at face value, while he uses them in a different sense, a sense that John's Christian readers understand. By this literary device—double meaning—the Gospel of John underlines the disparity between the perspective of Jesus and the world.

Moreover, in John, Jesus is often the aggressor, attacking the Jews—the sharpest charge being that they are of the devil (8:44). We can sympathize not only with the Jews of John but also with the Jews of today, who are offended by such a Jesus. Yet it must be said that because the Jews represent the unbelieving world, the Johannine Jesus would have said the same things about Greeks if the incarnation had occurred in Greece. If someone today were to claim for himself what John's Jesus claims, we would scarcely be less offended. We might not crucify him, but we might have him put into an institution.

The force of these observations is clear. The gospel is written in such a way that the reader of John faces the same decision about Jesus as did the Jews. Is he who he claims to be, and does he give what he claims to give, eternal life? Getting more historical information about Jesus, his family life, his education, or the context in which he lived does not make answering that question easier. John does not want us to correct the portrait of Jesus with historical facts, or even less to pity the Jews for not seeing who Jesus really is, but rather wants us to see ourselves in them, so that we are as confronted by the incarnate Logos as they were.

## III

In moving from Matthew and John to Paul, we not only step forty years closer to Jesus but change from narrative to analysis and argument. We look at an interpreter who was a contemporary of Jesus (though they seem never to have met) and who had been a zealous advocate of that form of Judaism that in Matthew and John produced Jesus' most persistent critics and foes, Pharisaism (Phil 3:4-6). Moreover, we recall that one of the points at issue between them was Jesus' rejection of the oral traditions, the unwritten law. Paul himself writes to the Galatians that he had been so extremely zealous for these traditions that he had tried to destroy the church before it got rooted too deeply (Gal 1:13-16). It is interesting to speculate what Paul the zealous Pharisee and Jesus would have said to one another had they met. Such speculation, however, I leave to novelists. Still, we expect that this ex-Pharisee would have a good deal to say about Jesus and Pharisaic Judaism. Of all the writers in the NT, he would know best where the shoe had pinched. In fact, however, he says not a word about our topic; at the same time, what he does say is important for it.

Paul wrote in the 50s, about a decade before the revolt against Rome that ended with the destruction of the temple. He seems not to have anticipated this uprising, to which Matthew and John could look back. Therefore there was nothing on Paul's horizon that he could regard as God's punishment of the Jews for rejecting Jesus. What Paul wrestles with in Romans 9–11 is the Jews' rejection of the gospel, not of Jesus. There is only one

passage in which it looks like Paul blames the Jews for Jesus' death and sees
in their fate God's punishment, namely, 1 Thessalonians 2:14-16. But I am
among those who regard this as a later addition to the text, a view not held
by everyone. In any case, in Paul's day the lines between church and synagogue were not yet hard. Jews who believed that Jesus was the Messiah were
still a sect within Judaism. The kind of expulsion from the synagogue that
John and Matthew assume had not yet been experienced widely. Above all,
Paul wrote for Christians in Anatolia, Greece, and Rome, and most of his
readers were Gentiles who, we may assume, had little knowledge of Judaism
in Palestine. The Judaism they knew was that of the Hellenistic synagogue,
which attracted Gentiles who accepted Jewish monotheism and ethics, but
not necessarily the Jewish rituals.

So it is understandable that whereas Matthew and John, who work with
traditions about Jesus, give at least some glimpses into the Judaism that Jesus
knew, Paul says not a word about it. Because the evangelists write the story
of Jesus' ministry, they must deal with his relation to Judaism because it is
unavoidable; since Paul does not write a story but interprets the meaning of
Jesus into new situations of his largely Gentile churches, he does not need to
deal with the topic directly—though at certain points he might have.

If we gather up the scattered references to Jesus in the seven undoubt-
edly genuine letters,[11] we get something like this: Jesus was a descendant of
David, born into Judaism ("under the law," Gal 4:4). He exercised his ministry
as a "servant of the circumcision" (Rom 15:8). Whether Paul knew that Judas
betrayed Jesus depends on how one translates the Greek verb *paredothē* in
1 Corinthians 11:23, where Paul repeats the tradition of the Lord's Supper.
The customary translation is "in the night when he was betrayed," but it
can also be rendered as "in the night he was handed over"—that is, by God,
to death. The same tradition has Jesus say that "this cup is the new covenant in my blood"—that is, in my death. A few chapters later, Paul repeats
another tradition, which says that "Christ died for our sins in accordance
with the scriptures" (1 Cor 15:3)." Paul knew, of course, that Jesus was crucified, that his body was buried, and that on the third day he was raised from

---

[11] The New Testament contains thirteen letters that claim Paul as their author. Because
of their differences in vocabulary, style, and content, few scholars today regard all of them
as genuinely from Paul. There is, however, agreement that Romans, 1 and 2 Corinthians,
Galatians, Philippians, 1 Thessalonians, and Philemon are genuine. There is wide, but not
universal, agreement that 1 and 2 Timothy and Titus were written much later by a disciple of
Paul. There is considerable disagreement over the genuineness of Ephesians, Colossians, and
2 Thessalonians.

the dead, as the old tradition also says (1 Cor 15:3-5). Of Jesus' teachings, he mentions only a few, one forbidding divorce (1 Cor 7:10-11) and the other that those who preach the gospel should get their living from it (1 Cor 9:14). (Some scholars find many more echoes of Jesus' teaching than these two.) Paul's letters have no reference to Jesus' preaching the kingdom of God, not a single hint that he had ever been in conflict with the Pharisees òr priests, not a single miracle story, not even one about healing on the Sabbath. Even when Paul discusses what a Christian may or may not eat (1 Cor 8, 10; Rom 14–15), he does not mention that Jesus too dealt with ritual-impurity or the possibility of being defiled by not observing the rules for ritual purity. In a word, Paul never mentions the message of Jesus or the Judaism in which it functioned. How do we explain this?

We cannot retrace Paul's thinking; the steps by which he came to his conclusions are his secret. What we can do, however, is to grasp his thought in such a way that we can understand why he did not seem to be interested in Jesus' own tensions with Judaism.

For Paul, the pivot on which the Christian understanding turns is Jesus' cross and resurrection. In his view, resurrection is not resuscitation. The coming alive again of a corpse is not resurrection, because it must die again. Rather, for Paul resurrection is the radical transformation of one's psychosomatic existence. Closely associated with it was the idea that the resurrection was one of the things to happen at the end, with the arrival of the age to come, the radical alternative to all of history. Today many of us have trouble with the idea of resurrection as such, wondering whether such a thing is possible. Paul's question, however, was whether it had happened in one case only—that of the crucified Jesus. If it had, then the new age had dawned. Moreover, the new age was, by definition, that state of affairs in which sin and death are overcome.

Moreover, for Paul sin and death enslave the self. In Paul's view, the human predicament is not that we commit sins and transgressions, violate rules of behavior. Rather, because we are human beings we are subject to sin and death before we commit any sin or transgression. Consequently, Paul is not interested in talking about individual sins and forgiveness of sins. What interests him is redemption, emancipation from the malign fate of sin and death. This is a human predicament, not a Jewish or Greek one. It is clear to Paul that obedience to the law of God cannot redeem the self from sin because the law makes us aware of sin (Rom 3:20). In fact, he implies that "law" is something to which we are also in bondage, be it the law of Moses or a Gentile moral law. For Paul, law is a structure of obligation.

In the case of the law of Moses, it was not an eternal law anyway, as the Pharisees taught, but something that God gave through Moses (Gal 3:17) in order to deal with human sin, but in the last analysis it is not able to do so. Sin is more powerful than law (Rom 8:3). Nor can obeying the law deal with death, even if the law were obeyed perfectly. The only way to be liberated from this bondage is by participating in the one event in which God broke the power of sin and death—Jesus and his resurrection. Whoever believes that God resurrected Jesus and is baptized becomes a participant in Christ, and whoever does this is emancipated from the tyranny of sin and death even though one still commits sins and must die (Rom 6:5-11). Paul can also put this in a different idiom and say that whoever entrusts his or her life to God on the basis of the gospel is rightly related to God (i.e., "justified"), or reconciled with God, thereby overcoming the hostility between creature and Creator (Rom 5:1, 9-11).

This very abbreviated summary of Paul's thought about redemption is enough to show why Paul was not interested in Jesus' conflicts with the Pharisees over the right way to obey the law. For Paul, we are not redeemed from sin and death by following Jesus, by heeding his teachings, nor are we freed from the tyranny of law as a way of life by imitating Jesus' own relation to the law. The only thing that frees us is trusting the gospel that God raised Jesus from the dead and participating in him by baptism. This is why for Paul Jesus is not a wise man, or a new Moses with a new law, or even the right interpretation of the old law, as for Matthew. That would still be law. In other words, redemption does not depend on what Jesus said and did or on our doing as he had said and done. Rather redemption depends on what God has done through Jesus' cross and resurrection to bring on the new age.

We can see why Paul treats the theme of "Jesus and Judaism" in a highly dialectical way. On the one hand, for Paul the phrase "Jesus and Judaism" makes sense not only because he knows that Jesus was a Jew, but also because he believes that Jesus is the Christ, the Messiah, the one in whom God's promise to Israel was kept. On the other hand, Paul became convinced that this promise keeping will extend the benefits (salvation) to the Gentiles, because Christ's resurrection signaled the coming of the new age for all creation. Those who believed that this has occurred and were made participants in Christ by baptism are redeemed from bondage to sin and death, whoever they may be. This redemption is not possible by obedience to Judaism's law. Moreover, Paul knows that Gentiles could become converts to Judaism (as in fact some did) and so become beneficiaries of God's promise to Abraham. However, that would not redeem them from sin and death any more than being obedient to the Torah would redeem Jews. By believing the good news about Jesus and being baptized, both Jew and Gentile were redeemed, both made recipients of God's promise and both made real children of Abraham (Gal 3:7, 14). Further, the fact that the Jesus-event occurred in Judaism does not make obedience to Judaism's Torah mandatory for all, but rather the opposite: redemption now is through faith and baptism.

In other words, Paul offers us an entirely different way of thinking about Jesus' relation to Judaism. It is different not only from that of Matthew and John, but also from our own concern to see the significance of Jesus by locating him historically in Judaism. For Paul, one discerns the saving significance of Jesus by thinking through the meaning of the Jesus-event as a whole, in its relation to Israel and Scripture *and* in relation to the human condition. Theologically, I believe that Paul's way is best.

## IV

It is clear, to begin with, that none of the NT authors we have looked at is interested in presenting a fair, historically accurate picture of Jesus in Judaism. Instead, each in his own way is interested in distinguishing Jesus from Judaism while at the same time insisting that he was part of it. None of them suggests that Jesus' Jewishness is something that must be overcome. Of the three writers we noted, only Paul's interpretive framework would be congenial to a historically accurate picture of Jesus' relation to Judaism, because while the significance of Jesus for the human condition does not depend on an accurate historical account of Jesus' ministry, it is congenial with it. In the case of Matthew and John, however, insisting on a historically sound picture of Jesus in Judaism, as we understand it, would require a complete rewriting of their gospels.

Must we, then, choose between a quest for an accurately reconstructed past (Jesus in Judaism) and the exegesis of the Gospels as we have them? By no means. Not if we think through the function of each of these enterprises.

I continue to believe that historically sound information about Jesus in Judaism is important not only with regard to Jewish-Christian relations, but even more with regard to the Christian community itself. Sound historical reconstruction of the past is a major way we have of testing all the things people say about Jesus. The conclusion of Matthew's Passion story suggests that he faced the same problem in his day. In any case, in our time we justify our own thought and action by appealing to Jesus—what he said and did, how he acted, and what he intended. A historically sound reconstruction of Jesus in Judaism is the only way we have of assessing whether these appeals are valid. For example, to justify our own revolutionary activity by appealing to Jesus the revolutionary is valid only if we can establish the probability that he was a revolutionary. In other words, we need the historical Jesus in Judaism to keep us honest.

Furthermore, keeping ourselves honest includes coming to terms with those elements of Matthew and John that are not historically accurate reports but that reflect the results of the growing tension between church and synagogue. That means coming to terms with our own past, with our own Christian history that forgot that the Matthean and Johannine picture had a particular historical context and is not constitutive of the gospel itself.

Interestingly enough, it is precisely the concern for our honesty and integrity that requires us also to interpret carefully the Gospels we have, which accent Jesus and Judaism. Why does Matthew, writing for a church that is increasingly Gentile, emphasize so much the difference between Jesus and the Pharisees? It is not only to account for Jesus' execution. He also emphasizes Jesus' criticism of the Pharisees because he sees the same dangers within the church. In other words, for Matthew the abuses of Pharisaism that Jesus attacks lurk also in the Christian. To miss this not only distorts the past, but fosters illusions about ourselves.

Finally, the interpretive frameworks of John and Paul, while quite different, nonetheless show that the formulation "Jesus and Judaism" is essential theologically if the integrity of Christianity is to be preserved. What is at stake here is not only the truth about Jesus but the truth about ourselves. In John's case, it has to do with ourselves as creatures who prefer darkness to light because our deeds are evil (John 3:19). That insight is valid only because a Jesus who confronts us as radically as the Johannine Jesus confronted the Johannine Jews is able to provide the radical alternative we need. In Paul's case, it has to do with ourselves as enslaved to sin and death. To the extent that insight is valid, only a Jesus who is God's act is able to redeem us. In this context what matters is not our agreement with John or Paul, but recognizing that an adequate theological grasp of the meaning of Jesus for salvation requires an interpretive framework that transcends what we usually mean by history.

# 6

# Anthropology and Soteriology
# in Johannine Christology

Whoever created the Fourth Gospel had the ability to draw its readers into a profoundly different "world" through simple, ordinary language used in extraordinary ways.[1] From the first line onward, one is challenged by arresting assertions that bend out of shape the customary meaning of common words. For example, Jesus claims to be "the living bread that came down out of heaven" (6:51) and that "those who eat my flesh and drink my blood have eternal life" (6:54). To express new thoughts John does not coin new words but combines old ones in such a way that understanding what is said requires not a lexicon but insight. This is true not only of nouns (bread, flesh), verbs (came down, eat), and adjectives (living, eternal) but also of prepositions, as when Jesus says, "I am in the Father and the Father is in me" (14:11). Indeed, this Gospel relies repeatedly on one preposition—ἐκ (of, from)—to express not only its Christology but also its anthropology and soteriology. For instance, Jesus tells "the Jews" that "He who is *of* God hears the words of God" (8:47 RSV). Although the whole of Johannine Christology,[2] anthropology, and soteriology does not flow through this one bunghole, enough of it does to justify considering it as an aperture into the Gospel's theology.

[1] See the suggestive study of John's language by Norman R. Petersen, *The Gospel of John and the Sociology of Light: Language and Characterization in the Fourth Gospel* (Valley Forge, Pa.: Trinity International, 1993). Petersen contends that John has created "an anti-language" in order to legitimate the community's identity as "an anti-society" (5); thereby Petersen carries forward the work of J. Louis Martyn and Wayne A. Meeks.

[2] For a useful overview and assessment of recent studies of John's Christology, see Maarten J. J. Menken, "The Christology of the Fourth Gospel: A Survey of Recent Research," in *From Jesus to Paul: Essays on Jesus and New Testament Christology in Honour of Marinus de Jonge* (ed. Martinus C. de Boer; JSNTSup 84; Sheffield: JSOT, 1993), 292–320.

In fact, by a particular construal of the Johannine "of-ness," Jeffrey Trumbower's *Born from Above* has challenged the predominant interpretation of John since Origen. Trumbower claims that John's "of" language expresses a dualistic anthropology of "fixed origins"; that is, not only do responses to Jesus disclose one's predetermined origin but *"these origins cannot change or be exchanged."*[3] Those who pass from death to life can do so only because they have the right origin to begin with. Thus John's anthropology is protognostic: like the Valentinians and *The Gospel of Truth* (cited repeatedly), John taught that the saved are predestined by nature, not by election as in Qumran, Paul, and Ephesians.[4] "The ability to achieve salvation . . . consistently depends on one's fixed origin. . . . From the author's point of view, all human beings do not start on an equal footing."[5] Given the consequences of such a reading, another look at the text is in order, though a full discussion of Trumbower's work cannot be undertaken here.

I

*John 1:12-13*

It is significant that the Johannine "of" language appears first in the prologue, in what appears to be the evangelist's explanatory comment (v. 12c) on the assertion (in 12a,b) about those who receive the Logos, because this puts us in direct touch with his "of" usage. One can expect that clarity gained here will guide one's reading of subsequent usages.

According to the inherited tradition in verse 12a, "to those who received him, he [the Logos] gave the power [ἐξουσία] to become God's children." Clearly, this status is the result of an event in which they became what

---

[3] Jeffrey A. Trumbower, *Born from Above: The Anthropology of the Gospel of John* (HUT 29; Tübingen: Mohr [Siebeck], 1992), 10; emphasis added. This monograph is a revised version of a 1989 dissertation supervised by H. D. Betz at the University of Chicago.

[4] Trumbower, *Born from Above*, 14.

[5] Trumbower, *Born from Above*, 22; see also 30. Trumbower agrees with Meeks' observation that the dualistic picture in John (believers vs. "the world") "is never rationalized by a comprehensive myth, as in Gnosticism" (Wayne A. Meeks, "The Man from Heaven in Johannine Sectarianism," *JBL* 91 [1972]: 68). But he undertakes to show that Meeks is wrong in saying that the believers' status "is a *conferred* one, not an ontological one." From Meeks' suggestion that "it is at least as plausible that the Johannine Christology helped to create some gnostic myths as that gnostic myths helped create the Johannine Christology" ("The Man from Heaven," 72), Trumbower infers that Meeks meant that "the Fourth Gospel may be pushing its inherited traditions in a 'gnosticizing' direction" (*Born from Above*, 55). But this is not Meeks' conclusion but Trumbower's: "The principal author of the Gospel, far from being a 'de-gnosticizer,' was actually interpreting his sources, like the prologue, in a gnosticizing direction" (*Born from Above*, 141; see also also 55).

they had not been before, or apart from, receiving him. That is, by believing in his name they acknowledge his identity and entrust themselves to him. Verse 13 explains this event by contrasting three aspects[6] of ordinary human generation of life ("not of [ἐκ] blood, nor of [ἐκ] the will of the flesh, nor of [ἐκ] the will of [a] man") with being "born/begotten[7] of [ἐκ] God." The point is not that these people were sired by God instead of by human parents. Rather, in receiving the Logos, in believing in his name, they are "begotten of God," so that they are simultaneously their parents' children and God's "children." Those who refused the Logos were begotten by parents only—of blood, of the will of the flesh, of the will of (a) man. Those who believe were begotten also in an entirely different way—namely, "of God."

Verse 13 provides a fine instance of the evangelist's use of language, for although "begotten" is used but once, it clearly has a dual meaning: the ordinary generation of human life, and the extraordinary act of God in generating another kind of life, not specified here but which the gospel will characterize as "eternal."

This passage presents Trumbower with a clear dilemma. With his right hand he grants that the text does imply that this begetting "of God" occurs in conjunction with believing, and that this was also the view of the hymn on which the evangelist comments. In other words, in both tradition and redaction, all persons do "start out on an even footing" but are differentiated by their response to the Logos. But letting this observation stand would vaporize his thesis about "fixed origins." Consequently, what the right hand granted, the left hand must take away: He claims that in adding 12c-13 the evangelist really meant to "designate the fixed category and provide an explanation for why certain people believe"—they were "born of God" before Jesus appeared on the scene.[8] However, as an "explanation" this simply self-destructs, for if this divine begetting does not interpret the believing/receiving and instead accounts for a fixed category to which one belongs prior to faith, then "begetting" loses its dual meaning.

More important is noting the import of this passage for Johannine Christology. (1) The act of God in begetting and the act of the Logos-Light in giving power to become God's children are two ways of saying the same

---

[6] Barnabas Lindars, however, suggested that the three phrases "cover the stages of reproduction in reverse order, in an attempt to trace it to its source" (*The Gospel of John* [NCB; London: Oliphants, 1972], 92).

[7] Since the point concerns the origin of life rather than the birthing process itself, "begotten" is preferable to the customary "born," retained by NRSV, NIV, and REB.

[8] Trumbower, *Born from Above*, 69.

thing. The work of the Son and the work of the Father are identical. This is a major theme in the gospel. Accordingly, Jesus can say, "I have shown you many good works from [of, ἐx] the Father" (10:32), as well as, "If I am not doing the works of my Father [τοῦ πατρός μου], then do not believe me" (10:37). (2) Receiving power to become God's children depends on believing in the name of the Logos (accepting his claims for his identity). He is able to give this power because of who he is. In the language of dogmatics, Christology (who Jesus is) makes possible soteriology (what he does); conversely, soteriology makes Christology necessary.[9] (3) Soteriology implies anthropology. Here, what the Logos gives deals effectively with the (unstated) human dilemma at its core—impotence, the inability to make oneself a child of God, and so overcome the limitations of being only "of" human parents.

## John 3:3-8

The "begetting" language reappears in the story of Nicodemus' rendezvous with Jesus, who makes it the pivot of the exchange by linking it with ἄνωθεν, which in John regularly means "from above" but which can also mean "again." Jesus, responding to Nicodemus' opening gambit, says, "Unless one is begotten[10] ἄνωθεν one cannot see the kingdom of God." Nicodemus, taking ἄνωθεν to mean "again," protests that it is impossible for a senior citizen to repeat birth from the mother's womb. Jesus now replies, "Unless one is begotten of [ἐx] water and Spirit[11] one cannot enter the kingdom of God."[12] The fact that one preposition ἐx governs both "water" and "Spirit"

---

[9] For the correlations of theology, anthropology, and soteriology with Christology, see chap. 1, "The Renewal of New Testament Christology."

[10] As in 1:13, here γεννηθῇ probably means "begotten" rather than "birth." Dorothy A. Lee's recent defense of "born" is quite unpersuasive (*The Symbolic Narratives of the Fourth Gospel: The Interplay of Form and Meaning* [JSNTSup 95; Sheffield: JSOT Press, 1994], 43–48). In making her case, she also contends that the "water" in v. 5 "refers metaphorically to the rupture of the amniotic sac in childbirth" (52), and she invents the "labor" of the Spirit in 1:13.

[11] Even if the evangelist originally wrote only of the Spirit, as Bultmann argued, every known text includes the reference to water, which makes it difficult to regard "born of the Spirit" as expressing the truly Johannine point of view before a traditionalist editor added the reference to baptism.

[12] According to Matt 18:3, Jesus said to his disciples, "Truly, I say to you, unless you change [turn] and become like children, you will never enter the kingdom of Heaven" (see also Mark 10:15; Luke 18:17). Barnabas Lindars has reconstructed the Greek form of the saying that came to John (but was not derived from Matthew): "John and the Synoptic Gospels: A Test Case," *NTS* 27 (1981): 287–94.

suggests that the nouns are not to be separated,[13] so that "water and Spirit" is a hendiadys[14] (two words for the same thing, as in "each and every").

Jesus continues, evidently with an explanation of the necessity of being begotten of water and Spirit, though the paratactic construction does not make this explicit with γάρ (because):

What is begotten of [ἐκ] flesh is flesh
and what is begotten of [ἐκ] the Spirit is Spirit.

This epigrammatic formulation of the principle that like produces like makes the contrast between flesh and Spirit absolute. Here, derivation— one's "of-ness"—determines not only one's "nature" but also one's (future[15]) destiny, for only the Spirit-begotten can enter the kingdom. No provision is made for adding or giving Spirit to flesh, as in the quotation of Joel 2:18 at Acts 2:17. Spirit is not something that flesh lacks, but its antithesis. The problem with flesh is not its behavior but its ontic status—what it is, the phenomenal (the non-Spirit). Consequently, also what flesh begets shares this flaw.

Jesus still is not finished: "Do not marvel because I said to you [sg.], You [pl.] must be begotten ἄνωθεν (v. 7)" and proceeds to use the dual meaning of Spirit (or wind) to assert that the Spirit's work can be recognized but not explained: just as one does not know the whence and whither of the πνεῦμα (wind) but knows it is blowing because one hears it, "so it is with everyone

---

[13] Luise Schottroff, on the other hand, not only regards "of water and" as an original part of the text but also infers from the absence of "water" in v. 8 that the evangelist takes up the tradition of rebirth through water (Titus 3:5) and quietly reinterprets it as derived from the Spirit (i.e., not sacramentally; "Heil als innerweltliche Entweltlichung," *NovT* 11 [1969]: 300). However, George R. Beasley-Murray is closer to the probable point: "The *whole* expression . . . defines the manner in which one is born from above" (*John* [WBC 36; Waco, Tex.: Word Books, 1987], 48). Xavier Léon-Defour thinks that the "and" (καί) is epexegetical: water that is Spirit ("Towards a Symbolic Reading of the Fourth Gospel," *NTS* 27 [1981]: 450). On the other hand, Udo Schnelle distorts the meaning when he says that "of water and Spirit" refers to an "all-embracing new creation that is *accomplished* in baptism with water and *leads to* a life filled and determined by the Spirit" (*Antidocetic Christology in the Gospel of John* [Minneapolis: Fortress, 1992], 186; emphasis added). What Schnelle says may well be true of the Johannine community, but that is not what the *text* says.

[14] So also James D. G. Dunn, *Baptism in the Holy Spirit: A Re-Examination of the New Testament Teaching on the Gift of the Spirit in Relation to Pentecostalism Today* (Philadelphia: Westminster, 1970), 192; and Charles H. Talbert, *Reading John: A Literary and Theological Commentary on the Fourth Gospel and the Johannine Epistles* (New York: Crossroad, 1992), 99.

[15] Since this is the only passage in John in which "the kingdom of God" is mentioned, it is difficult to discern whether seeing/entering the kingdom occurs now or in the future.

who is begotten of [ἐκ] the πνεῦμα [Spirit]" (v. 8).[16] The Spirit's action is inexplicable precisely because, being ἄνωθεν, it is not subject to explanations, which pertain to the domain of flesh.

What Jesus tells Nicodemus reformulates and amplifies what was signaled by the prologue in 1:12-13.[17] It is only natural, then, for Trumbower to say that "when . . . Jesus tells Nicodemus 'unless one is born ἄνωθεν, one cannot see the kingdom of God,' he means one must belong to a fixed category of persons. . . . Nicodemus does not and cannot belong to this category . . . because they exist as a category before Jesus' coming and their membership list does not grow or shrink with Jesus' advent."[18] Trumbower's exegetical warrants for this interpretation are not convincing. (1) In order to say that in verse 3 Jesus speaks generally instead of addressing Nicodemus ("unless one is begotten . . ."), Trumbower ignores the first part of the verse: "Jesus . . . said *to him*, 'Amen, amen, I say *to you*.' " (2) Trumbower grants that the begetting by water and Spirit refers to a *re*birth, "but it is not a rebirth in which Nicodemus can participate." Why not? Because Trumbower, ignoring John's penchant for paraphrase, distinguishes "seeing" the kingdom (v. 3) from "entering" it (v. 5). This allows him to infer that "[fixed] birth from above is necessary 'to see' initially; subsequent rebirth from [water and] spirit is necessary to enter." Indeed, "such rebirth accrues automatically to those from above"[19]—said to be confirmed by Jesus' promise of the Paraclete whom the world cannot receive (14:16-17). But this has nothing to do with rebirth. (3) It may well be that subsequent references to Nicodemus (7:48-51; 19:39) indicate that he "is stuck in the realm of the flesh," but in no way does that confirm the claim that "he is outside the pale; he is not and *cannot be* born 'from above.' "[20]

The function of the stark contrast between flesh and Spirit in verse 6 is not to explain why Nicodemus is in a hopeless situation but rather to underscore the necessity of being begotten ἄνωθεν, because what is of flesh cannot escalate itself into Spirit. In other words, verse 6 is the Johannine equivalent of 1 Corinthians 15:50: "flesh and blood cannot inherit the

---

[16] The comparison does not imply that "those of the flesh (earth) may indeed have some experience of spiritual things," as Jerome H. Neyrey infers ("John III: A Debate over Johannine Epistemology and Christology," *NovT* 23 [1981]: 115–27 [120]).

[17] Neyrey provides a convenient table of parallels between the prologue and John 3 ("John III," 125).

[18] Trumbower, *Born from Above*, 72.

[19] Trumbower, *Born from Above*, 74.

[20] Trumbower, *Born from Above*, 73; emphasis added.

kingdom of God." Whereas for Paul the solution is the ontic transformation of perishable flesh and blood into an imperishable mode of existence, an event expected at Christ's Parousia. John's solution is another "begetting," a categorically different "of-ness" that can occur in the present. While Paul too affirms a decisive change in the believer's present (new creation), he nonetheless distinguishes it clearly from the future transformation. For John, however, this change occurs now in one's positive response to the Redeemer because it is not an ontic transformation but an existential one pertaining to the whence of one's life. Consequently, what is stated formally as a requirement ("unless," vv. 3, 5; "you must," v. 7) actually formulates the gospel, since the requirement implies that the totally different "of-ness" is possible now.

In a word, the exchange with Nicodemus indicates that being begotten of the Spirit = being begotten of water and the Spirit = being begotten from above = being begotten of God = believing in his (Christ's) name = receiving the Logos-Light = receiving power to become children of God. Precisely because derivation is destiny, a change in "of-ness" is required and possible. Were this not the case, we would expect John 3:17 to say that God sent the Son into the world "so that those begotten of God would be saved through him."

## John 3:31-32a

To a passage concerned with Jesus' superiority over John (3:22-30) the evangelist appends the narrator's commentary (vv. 31-36),[21] which concludes this section by looking ahead (cf. v. 34 and 8:26) and back (cf. v. 36 and vv. 16-18). Here for the first time the reader finds that "of" language, used previously to express Johannine anthropology, is also used to formulate Christology. The passage can be rendered as follows:

> He who comes ἄνωθεν is above [ἐπάνω] all;
> He who exists of the earth [ὁ ὢν ἐκ τῆς γῆς]
>     is of [ἐκ] the earth and speaks of [ἐκ] earth;
> He who comes from [ἐκ] heaven is above all
>     and testifies to what he has seen and heard [there].

---

[21] That vv. 31-36, like vv. 16-21, are not to be taken, respectively, as the continuation of the Baptist's words to his disciples and of Jesus' word to Nicodemus is generally acknowledged, though there is no marker in the text to indicate this shift. Lee, however, asserts that both passages "make most sense if Jesus . . . is regarded as the speaker" (*The Symbolic Narratives*, 38).

The fact that the passage does not argue *for* the descent-ascent pattern of Christology but *from* it shows that it is taken for granted. It is also assumed that its pattern applies only to Jesus. Consequently, Jesus' coming "from above" (ἄνωθεν) can imply that he is superior to everyone else. Accordingly, even though John the Baptist was sent from God to be a witness to the light (1:6-8, 15, 19-34; 3:25-30), he still was an earthling ("of the earth"[22]), and his testimony was only "of earth" because it cannot transcend its whence, for derivation is decisive. Moreover, once derivation (ἐκ) is construed spatially (ἄνωθεν), it can also be used to refer to the Son's descent from heaven. Consequently, the testimony of Jesus, who is not an earthling because of his derivation ἄνωθεν (= coming from [ἐκ] heaven), concerns "heavenly things" (3:12), "what he has seen and heard" there (even though he never conveys privileged information)—namely, "the words of God" (v. 34). In short, this passage is a commentary on 1:18: only the Son, who is in the Father's lap, has made God known because his unique derivation qualifies him to do so.

Although derivation, expressed in "of-ness" language, is used in both Christology and anthropology, it is used in a spatial sense (as in 3:31, "he who comes ἐκ heaven") only in christological and soteriological statements. The bread discourse in John 6 shows this usage repeatedly (e.g., "I am the living bread which has come down from heaven [ὁ ἐκ τοῦ οὐρανοῦ καταβάς]," verse 51; see also verses 32, 33, 41, as well as verse 38, where some manuscripts read ἐκ instead of ἀπό, printed in Nestle-Aland [26th ed.]). In other words, "of-ness" is combined with the descent-ascent pattern only in the case of Christ because preexistence pertains only to him. This is confirmed by the fact that also πόθεν ("from where?") is used in the pregnant sense only of Christ. Thus he says, "I know from where [πόθεν] I have come and where [ποῦ] I am going" (8:14). In interrogating the formerly blind man "the Jews" admit that they do not know Jesus' "whence," to the man's amazement (9:29-30). On the other hand, it is Johannine irony that has "the Jews" know exactly where he is from; they rely on this knowledge to disqualify him from being the Christ, whose "whence" is unknown (7:27-28; see also 6:24, where knowledge of Jesus' parentage is the basis of their rejecting his claim to have descended ἐκ heaven). It is not accidental that also Pilate asks, "Where are you from?" (πόθεν, 19:9). In other words, Jesus' true "whence" is either not known or used against him, because his claim about his derivation (his ἐκ) is not accepted. This becomes particularly evident in John 8.

[22] Probably the text uses "earth" instead of "world" in order to avoid saying that John the Baptist was "of the world," a formula with negative meaning (see pp. 82–87 below).

*John 8:21-24, 42-44a, 47*

In chapter 8 Jesus' bitter controversies with "the Jews" repeatedly concern his "of-ness." Moreover, here the anthropological, soteriological, and christological uses reinforce one another. The first controversy of concern here[23] (8:21-24) can be set out as follows:

Jesus:      I am going away, and you will search for me,
            but you will die in your sin.
            Where I am going, you cannot come.

The Jews:   Is he going to kill himself? Is that what he means . . . ?

Jesus:      You are from below [ἐκ τῶν κάτω ἐστέ],
            I am from above [ἐκ τῶν ἄνω εἰμί];
            You are of this world [ἐκ τούτου τοῦ κόσμου ἐστέ],
            I am not of this world [οὐκ ἐκ τοῦ κόσμου τούτου].
            Therefore[24] I told you that you will die in your sins,
            for unless you believe that I AM, you will die in your sins.

Here Jesus appropriates and interprets the narrator's language in 3:31-32a in order to comment on his death as his departure and return to the Father in heaven.[25] The ἐκ τῶν ἄνω ("from above") here is clearly synonymous with the ἄνωθεν used there. Moreover, "of-ness" (English usage requires that here ἐκ be rendered "from") is first construed spatially (below/above), thereby replacing the narrator's earth/heaven, then is given a distinctly Johannine interpretation as "this world"/"not this world." The text does not simply

---

[23] Chapter 8 has three controversies (8:12-20, 21-30, 31-59), which continue those begun at 7:14; they occur during Tabernacles and take place in the temple (7:14; 8:20, 59). For an analysis of the chapter that emphasizes both its function and forensic character, see Jerome H. Neyrey, *An Ideology of Revolt: John's Christology in Social-Scientific Perspective* (Philadelphia: Fortress, 1988), 37-58, 233-36. Neyrey claims that here "Jesus conducts a trial in which some people are formally charged, tried, convicted, and sentenced" (37).

[24] NRSV, following p[66] ℵ a e sy[s.p], omits "therefore" and reverses the last two lines. Even without "therefore" the function of the statement remains unchanged.

[25] For a discussion of this Johannine way of referring to Jesus' death, see Godfrey C. Nicholson, *Death as Departure: The Johannine Descent-Ascent Schema* (SBLDS 63; Chico, Calif.: Scholars Press, 1983). Petersen could easily have included "departure" in the following apt statement: " 'Exaltation,' 'glorification,' 'resurrection,' and 'ascent' all have different meanings, denotations, and referents in everyday language, but in John's special language [supra, n. 1] they refer to the same thing, which is none of the things the words conventionally denote. For this reason we cannot pin down their Johannine meaning and reference in anything but the minimal structural sense of the Word's return from its incarnation" (*Gospel of John*, 47).

paraphrase "below" as "this world" (= the earth), as C. K. Barrett says,[26] but interprets "below" anthropologically.

In John, "world" often refers to humanity in need of salvation. It is the skewed and hostile human "world" that God loves enough to send the Son into in order to save it (3:16-17).[27] The anthropological meaning of "world" is manifest in the fact that frequently it is personified and thus is the subject of verbs normally used of humans: The world "did not know" the Logos (1:10) or the Father (17:25); it cannot "receive" the Spirit (14:17), and the peace that it "gives" differs from that which Christ gives (14:27); soon it will no longer "see" Jesus (14:19) but will "rejoice" when he is gone (16:20). It "hates" both Jesus and the disciples (15:18; 17:14). Nonetheless, the Christ-event occurred so that it would "believe" (17:21) and its sins be "taken away" (1:29).

Here, however, Jesus does not speak simply of "the world" but pointedly of "this world," an expression that reflects "this age" (αἰὼν οὗτος; העולם הזה), frequently found in apocalyptic thought, where it is contrasted with "the age to come," as in Matthew 12:32.[28] Like עולם, αἰών ("aeon," "age") in such contexts refers not to a discrete historical period (e.g., the Roman era) but to time-space as a totality, viewed from the standpoint of the future aeon/age from which it differs categorically. The age to come is not the outgrowth of the past and present but the God-given eschatological alternative to it. To speak holistically of all human experience on this side of the divide as "this age" is therefore to disparage it because of its flawed character, as seen in light of its flawless replacement. This devaluation of the present in light of the radically different future is implied in the phrase even if it is not paired explicitly with "the age to come." Thus Paul can speak disparagingly of "the wisdom of this age" (1 Cor 2:6); he can also substitute "world" for "age" in order to write of "the wisdom of this world" (3:19). Why neither Paul nor John uses "the age/world to come" need not be probed here. What must be

---

[26] C. K. Barrett, *The Gospel according to St. John: An Introduction with Commentary and Notes on the Greek Text* (2nd ed.; Philadelphia: Westminster, 1978), 341.

[27] Paul, too, can use "world" to refer to humanity (2 Cor 5:19). John, however, shows no interest in the redemption of the nonhuman creation that is in bondage to death, as does Paul (Rom 8:18-25).

[28] While John Ashton rightly notes that the Fourth Gospel prefers "this world" to "this age," strangely he does not see that the former was influenced by the latter, even though the temporal (future) aspect is missing (*Understanding the Fourth Gospel* [Oxford: Oxford University Press, 1991; repr., 2007], 207–8). At the same time, Ashton concedes (in another context) that "one is forced to pay attention to a possible apocalyptic background" of John (307 n. 36). His chapter, "Intimations of Apocalyptic" (307–29), limits the two-ages motif to "the age of concealment" and "the age of disclosure" (311)—surely too restricted.

noted, however, is that in John "this world" is so estranged from God that it is subject to a malign power called "the ruler of this world" (John 12:31; 14:30; 16:11). Evidently, in the Johannine community the somber colors of "this world" have bled into the coloration of "the world."

The foregoing considerations, abbreviated though they are, indicate that when Jesus says, "You are of this world," he is not simply identifying his opponents as earthlings or even as denizens of the known solar system. Rather, he is making an anthropological accusation about the derivation of their real "nature"; he is identifying the hostile "whence" that accounts for their obduracy, for their not knowing either him or the Father (8:9), and for their not understanding that his words about the sender are about the Father (8:27). Their resistance to him actualizes and demonstrates their "of-ness." They do not realize this, so he makes this disclosure part of his word.[29] At this point Bultmann's famous contention—that as the Revealer Jesus reveals only that he is the Revealer—sells the Fourth Gospel somewhat short.

On the other hand, Bultmann rightly saw that when Jesus amplifies his terse christological assertion ("I am not of this world") by speaking of his relationship to the sender (8:2, 6, 28-29), he does not provide positive information about his own "of-ness" in order to transmit knowledge about another world but grounds his mission's character and warrant. In John, Jesus is God's Son sent into the world, who during his sojourn in it as an unlettered Nazarene of known parentage was not "of this world." He was a "stranger from heaven."[30] The effectiveness of his mission depends precisely on being "not of this world," for only so could he be simultaneously not part of the human dilemma and truly obedient to the one who sent him into it. Jesus' "of-ness" is as essential to Johannine Christology as his opponents' "of-ness" is for its anthropology.

---

[29] Luise Schottroff, on the other hand, insists that in John the dualistic understanding of "world" exists only in connection with the refusal of revelation, that there was no "world" before the revelation. She appeals to 9:41 and especially to 15:22 in support: "If I had not come and spoken to them, they would not have sin" (also 15:24). But her interpretation implies that Jesus' word creates "the world" in the act of his speaking, which overlooks the point that God loved the world so that it might be saved, implying that it needed salvation before the Son arrived (*Der Glaubende und die feindliche Welt: Beobachtungen zum gnostischen Dualismus und seiner Bedeutung für Paulus und das Johannesevangelium* [WMANT 37; Neukirchen: Neukirchener Verlag, 1970], 229–30).

[30] The phrase is taken from the subtitle of Marinus de Jonge's volume of collected essays, *Jesus, Stranger from Heaven and Son of God: Jesus Christ and the Christians in Johannine Perspective* (SBLSBS 11; Missoula, Mont.: Scholars Press, 1977).

Especially fascinating in 8:21-24 is the way (a) Jesus interprets the "of-ness" anthropology further and (b) links it with Christology in order to confront opponents with a decision freighted with ultimate consequences. (a) In verse 21, sandwiched between Jesus' two assertions about what will follow his departure ("you will search for me" and "you cannot come") is the dire prediction, "and you will die in your sin." Despite the severity of this promise, "the Jews" ignore it and instead wonder if Jesus is planning suicide (cf. 7:32-36). Jesus will not be deflected from his prediction (made three times). After interpreting "from below" as "you are of this world," he adds, "therefore I told you that you would die in your sins." Here he interprets their being "of this world" by specifying the resultant destiny. They are "in" sin/sins, not because they are earthlings, but because sin characterizes "this world" that they are "of." In other words, they will die in their sins because, being of this world (= from below), they cannot follow Jesus when he departs for the world he had left.

(b) Jesus' last word, however, states the condition on which the alternative destiny depends:[31] namely, accepting his christological claim—"believe that I AM"—the enigmatic appropriation of God's own self-proclamation in Isaiah 43:10.[32] Those who believe what Jesus says about himself—John's "high" Christology—will not die in their sins because believing this makes them no longer "of this world."[33] Accordingly, they will be able to go where he goes—exactly what Jesus promises the disciples (John 13:33, 36; 14:2-3), even if he speaks also of his coming to them (14:18, 23, 28; 16:16).

Given the intimate correlation of soteriology and anthropology with Christology, this passage casts light on "of-ness" because it is by believing a christological assertion that one ceases to be "of this world." Understanding this connection entails grasping what is implied in believing Jesus' claim

---

[31] Trumbower recognizes this implicit invitation to believe but appeals to the "above" language in v. 23 to say that the evangelist has already "stated his ultimate attitude that belief is impossible for them" (*Born from Above*, 87). It is one thing, however, to regard v. 23 as expressing a "boundary between Jesus and these Jews . . . in terms of origin"; it is another to say that the boundary cannot be crossed, that their "of-ness" is immutable.

[32] For a recent, succinct overview of the background of the I AM formula, see Neyrey, *Ideology of Revolt*, App. 1. This absolute use must be distinguished from that which includes a predicate, as in "I am the bread of life."

[33] Given the Johannine penchant for paraphrase, one would not err in inferring that the "ideal reader" (the one who makes all the appropriate moves in reading the text from the beginning) is expected to see an allusion to the Baptist's identification of Jesus as "the Lamb of God who takes away the sins of the world" (1:29); that is, by believing in Jesus as I AM, one's sins are taken away.

to be I AM (ἐγώ εἰμι). To begin, it is to acknowledge that Jesus is the phenomenal, temporal mode of the eternal (nontemporal) divine reality itself, so that the response to Jesus is a response to God the Creator on whom all that is is contingent, and who by definition is "not of this world." Further, one cannot acknowledge that this reality is present without being shaped by it, for to acknowledge its presence is to avow one's contingency on it. To say "yes" to this reality's self-presentation is to place oneself deliberately at its disposal, to open one's existence to its influence; it is to affirm that one's true life is derived from the nonphenomenal, nontemporal other instead of from the phenomenal and transient. Moreover, it is to see that being "of this world" is likewise a matter of believing, of trusting that its implicit and explicit self-presentation is sufficient, valid, and trustworthy enough to obey. Indeed, it is precisely in being confronted by the self-presentation of the other-as-Jesus that one is confronted also by the extent to which one is "of this world." Given the character and power of "this world," such confrontation is necessary if one is to see the situation clearly enough to grasp the possibility of being free from it.

This analysis of "of-ness" is confirmed in the latter half of chapter 8, which contains Jesus' most drastic polemic against the very Jews who, despite believing in him (vv. 30, 31), nonetheless reject his promise of freedom, claiming that as Abraham's descendants they have never been enslaved. Jesus, however, sets up the following dispute by pointing out that whoever sins is a slave of sin,[34] that their refusal of his word contradicts their claim to be Abraham's seed, and that just as he reflects his Father so also they reflect theirs (vv. 34-38). They respond, "Abraham is our father," but Jesus replies that what they do (seek to kill him, v. 40; cf. v. 59) shows that this is not the case but, rather, exposes who their father really is. It is at this point that the "of-ness" language reappears.

The Jews:    We are not bastards (begotten of [ἐκ] fornication).

Jesus:       If God were your Father, you would love me,
             for I came out from God [ἐκ τοῦ θεοῦ ἐξῆλθον]
             and now I am here. . . .
             Why do you not understand my speech [λαλίαν]?
             Because you cannot hear[35] my word.

[34] Although Trumbower does not actually say so, in his reading of John the saying would mean that one sins because one is a slave of sin, a member of a fixed category. In that case would not the text say, "Whoever is a slave of sin sins"?

[35] NRSV's rendering of "hear" as "accept" is a significant correction of RSV's "bear to hear," for the point concerns their inability to hear (= hearken), not emotional resistance.

> You are of [ἐκ] your father, the devil,
> and you want to do the desires of your father. . . .
> He who is of [ἐκ] God hears the words of God.

Jesus' brutal attack (doubtless reflecting the invective of Jewish-Christian polemic against non-Christian Jews) is based on the previously noted principle that like produces like, here expressed as "like father, like son." Consequently, "of-ness" implies not only the point of origin (derivation) but also the reproduction of its character. In other words, by construing "of-ness" as paternity, one can argue in both directions: one can infer the identity and character of the father from the behavior of the children, and one can attribute the character of the father to the children. Accordingly, since Jesus' opponents' father is the devil, a murderer (v. 44), they seek to kill him (vv. 40, 59). Likewise, because the devil, being "a liar and the father of lies," has "no truth in him" (v. 44), it is inevitable that they do not believe Jesus, precisely because he tells the truth (v. 45). Conversely, were he to deny that he knows the Father, he would be a liar too (v. 55). Their claim to have God as their Father is annulled by their refusal to love his emissary, who is "of God" (vv. 41-42). In addition, whereas Jesus always does what is pleasing to his Father (v. 29), his opponents willfully actualize the desires of their father, the devil (v. 44). They are not acting under constraint but as willing servants—the most insidious consequence of their "of-ness."

## John 18:36

Jesus' most frequently cited "of" saying was spoken to Pilate: "My kingdom[36] is not of [ἐκ] this world. If my kingdom were of [ἐκ] this world, my staff [ὑπηρέται] would be fighting so that I would not be handed over to the Jews. But now [NRSV: as it is] my kingdom is not from here [ἐντεῦθεν]." He could just as well have said that it is ἄνωθεν ("from above"); but in this trial, in which the judge is judged by the accused, it is enough to say what Jesus' kingdom is not "of"—"this world," where power is based on might.[37]

---

[36] Dorothy A. Lee offers no reason for regarding this phrase as another reference to "the kingdom of God" (John 3:5; *Symbolic Narratives*, 45). The two should not be fused without evidence.

[37] Trumbower, *Born from Above*, 14. Petersen uses Jesus' statement to illustrate the point that "anti-languages are not different *languages*; they are languages that differ from an everyday language as a special use of *that* language." Thus Jesus "accepts Pilate's notion of 'King of the Jews' but denies its everyday referent by implying another one that is *opposed* to it. . . . The political referent is displaced by another that is semantically constituted by its otherness— '*not of this world.*' Jesus does not point to a new concrete referent" (*Gospel of John*, 89).

Consequently, Jesus' supporters do not engage in armed struggle on his behalf, for that would imply that his kingship is contingent on their success—that is, ἐντεῦθεν (from here) after all.

## II

Several questions will help us consolidate these observations: What, then, does it mean to be "of," whether "of God" or "of the world"? Why is so much emphasis placed on one's derivation? What is implied about the self, and about Christology, in John?

To begin with, "of-ness" implies that what is decisive about a person is neither self-generated nor self-defined; to the contrary, one is wholly contingent at the center where the self is constituted. An anthropology based on an autonomous self is precluded. In John, speaking of derivation is itself a way of making an anthropological statement. Indeed, Jesus' repeated insistence that he does not act or speak on his own (5:19, 30; 7:16-18; 8:28, 42) shows that exactly the same holds true of "of" language in Christology as well. This is why Jesus' dictum, "The one who hears the words of God is of God" (8:47), applies to him as well as to those of his hearers who accept his word.

In the juxtaposition of "I am from above" and "I am not of this world," the second claim interprets the first, showing that "of-ness" means more than point of origin. It also determines both what is actualized and the form of the actualized, as noted in the use of "of-ness" in conjunction with paternity. But "of-ness" language appears in other contexts as well because it is based on the principle of replication. Accordingly, it is virtually inevitable that the Jesus who says, "I have come out from God [ἐκ τοῦ θεοῦ ἐξῆλθον] and [now] I am here" (8:42), will also say, "The one who has seen me has seen the Father" (14:9). Nor is it surprising that the one "of God" appropriates the divine "I AM" to assert his identity. So, too, "this world" expresses itself in those who are "of" it: they "judge according to the flesh" (8:15) and so either cannot understand Jesus or reject his claims when they do.

Useful as "of-ness" is for formulating both anthropology and Christology in John, it nevertheless does not dissolve the distinction between the Savior and the saved, because only in the case of the former does "of-ness" refer to a preexistent state. Consequently, when Jesus says he is "not of this world" (17:14, 16), he means that on earth he maintained his unique derivation by not deriving the warrant for his life from "this world" but instead by pleasing the One who sent him. For the disciples, however, their being "not of this world" is a status acquired. As a result they do not share Jesus' ontic "of-ness" but its consequences: the world hates both the inherently alien Jesus, whose "of-ness" was maintained, and those made aliens by acknowledging the "of-ness" of Jesus. Never does Jesus usurp God's role as the One in whom one's "of-ness" is to be grounded; instead, he is the one through whom this God-grounded "of-ness" is effected.

Instead of imparting his own "of-ness" as the Son (υἱός), Jesus makes it possible for believers to "become" God's children (τέκνα) by being "begotten" of God. Jesus never says they are "begotten of me" or that they are "of me." When he implies that they are "of" his flock (10:26), he refers not to their derivation but to their participation in a community, just as Nicodemus is "of the Pharisees" (3:1). To express Jesus' intimate relation to believers, John uses "in" language (e.g., "I am the vine, you are the branches; those who abide in me and I in them bear much fruit," 15:5).

Jesus is the only character in the gospel who uses "of" language in the sense reviewed here. The disciples hear it but do not repeat it, nor do his opponents pick it up in order to contest it. It is part of Jesus' distinctive revelatory proclamation, reinforced by the narrator's use in the prologue and at 3:16-21, 31, both of which inform the reader of the transhistorical basis on which Jesus can use this language. Likewise, the narrator's comment at 2:25 signals the mundane basis: Jesus did not entrust himself to those who believed because of his signs, for "he knew what was in everyone" (= he knew that their "of-ness" had not been changed by such faith).

John's relentless dualism, which precludes shades of gray between the black and white alternatives, also makes no allowance either for extenuating circumstances or for oscillation—now more "of" flesh, now more "of" the Spirit. It is either/or, all or nothing, because what is in view is that which defines the existence of the self. Thereby John's dualism is focused on the individual in such a way that what is called for, explicitly or not, is a decision: either to deny the validity of Jesus' construal of one's condition (and thereby to remain determinedly in it) or to affirm that Jesus is right and so have the grounding of one's existence reconstituted, a change so radical that the appropriate metaphor for it is being "begotten of God." What the Gospel, like its protagonist in its narrative, asks from the reader is not the mind's assent to a dualistic worldview but a decision about one's existence, as Bultmann saw in characterizing this dualism as a "dualism of decision." Accordingly, John shows no interest in accounting for the alienation of creation into "this world." Nor does the Gospel encourage the readers (or the characters in the story) to see themselves as victims of fate or as the captives of a malign power, for that would shunt responsibility away from the self who must decide. Nor is Jesus' saying "You are of this world" either a condescending observation or an explanation[38] voicing the standpoint of an elite. It is, rather, a word whose confrontational character is required if the self's derivation is to be reconstituted and not merely improved.

---

[38] According to Trumbower, the evangelist appealed to "fixed origins" to explain ret-rospectively the phenomenon of belief and unbelief (*Born from Above*, 85, 105). At the same time, "by not immediately disclosing the true fixedness and determined quality of the hos-tile Jews' response, the author has left room for an outsider reading the gospel (perhaps a Jew!) to change his response and join the Johannine community (5:34), but he has also left no doubt in the mind of the insiders who read the gospel that the reason so many reject Jesus has to do with their fixed spiritual origin (8:43-47)" (128). In other words, Trumbower reads the gospel's statements addressed to outsiders as having the same function as 1 John 2:19 has for insiders: a rationalizing of the fact that the schismatics departed because they were not part of the church in the first place (83). Were that the case, one would expect John 6:66-67 to read differently: there the gospel not only reports the defection of many disciples but also has Jesus respond to their departure. This would have been an excellent point at which Jesus could have explained that they had not been "born of God" to start with. In other words, Trumbower overlooks a rather elemental point: that nowhere in John does "of-ness" language appear in contexts in which Jesus or the narrator explains to the reader either the acceptance or rejection of Jesus.

# 7

# Christology, Soteriology, and the Praise of God in Romans

Paul's letters surprise us repeatedly, partly because what has seemed relatively clear often turns out to contain problems that require a solution before the passage can be interpreted convincingly, and partly because pursuing them implicates themes whose construal determines the way the entire letter is understood. Romans 15:7-13 is such a passage. In it Paul puts an intramural Christian problem in the context of Christology, soteriology, and the praise of God.

We expect this paragraph to be especially important because it concludes the letter's theological/ethical core. Just as 1:16-17 opens the argument and paraenesis, so also 15:7-13 closes it;[1] this core is "framed" by a discussion of Paul's relation to the readers (1:8-15; 15:14-33). There are other "concluding" paragraphs within this core (8:31-39 and 11:33-36 being notable examples); indeed, 15:1-6 is another, as we shall see. However, whereas their horizon is the subject matter that precedes immediately, the horizon of 15:7-13 is nothing short of the entire argument. Moreover, given this paragraph's function as the capstone of the argument/paraenesis, as well as the care with which the entire discussion is crafted, we also expect this paragraph to be free of problems that might inhibit its effectiveness. Yet, on closer examination, we are surprised that everything is not as smooth and clear as we expect.

---

[1] The paragraph is surely more than an addendum (*Ahang, bzw., Nachtrag*), as Dietrich-Alex Koch says (*Die Schrift als Zeuge des Evangeliums. Untersuchungen zu Verwendung u.z. Verständnis der Schrift bei Paulus* [BHT 69; Tübingen: J. C. B. Mohr, 1986], 281).

I

More important than this paragraph's formal function in the structure of the letter is its material role in relation to the letter's occasion and purpose, on the one hand, and to the question of its literary integrity (and therefore its history), on the other. The two issues are intertwined.

We are surprised, to begin with, by the fact that the content of this paragraph appears to have been anticipated, even in the sequence of themes, by the paragraph that precedes it (15:1-6).

| exhortation | vv. 1-2 | v. 7 |
|---|---|---|
| Christ | v. 3a | vv. 8-9a |
| Scripture | vv. 3b-4a | vv. 9b-12 |
| hope | v. 4b | v. 13 |
| praise of God | v. 6 | vv. 9-11 |

Having written verses 1-6 as the climax of the word to the "weak" and the "strong," why does Paul begin afresh to treat the same themes in verses 7-13, especially having ended the previous paragraph with a hortatory benediction (vv. 5-6)?[2] Since a transition from verse 6 to verse 14 would have been just as smooth as between verse 13 and verse 14, it can scarcely have been Paul's concern for stylistic felicity that prompted him to add verses 7-13. Either he had something else in mind to say, suggested by the greater attention paid to Scripture,[3] or someone else is responsible for the juxtaposition of these two paragraphs. In any case, one thing must be emphasized: the relation of these two paragraphs to each other is the same regardless of who juxtaposed them.

Given the well-known and complex history of the text of Romans, one cannot exclude a priori either of the two ways of holding someone other than Paul responsible for the phenomenon before us—the one that regards verses 7-13 as an interpolation, as do Pallis and O'Neill,[4] the other that sees the paragraph as part of a genuine Pauline letter placed here by the editor who created the letter we have, as do Schmithals and his predecessors.[5]

---

[2] William Sanday and Arthur C. Headlam are content to say that in vv. 7-13 Paul generalizes. See *A Critical and Exegetical Commentary on the Epistle to the Romans* (ICC; Edinburgh: T&T Clark, 1895).

[3] So Koch, *Die Schrift als Zeuge*, 282.

[4] Alexander Pallis, *To the Romans* (Liverpool: Liverpool Booksellers, 1920), 152; John C. O'Neill, *Paul's Letter to the Romans* (Harmondsworth, U.K.: Penguin, 1975), 240.

[5] Walter Schmithals' views about Rom 15:1-13 are an essential part of his imaginative (some would say imaginary) reconstruction of the literary prehistory of our Letter to the

Despite evidence for interpolation throughout the entire letter,[6] here one should hold Paul himself responsible until there is clear reason to judge otherwise.

Romans 15:7 begins with διὸ προσλαμβάνεσθε ἀλλήλους, which clearly requires of both the "weak" and the "strong" what 14:1, which opens the discussion abruptly, requires only of the latter: τὸν δὲ ἀσθενοῦντα τῇ πίστει προσλαμβάνεσθε. The identity of these two groups continues to be debated because Paul himself does not provide the information we deem essential. Commonly, the "weak" are viewed as scrupulous, law-observant Jewish Christians (at least predominantly) and the "strong" as Gentile, perhaps, Paulinist, believers who are hectoring the former to join them in developing an ethos based on freedom from the law. Given the prominence of the "Jew-Gentile" theme in Romans, this identification may well be correct— so long as one does not impose it rigidly. Still, the remarkable thing is that Paul himself neither states such an identification (strictly speaking the "we who are strong" in 15:1 precludes it), nor argues his exhortation on this basis. What makes our paragraph potentially important for the interpretation of chapters 14–15 is the fact that here, and only here, does the text speak of Jews and Gentiles. Indeed, apart from the initial and final sentences (vv. 7, 13), the theme of Jew and Gentile dominates the whole paragraph. In other words, the juxtaposition of the Jew-Gentile theme in verses 8-12 with

---

Romans, in *Der Römerbrief als historisches Problem* (Gütersloh: Gerd Mohn, 1975). He calls attention not only to a formal similarity between vv. 5-6 and 13 but also to the fact that such benedictions normally appear near the end of a Pauline letter and are never duplicated (154–56). He also contends that 15:1-6 and 8-13, taken in themselves, have nothing to do with one another (157–58). He also thinks that the editor shifted v. 7 from its original position after 4a (4b being redactional) in order to provide a connecting link to vv. 8-13, which originally followed 11:36 (but continued the thought of 11:32). Thus Rom 12:1–15:4a, 5-6, 7 + 15:14-32 + 16:21-23 + 15:33 once constituted Paul's Second Letter to the Romans (157–62), written shortly before going to Jerusalem. The first letter consisted of 1:1–4:25 + 5:12–11:36 + 15:8-13. Romans 16:1-20 was originally destined for Ephesus. Our Romans also includes fragments of genuine letters originally sent to Thessalonica, as well as nongenuine passages and redactional comments. (See 210–11 for a summary.) Schmithals generally follows Friedrich Spitta, whose turn-of-the-century views he summarizes. See also Rudolf Schumacher, *Die beiden letzten Kapitel des Römerbriefes: Ein Beitrag zu ihrer Geschichte u. Erklärung* (Münster: Aschendorff, 1929).

[6] See, e.g., Rudolf Bultmann, "Glossen im Römerbrief," *Exegetica* (ed. E. Dinkler; Tübingen: J. C. B. Mohr, 1967) 278–84; originally published in 1947; Leander E. Keck, "The Post-Pauline Interpretation of Jesus' Death in Rom 5, 6-7," *Theologia Crucis—Signum Crucis* (ed. C. Andresen and G. Klein; E. Dinkler Festschrift; Tübingen: J. C. B. Mohr, 1979), 237–48; repr. in Keck, *Christ's First Theologian*, 233–44; idem, "Romans 15:4—An Interpolation?" In *Faith and History: Essays in Honor of Paul W. Meyer* (ed. John T. Carroll, et al.; Atlanta, Ga.: Scholars Press, 1991; repr., Eugene, Ore.: Wipf & Stock, 2004), 125–36.

verse 7, which links the whole paragraph to the preceding discussion of the "weak" and the "strong," warrants the inference that the ἀλλήλους refers to the Jewish and Gentile Christians. But still, an inference, no matter how valid, is not yet evidence.

The inference, however, is consonant with a coherent interpretation of the whole. Romans 15:1-13 wants the reader to infer that the "weak" (Jewish) Christians will praise God among "strong" Gentile (Christians), and that the latter will join their Jewish fellow believers in praising God, thereby overcoming the tension between them.[7] This, too, is an inference, which Zeller calls "a nice idea" but not one stated in the text. The frustrating fact is that apart from the repetition of προσλαμβάνεσθε in verse 7,[8] nothing in our paragraph expressly links it with the foregoing discussion of the "weak" and the "strong."[9] The link is in the mind of the reader, and it is the juxtaposition of themes that suggests it.

If at this point the letter had literary integrity, then it was Paul who brought the discussion of the "weak" and the "strong" to its conclusion by implicitly relating it to the Jew-Gentile theme in the rest of the letter. Then, moreover, 15:1-13 as a whole can be brought into a discussion of the letter's occasion and Paul's purpose in writing. Otherwise, in making the inference the reader is fulfilling the desire of the editor (or interpolator), and then 15:1-6 might still be a clue to the occasion that prompted Paul to write, but 15:7-13 would disclose nothing of either his purpose in doing so or the context in which he placed his admonition. Schmithals sees this clearly. A closer examination of verses 7-13 is required before that question can be adjudicated properly.

## II

Romans 15:7-13 contains four types of material: (a) an exhortation with a soteriological warrant (v. 7); (b) a christological assertion (vv. 8-9a); (c) a fourfold scriptural warrant for the christological assertion (vv. 9b-12); and (d) a hortatory benediction (v. 13).[10] What is surprising is not this diversity but the unexpected rationale, or lack of it, that unites these materials.

[7] See Paul S. Minear, *The Obedience of Faith* (SBT 2/19; Naperville, Ill.: Alec R. Allenson, 1971), 10–11.

[8] Dieter Zeller, *Juden und Heiden in der Mission des Paulus: Studien zum Römerbrief* (Stuttgart: Katholisches Bibelwerk, 1973), 218–19.

[9] Schmithals puts it sharply: in 14:1–15:6 there is no mention of Jew and Gentile; in 15:8-13 we do not meet the "strong" and the "weak" (*Der Römerbrief*, 157).

[10] See Robert Jewett, " 'The Form and Function of the Homiletic Benediction," *ATR* 51 (1969): 18–34.

Apart from the benediction, which is loosely attached grammatically to the preceding elements by a postpositive δέ (as also in v. 6), each element is linked explicitly to the one that precedes it by a series of terms whose function is to create a coherent flow of thought:

| | |
|---|---|
| vv. 5-6 | hortatory benediction |
| v. 7a | διό + imperative: |
| v. 7b | καθώς + soteriological warrant |
| vv. 8-9a | γάρ + christological warrant |
| vv. 9b-12 | καθώς γέγραπται + scriptural warrant |

This formal, grammatical coherence, however, appears to be poorly supported by the material content. (a) To begin with, since the content of the preceding benediction in verses 5-6 and that of the closely linked imperative in verse 7 concerns the readers' unity (ὁμοθυμαδόν, προσλαμβάνεσθε ἀλλήλους), one expects the supporting warrants to say something like: Christ, too, welcomed diverse persons, and this accords with Scripture, which also speaks of God's welcoming diverse persons. Instead, verses 7-13 pick up the theme of the benediction's purpose clause, the glorification of God (εἰς δόξαν τοῦ θεοῦ, v. 7; δοξάσαι τὸν θεόν, v. 9a; and all scriptural quotations paraphrase the theme of glorifying God. Nothing more is said of the attitude of one group to the other, and the focus shifts to Jews and Gentiles. (b) Moreover, the christological warrant in verse 8 does not continue the theme of what Christ did (προσελάβετο ὑμᾶς) but states his function vis-à-vis Jews and Gentiles. Furthermore, of the four quotations adduced in support of the Gentiles' praise of God, only the first three explicitly speak of this, and of these only the second and third actually summon the Gentiles to praise. The first has the speaker himself do the praising, and the fourth shifts to two other themes: the Davidic ruler of the Gentiles and their hope in him. (c) Finally, although the theme of hope in verse 12 is continued in the concluding benediction (v. 13), it speaks of neither Jew nor Gentile but of an unspecified "you." How does one account for such a strange paragraph, located at such a strategic place? Clear examination of each of its components should help us move forward.

### III

*The exhortation and its soteriological warrant*

Verse 7 is relatively free of problems. The reciprocal welcome urged here, while going beyond 14:1 where the "strong" are to welcome the "weak," has been anticipated negatively at 14:3 (μὴ ἐξουθενείτω, μὴ κρινέτω) and warranted by God's welcome (προσελάβετο), not by Christ's as here.[11] In verse 7 the readers[12] are not so much urged to imitate Christ's welcoming them as to act in a way that is consistent with it.[13] The concluding εἰς δόξαν τοῦ θεοῦ probably goes with the imperative (welcome one another for the glory of God[14]) rather than with the indicative (Christ welcomed you for the glory of God).[15]

Although the glorification of God is both a major theme of the paragraph and the link to verse 6, there are subtle differences in the ways in which it is expressed. In verses 5-6, the glorification of God is homological, a verbal act (ἐν ἑνὶ στόματι) that is to result from a christomorphic common mind (τὸ αὐτὸ φρονεῖν ἐν ἀλλήλοις κατὰ Χριστὸν Ἰησοῦν), which God is asked to give (ὁ δὲ θεὸς . . . δῷν). In verse 7 it is the goal of a moral act that reflects the soteriological experience. In terms of Christian dogmatics, in verses 5-6 it results from sanctification, but in verse 7 it reflects justification.[16]

---

[11] This shift from God to Christ cannot be adduced as evidence of interpolation because in other places as well Paul has Christ do on one page what God does on another. See, e.g., Rom 14:10 and 2 Cor 5:10. The same sort of pattern applies to Christ and the Spirit (see, e.g., Rom 8:27, 34).

[12] If in v. 7 one reads ημας; with BD*P and so on, as well as with the pre-Vulgate and the Sahidic, then Paul would include himself. Better attested, however, is υμας (א ACD² FG lat sy Bo), and is to be preferred. O. Michel (Der Brief an die Römer [5th ed.; KEK; Göttingen: Vandenhoeck & Ruprecht, 1978], 447 n. 19), however, follows Heinrich Schlier (Der Römerbrief [HTKNT; Freiburg: Herder, 1977], 424) in thinking that ημας might be original, even though it sounds "doxological." Zeller's restriction of the ημας to the Gentile Christians in Rome (even though they are not simply equatable with the "strong") is one wholly unconvincing result of his construal of v. 8.

[13] Here καθώς does not have its usual comparative sense but indicates that what follows is a warrant for the imperative. So also C. E. B. Cranfield, A Critical and Exegetical Commentary on the Epistle to the Romans (2 vols.; ICC; Edinburgh: T&T Clark, 1975–1979) 2:799, following Ernst Käsemann, Commentary on Romans (trans. G. W. Bromiley; Grand Rapids: Eerdmans, 1980), 385.

[14] So also H. W. Schmidt, Der Brief des Paulus an die Römer (Berlin: Evangelische Verlagsanstalt, 1966); J. Murray, Romans (2 vols.; NICNT; Grand Rapids: Eerdmans, 1967) gives no reason for rejecting this construction. Westcott-Hort inserted a comma before the prepositional phrase.

[15] So Michel (who does not comment), followed by Cranfield, who finds this construal more appropriate.

[16] Käsemann, who is sensitive to the problems of the passage, sees here evidence that justification by faith is "the theme of the epistle so that exhortation is sustained and surrounded by it" (Romans, 384).

*The christological warrant (vv. 8-9a)*

The serious problems begin here, where a different theme is introduced formally by λέγω γάρ.[17] It is this γάρ that makes what is said about Christ the warrant for the exhortation in verse 7.

Exactly what is said about Christ depends on how one construes the syntax of the complex sentence. There are two major possibilities.[18] According to the first, λέγω governs two clauses that begin with accusatives, thereby making Paul say two things, one about Christ's relation to Jews and the other about the Gentiles' glorification of God.

λέγω γάρ    (1) Χριστὸν διάκονον γεγενῆσθαι περιτομῆς
                 ὑπὲρ ἀληθείας θεοῦ
                 εἰς τὸ βεβαιῶσαι τὰς ἐπαγγελίας τῶν πατέρων
          (2) τὰ δὲ ἔθνη ὑπὲρ ἐλέους
                 δοξάσαι τὸν θεόν.

On this basis, the two ὑπέρ phrases are emphasized and contrasted, and δέ is consequently regarded as "but."[19] However, this makes the purpose clause (εἰς τὸ βεβαιῶσαι κτλ.) virtually a parenthesis[20] (and it appears to be more important than that). The main difficulty is that this construal merely juxtaposes two assertions, with the result that it remains unclear how this statement as a whole warrants verse 7—a difficulty exacerbated by the initial quotation that follows. Indeed, Zeller concludes that verses 8-12 explain only 7b.[21] In other words, it has Paul make a series of statements that, despite explicit connecting links, are in substance disconnected:

1. Welcome one another for the glory of God as Christ welcomed you,
2. because I declare
   (a) [that] Christ became a servant of the circumcision for the sake of God's truthfulness (in order to confirm the promises of the fathers)

[17] Cranfield rightly observes that λέγω γάρ "here introduces a solemn doctrinal declaration" (*Romans*, 2:740).

[18] Cranfield discusses four others in *Romans*, 2:742–44.

[19] So Marie-Joseph Lagrange, *Saint Paul Épitre aux Romains* (Ebib; Paris: J. Gabalda, 1922) followed by Zeller, *Juden und Heiden*, 219. Accordingly, Paul contrasts the "*economie de promisse*" with the "*economie de misericorde.*" Zeller must, therefore, conclude that this passage shows how little the call of the Gentiles can be subsumed under God's covenant of faithfulness—precisely opposite the view being developed in this discussion.

[20] As Käsemann admits, citing Zeller (who cites Lagrange).

[21] Zeller, *Juden und Heiden*.

(b)  but [that] the Gentiles glorify God because of his mercy,
(c)  as it is written, "I will confess you among the Gentiles," and so on.

The second possibility has its eye on neither the two clauses introduced by the accusatives Χριστόν and τὰ ἔθνη nor on the two ὑπέρ phrases, but on the three infinitives (γεγενῆσθαι, βεβαιῶσαι, δοξάσαι) and regards the latter two as explicating the first. Moreover, it assumes that εἰς τό governs two infinitives, thereby having Paul make one complex assertion:

λέγω γὰρ
    Χριστὸν διάκονον γεγενῆσθαι περιτομῆς . . . θεοῦ
        εἰς τὸ βεβαιῶσαι τὰς ἐπαγγελίας . . .
        τὰ δὲ ἔθνη . . . δοξάσαι τὸν θεόν.

On this basis, Christ's becoming a servant of the circumcision has a dual purpose (δέ now regarded as "and"): confirmation of the promises and evocation of the Gentiles' glorification of God. On the whole, the second construal is preferable,[22] though a completely problem-free solution is not likely.

Some modern versions prefer to paraphrase Χριστὸν διάκονον γεγενῆσθαι περιτομῆς. The New Jerusalem Bible, for instance, has "Christ's work was to serve the circumcised," thereby substituting a statement about the work of Christ for his person. More subtle is the result of adopting the aorist infinitive reading γενέσθαι (BC*D*G) instead of adhering to the more difficult (!) perfect infinitive (γεγενῆσθαι), thereby substituting a simple historical event for a more complex transhistorical perspective: Christ has become and continues to be a servant of the circumcision.[23] Why NAS, and de Jonge,[24] have "a servant *to* the circumcision" (emphasis added) is neither clear nor convincing,[25] and KJV's "minister of the circumcision" is quite misleading and wholly un-Pauline. It is unlikely that the phrase means

[22] Michel (*Römer*, 448 n. 22) thinks the second possibility has the advantage of style, the first the advantage of context. NEB follows the second.

[23] For this very reason, Theodor Zahn's commentary prefers the aorist (*Der Brief des Paulus an die Römer* [Leipzig: Deichert, 1910]).

[24] Marinus de Jonge, *Christology in Context: The Earliest Christian Response to Jesus* (Philadelphia: Westminster, 1988), 88.

[25] Sam K. Williams gets it right. The point is not that the Jews were objects of Christ's service (as Weiss' commentary says), rather the genitive points to origin (and, I would add, belonging), as in Rom 1:3; 9:5; Gal 4:4 ("The 'Righteousness of God' in Romans," *JBL* 99 [1980]: 286–87). See also Bernhard Weiss, *Der Brief an die Römer* (Göttingen: Vandenhoeck & Ruprecht, 1899).

more than that Christ became a servant who belongs to the Jewish people.[26]

The next phrase shows what Paul took the clause to mean. The incarnation occurred in a Jew ὑπὲρ ἀληθείας θεοῦ, a clear cross-reference to Romans 3:4, where the truthfulness of God refers to God's faithfulness.[27] To this faithfulness the purpose clause refers: εἰς τὸ βεβαιῶσαι τὰς ἐπαγγελίας τῶν[28] πατέρων. This confirmation, however, includes the Gentiles[29] as equal beneficiaries (as in 4:12-25): τὰ δὲ ἔθνη ὑπὲρ ἐλέους δοξάσαι τὸν θεόν (for Zeller's contrary view, see n. 12 above). In other words, Christ's Jewish identity is significant for the current positive Gentile response to the gospel. Had he not been a Jew, the promise that Gentiles would be blessed through Abraham could not have been kept, and this would have violated the integrity, the fidelity, and the truthfulness of God.[30] This understanding of the matter is said to be supported by Scripture.

## The scriptural warrant (vv. 9b-12)

There follow four quotations, taken from Psalm 17:50 (= 2 Sam 22:30); Deuteronomy 32:43; Psalm 117:1; and Isaiah 11:1, 10, respectively, each distinguished from its neighbor by a form of καὶ πάλιν, not simply combined to form a single "passage" as in Romans 3:10-18.[31] Only in the case of Isaiah is the source identified; deviations from LXX are minor.[32]

Still, there are problems. (a) Given the customary καθὼς γέγραπται, the reader expects that all of the quotations will speak of the Gentile praise of God. As already noted, this appears only in the second and third, while in the first it is the speaker who does so, albeit in a Gentile context (ἐν ἔθνεσιν). The fourth quotation says something quite different. There is one word, and one word only, that connects all four quotations: ἔθνη.

---

[26] Cranfield denies the force of the contrary considerations he cites when he maintains that this alludes to the Isaianic Servant (*Romans*, 2:741 n. 3). In view of Cranfield's concession that "no word of the διακονεῖν group is ever used in the LXX in the Servant Songs," Michel's "διάκονος = עֶבֶד" must be rejected.

[27] See Richard Hays, "Psalm 143 and the Logic of Romans 3," *JBL* 99 (1980): 107–15.

[28] One expects "promises *to* the fathers." Does Paul use the genitive instead because in 9:4 he had written, "to them belong (ὧν) the sonship . . . and the promise"?

[29] Schmidt is right on target in rejecting all interpretations that restrict the scope of the βεβαίωσις to the Jews (*Römer*, 240).

[30] Zeller is surely wrong in saying that v. 8 has a concessive sense, even though Christ became a servant of the circumcision (*Juden und Heiden*, 221).

[31] See my "The Function of Rom 3:10-18," in *God's Christ and His People* (Nils Dahl Festschrift; Oslo: Universitets Forlaget, 1978), 141–57.

[32] O'Neill's claim that this use of the LXX shows that the passage is interpolated because Paul made his own translation (*Paul's Letter to the Romans*, 240) is not convincing.

(b) However, the appearance of ἔθνη throughout poorly conceals the lack of a coherent rationale governing either the sequence or the substance of all four quotations. The sequence of the first three is governed by the idea of the universalizing of the praise of God: confession and praise of God (by a Jew?[33]) among Gentiles leads to a summons to them to join God's people (λαὸς αὐτοῦ) in rejoicing, which leads to an exhortation to all peoples (πάντες οἱ λαοί) to praise God. These three quotations, in this sequence, support the Gentile praise of God in verse 9a, but not a syllable in them prepares the reader for the fourth, which abruptly introduces the idea of the Davidic ruler[34] of Gentiles, and the Gentiles' hope in *him* (not in God!).[35] Indeed, the parity between Jew and Gentile,[36] manifest in the first three quotations (albeit in accord with "to the Jew first") is displaced here by the subjection of the Gentiles to the Jewish Messiah.
(c) Despite the internal coherence of the first three quotations, the connection between the series and verse 9a is awkward because it is not clear who is the subject of verbs ἐξομολογήσομαι and ψαλῶ. Käsemann's proposal that Paul alludes to himself[37] is difficult to accept, but the alternative—that it refers to Christ—is even less satisfactory if taken to refer to the ministry of Jesus.[38] In fact, the transition from verse 9a to Scripture would be

[33] Koch sees the first quotation as being concerned with God's relation to Israel in contrast with the concern of the second and third, which is oriented to Gentiles (*Die Schrift als Zeuge*, 282 n. 25).

[34] Commentators agree that here ῥίζα (root) should be taken to mean "shoot"—i.e., "scion."

[35] Cranfield (*Romans*, 2:747), however, says that this last sentence "makes a fitting conclusion" to the whole series, and Koch claims that *only* the fourth quotation corresponds to the orientation of the quotations that precede it. "Beobachtungen zum christologischen Schriftgebrauch in den vorpaulinischen Gemeinden," *ZNW* 71 (1980): 175. Later, in *Die Schrift als Zeuge* (283), he claims that v. 12 states the presupposition of vv. 9-11, thereby obscuring the difference between the fourth quotation and the other three.

[36] Zeller (*Juden und Heiden*, 221) rightly sees that the Gentiles are not incorporated into Israel. Did Paul overlook the tension between this passage and his analogy of the olive tree in 11:17-24?

[37] Rolf Dabelstein thinks that Paul is the subject not only in v. 9 but also in vv. 10-11 (*Die Beurteilung der "Heiden" bei Paulus* [Frankfurt: Peter Lang, 1981], 108).

[38] Weiss' commentary, *Der Brief an die Römer*, regards the subject as Christ, present among Gentile Christians. Adolf Schlatter (*Gottes Gerechtigkeit* [2nd ed.; Stuttgart: Calwer Verlag, 1952], 383) agrees that it is Christ, but says that the church's confessing and singing are the work of Christ. Koch (*Die Schrift als Zeuge*, 282 n. 24) rejects this identification because it is unlikely that Paul would have included Christ in the church's praise, but he also doubts that the subject is Paul. What Bo Frid ("Jesaja und Paulus in Rom 15, 12," *BZ* 27 [1983]: 241 n. 5) means by saying that it is as a Jew among Gentiles that Christ is a servant of the circumcision is not clear.

smoother without the first quotation; yet, the three quotations have a clear rationale holding them together. (d) According to verses 8-9a, the Christ-event has a dual purpose (confirmation of the promises and evocation of Gentile praise), but the former theme is absent from the first three quotations. However, the chief promise (a Davidic Messiah) appears in the fourth quotation. From the standpoint of "promise," the whole paragraph would have a clearer coherence without the first three quotations in verses 9b-11, which dominate the whole.

## The hortatory benediction (v. 13)

The formal structure of this benediction is virtually identical with that of verses 5-6.[39] Interestingly, here the transition from verse 12 is smooth, for the benediction picks up the theme of hope. Equally interesting is the fact that it does not mention Christ at all (contrast with v. 5).

One way of accounting for these puzzling phenomena has not, to my knowledge, been explored[40]—that they result from the use of two previously independent pieces of tradition. This possibility may prove to be the key to the passage. In fact, all the difficulties can be accounted for by this hypothesis.

## IV

The hypothesis can be stated succinctly: It was Paul himself who created the text before us, and he did so by inserting the threefold quotation into a tradition that consisted of verses 8 and 12, and by adding phrases designed to bind the resulting paragraph to its larger context—namely verse 9, as well as by inserting verse 12. The Pauline character of these phrases argues against the hand of an interpolator or editor.

---

[39] The variants πληροφορησαι εν παση χαρα και ειρηνη (B) and πληροφορησαι παση χαρα και ειρηνη (FG) are difficult to explain. The omission of εν τω πιστευειν (DFG bm) is probably accidental (so also Cranfield, *Romans*, 2:748 n. 4), as is the omission of εις το περισσευειν (B 945 2495).

[40] Wilckens (*Der Brief an die Römer* [EKKNT 6; Zurich: Benziger Verlag, 1978], 1:108) mentions the possibility that verses 9b-12 are an originally independent catena and observes that this would account for the fact that its scope does not agree with the dual purpose of the Christ-event in vv. 8-9a. However, he does not reckon seriously enough with the possibility that also vv. 8 and 12 also constitute a piece of tradition. Koch thinks that in v. 12 Paul is following a Christian tradition (which rests on Jewish tradition) of interpreting Isaiah 11:10 christologically, but he does not pursue the matter ("Beobachtungen," 186). In *Die Schrift als Zeuge* (283 n. 27) he repeats this view and rejects Wilckens' suggestion as bereft of any evidence.

One tradition, probably formed in Hellenistic Jewish Christianity, consisted of the following:

Χριστὸν διάκονον γεγενῆσθαι περιτομῆς
εἰς τὸ βεβαιῶσαι τὰς ἐπαγγελίας τῶν πατέρων,
καθὼς γέγραπται.
    ἔσται ἡ ῥίζα τοῦ Ἰεσσαί,

καὶ[41] ὁ ἀνιστάμενος ἄρχειν ἐθνῶν.
ἐπ᾿αὐτῷ ἔθνη ἐλπιοῦσιν.

The tradition made the legitimacy of Gentile Christianity conditional on acceptance of Jesus' Davidic messiahship, not unlike what we find later in Matthew. This perspective is consonant with the christological tradition that Paul cites, and also modifies, at the beginning of the letter (1:3-4). Paul probably assumed that both of these traditions were known in Rome.

All that remains of the other tradition[42] is the threefold quotation in verses 9b-11, which probably had a prefatory statement that Paul omitted. The distinctive content of this threefold quotation now emerges more clearly. Unless Paul had previously assembled these texts to support his self-interpretation, it is unlikely that the "I" in ἐξομολογήσομαι and ψαλῶ refers to the apostle himself. Rather, it probably refers to Christ[43]—that is, to the preexistent Christ's declaring in advance the purpose of his impending incarnation.[44] Nowhere else does Paul write of the incarnation in the first person. In the New Testament only Hebrews 2:12-14 does so, and there too the author uses three quotations from Scripture. Whereas the quotations in

---

[41] Frid ("Jesaja und Paulus," 239) rightly sees that καί is not a copula here, but represents the Hebrew אשר and should be rendered "even he who."

[42] Although Barnabas Lindars assumes that Paul assembled the quotations, he calls attention to generally overlooked data that might be evidence that the compiler regarded all three quotations as coming from the Psalter. (a) In the Catena, Deut 32:43 (LXX) stands between Psalms 17:49 and 117:1. (b) In LXX, Deut 32 (the Song of Moses) is included in the *Odae*, which follows the Psalms. Lindars infers that "it is probable that it already stood in the previous Jewish text as an additional hymnary for liturgical use." (c) Hebrews 1:6 also cites Deut 32:42, but in a form "which has an exact parallel only in the reading on the *Odae*. There also the quotation occurs in a catena of Psalm verses" (*New Testament Apologetic: The Doctrinal Significance of the Old Testament Quotations* [Philadelphia: Westminster, 1961], 244–45).

[43] One should not confuse this confession with the "good confession "Jesus made before Pilate, according to 1 Tim 6:13.

[44] So too A. T. Hanson, who also says that for Paul the Psalms "are the vehicle by which the Messiah is to praise God in the church (Rom. 15:11)" (*Studies in Paul's Technique and Theology* [London: SPCK, 1974], 171.)

Romans focus on the consequences for Gentiles of Christ's work, those in Hebrews express the three stages of the Christ-event itself. Outside the NT the gnostic Naassene hymn also presents the incarnation in first person, though without relying on biblical quotations.[45]

In using the threefold quotation, Paul's interest is not in the "I" but in the rationale of the whole: through Christ the Gentiles join in the praise of God. Consequently he writes τὰ δὲ ἔθνη . . . θεόν to connect the quotations with the Hellenistic Jewish–Christian tradition, which asserts the confirmation of the patriarchal promise. Moreover, by inserting the triple quotation into the Jewish–Christian tradition, Paul gives a new interpretation to its quotation of Isaiah 11:10 (καὶ ὁ ἀνιστάμενος ἄρχειν ἐθνῶν, ἐπ'αὐτῷ ἔθνη ἐλπιοῦσιν). He deprives it of its imperialistic messianism, on the one hand, and assures its universal religious/soteriological meaning on the other— that is, he takes ἀνιστάμενος to refer to Christ's resurrection,[46] and his ἄρχειν to his universal lordship. These hermeneutical moves are consistent with those made in Romans 1:3-4—the Christ-event is interpreted by incorporating its messianic/Davidic dimensions into a wider context based on the meaning of the resurrection.

V

The resulting rationale and content of this passage, despite its various difficulties, form a fitting and effective climax to the theological/ethical core of Romans. In the first place, whatever the exact ethnic identity of the "weak" and the "strong" may have been, verse 6 clearly sees the ultimate purpose of their requisite unity in Christ as their united praise of God. Romans 15:7-13, then, expands this unity by showing that it is not simply a mutual,

---

[45] But Jesus said, "Father, behold.
Pursued by evils here upon earth
There roams the (work) of thine own breath;
. . .
Therefore send me, Father;
Bearing seals I will descend,
I will pass through all the Aeons,
I will disclose all mysteries . . .
Awaking gnosis I will impart.' "
(From Werner Forester, *Patristic Evidence* [vol. 1: *Gnosis*; Oxford: Clarendon, 1972], 282).

[46] Why Cranfield (*Romans*, 2:747 n. 4) rejects this as "hardly likely" is not clear. Wilkens assumes that Paul sees here an allusion to Christ's resurrection, as does Käsemann. Dietrich-Alex Koch rightly asserts it ("Beobachtungen," 185).

intramural accommodation to be reached in Rome, but a local instance of God's saving purpose in Christ—the eschatological unity of all people, concretely Jew and Gentile. By coming back to this theme, Paul draws a thread through the entire letter and shows that in Scripture God has indeed promised in advance the gospel for all humanity (1:2).[47]

Second, the theme of the universal praise of God is, in Paul's view, much more than a rhetorical flourish. It is the actual, material, soteriological alternative to the root problem of humanity: not giving praise to God or honoring God. The indictment of the Gentiles in 1:21 (γνόντες τὸν θεὸν οὐχ ὡς θεὸν ἐδόξασαν ἢ ηὐχαρίστησαν) and that of the Jews in 2:23 (ὃς ἐν νόμῳ καυχᾶσαι, διὰ τῆς παραβάσεως τοῦ νόμου τὸν θεὸν ἀτιμάζεις;) is basically the same. Moreover, in the next verse the stinging indictment, quoting Isaiah 52:5 (the name of God is blasphemed among the Gentiles because of you) is precisely what is overcome when the Gentiles join the people of God in praising God as a result of Christ.

---

[47] Richard Hays sees this, too, and goes on to observe, "In Romans, Paul cites Scripture not as a repository of miscellaneous wisdom on various topics but as an insistent witness to one great truth: God's righteousness, which has now embraced Gentiles among the people of God, includes the promise of God's unbroken faithfulness to Israel. Virtually every text that Paul cites or alludes to is made to circle around this one theme" (*Echoes of Scripture in the Letters of Paul* [New Haven: Yale University Press, 1989], 73). Hays, however, does not see the inner tensions of the passage discussed here.

# 8

# "Jesus" in Romans

Before one can speak in a truly historical way about Jesus *and* Paul,[1] it is essential to understand "Jesus" *in* Paul. This entails discerning both the "Jesus" to whom Paul refers and accounting for the ways in which he refers to him. Otherwise one subtly insinuates into the discussion modern perspectives, which tend to insist either that Paul had little interest in "the Jesus of history" or that his letters reflect a quite ample knowledge of Jesus—that is, knowledge of the early Jesus traditions as they have been recovered by critical analysis.[2] It is, of course, legitimate to reconstruct the history of the Jesus traditions and then to ascertain, as best one can, their relation to what Paul appears to have known of them, but such inquiry should be undertaken after "Jesus" *in* Paul's thought and mission has been grasped as clearly as possible. In other words, the "Jesus *and* Paul" question is skewed whenever the quantitative issue—How much did Paul know about Jesus?—is allowed to dominate; moreover, what moderns refer to when they speak of Jesus is to be distinguished clearly from the "Jesus" to whom Paul refers. The Letter to the Romans, written for congregations who

---

[1] The vast amount of literature on the subject which scholars have produced has been surveyed and discussed frequently. See, e.g., Victor Paul Furnish, "The Jesus-Paul Debate: From Baur to Bultmann," *BJRL* 47 (1965): 342–81; J. W. Fraser, *Jesus and Paul: Paul as an Interpreter of Jesus from Harnack to Kümmel* (Abingdon, U.K.: Marcham Press, 1974); Friedmann Regner, *"Paulus und Jesus" im 19. Jahrhundert: Beiträge zur Geschichte des Themas "Paulus und Jesus" in der neutestamentlichen Theologie* (Göttingen: Vandenhoeck & Ruprecht, 1977).

[2] See, e.g., Dale C. Allison Jr., "The Pauline Epistles and the Synoptic Gospels: The Pattern of the Parallels," *NTS* 28 (1982): 1–32; Peter Stuhlmacher, "Jesustradition im Römerbrief?" *TBei* 14 (1983): 240–50; Nikolaus Walter, "Paulus und die urchristliche Jesustradition," *NTS* 31 (1985): 498–522.

had no memory of Paul's teaching, is especially useful for this investigation because this letter disallows one line of argument—that Paul need not have written much about Jesus because he had already shared his knowledge as part of his preaching and teaching. At the same time, Paul emphasizes "Jesus" as he makes a case for his grasp of the gospel. Since he is writing to believers, he can also assume that his Roman readers already are informed about Christ, though whether what they knew without Paul coincided with what the Corinthians knew through him is yet to be discerned. In any case, Paul could assume a deposit of tradition which he had not made.

In developing his argument, then, he could bring to bear the persuasive power of his logic, his own understanding of "Jesus," and the readers' knowledge of Christ. By looking closely at Paul's argument, therefore, one should be able to distinguish the Christ assumed to be known in Rome from the "Jesus" Paul's argument requires. However, if such a distinction cannot be made, then one may conclude that Paul assumed that his "Jesus" and that of the readers are identical. That such a conclusion would be significant for the history of early Christology is evident. Be that as it may, analyzing "Jesus" in Romans should provide some clues to both "Jesus" in Paul and to "Jesus" in Rome.

We will begin by surveying Paul's references to "Jesus," noting first what we do not find, then his characteristic expressions (I). Then we will attempt to discern what Paul assumes is known about "Jesus" in Rome (II). After that we will explore what appears to be Paul's distinctive accent (III). Concluding remarks will suggest implications for further work (IV).

I

There are four things that the reader of Romans will find with reference to "Jesus." First, Paul does not deem it necessary for his argument to refer to a single thing that "Jesus" did or said. There is not even an explicit reference to the cross (apart from the oblique allusion in συνεσταυρώθη in 6:6). Where he does refer to "Jesus" he does not mention a Jesus tradition; conversely, where scholars, like Dale Allison, find allusions to Jesus traditions (Rom 12–14), there is no reference to "Jesus" apart from 13:14—"Put on the Lord Jesus Christ." Romans 14:14 is famous precisely because it is not clear whether being "persuaded in the Lord Jesus that nothing is unclean in itself" refers to a tradition that came to Paul (a variant of what is now in Mark 7:1-23) or Paul's inference.[3] In any case, he does not say that he is persuaded *by* Jesus.

[3] In adjudicating the question one should avoid converting the consonance between the Jesus tradition and Paul into his knowledge of and allusion to it, because the points

Second, nowhere does Paul explicitly appeal to traditions, as he does in 1 Corinthians 11:23-25; 15:3-8, though it is reasonably clear that he includes them in his text. The evidence is strongest for the use of traditions in 1:3-4; 3:24-26; 10:9, although other passages (like 4:24-25; 8:34) have been identified as well. The only authority that Paul cites explicitly is Scripture. Romans may well include confessional traditions about "Jesus" and allude to traditions of Jesus' teachings, but Paul is as unconcerned with identifying the one as the other: this implies that the greater the evidence that he is using traditions, the more likely that he assumes that his readers will recognize them.

Third, although Paul states that "Jesus" was a descendant of David and that Christ had been a minister of Israel (1:3-4; 15:8), and although chapters 9–11 wrestle with the Jews' refusal of the gospel, he never says that the Jews refused Jesus. Indeed, apart from 9:5 and 10:4-9 he wrestles with the meaning of Israel without referring to "Jesus"; conversely, when he expounds the meaning of "Jesus" he says nothing about Israel until the complex paragraph in 15:7-13 (see preceding chapter).

Fourth, although the heart of Paul's gospel is the "Jesus"-event, he never uses the man's proper name in conjunction with εὐαγγέλιον;[4] his phrase is εὐαγγέλιον τοῦ Χριστοῦ (15:19)[5] or τοῦ θεοῦ (1:1; 15:16; see also 2 Cor 11:7; 1 Thess 2:2, 6, 9).[5]

On the other hand, one finds that Paul refers to "Jesus" in a number of characteristic ways, beginning with the fact that the overwhelming number of references to "Jesus" mention "Christ" absolutely, as if it were a proper name. Only in 9:5 does ὁ Χριστός retain its meaning as a title or office.[6] Indeed, so dominant are the references to "Christ" alone (34 times)

---

registered by the tradition and by Paul are not identical. Moreover, Heikki Räisänen rightly observes that "the οἶδα καὶ πέπεισμαι clause would be a very surprising formula to introduce a quotation from *verba domini*"—or, one might add, an allusion (*Paul and the Law* [WUNT 29; Tübingen: Mohr Siebeck, 1983], 247). Even if Paul had in mind a Jesus tradition, he clearly does not point his readers to it. In fact, being "persuaded in the Lord Jesus" is *his* warrant, not one that he assumes is shared also with the readers.

[4] Second Corinthians 11:8 does use "another Jesus" in the same breath as "another gospel" and "another Spirit" as part of Paul's taunting the readers for receiving his rivals. Even so, Paul never writes "the gospel of Jesus."

[5] See also 1 Cor 9:12; 2 Cor 2:12; 9:13; Gal 1:7; Phil 1:27; the context prompted "the gospel of the glory of Christ" in 2 Cor 4:4. The more elaborate "the gospel of our Lord Jesus Christ" (2 Thess 1:8) and "my gospel and the kerygma of Jesus Christ" (Rom 16:25) are found only in nongenuine texts.

[6] See Nils A. Dahl, "The Messiahship of Jesus," in *The Crucified Messiah* (Minneapolis: Augsburg, 1974), 37–47.

that the fuller phrases stand out: Jesus Christ, Christ Jesus, Christ Jesus our Lord.[7] The tradition cited in 1 Corinthians 15:3-8 shows that using "Christ" as a proper name did not begin with Paul; he evidently assumes that this usage is known and accepted also in Rome. The ways in which Paul uses "Christ" in Romans are to be noted as well. He eschews it as the subject of verbs in the present tense, though twice ἐστίν is to be supplied: at 8:10 (εἰ δὲ Χριστὸς ἐν ὑμῖν) and at 10:4 (τέλος . . . νόμου Χριστός) and once it has a future sense: Χριστὸς . . . οὐκέτι ἀποθνῄσκει (6:9). Everywhere else in Romans it is the subject of verbs that refer to past action, most frequently ἀπέθανεν (5:6, 8; 14:19)[8] Only once in the uncontested letters does Paul write "Jesus died"— in 1 Thessalonians 4:14, which might be traditional language.[9]

On the other hand, Κύριος, when used absolutely, does retain its titular meaning: Paul's διὰ Χριστοῦ has no counterpart in διὰ Κυρίου. More intriguing, however, is something else: in view of the diverse uses of "the Lord" in Paul's other letters,[10] in Romans this usage is reduced

---

[7] Interestingly, neither Paul's reference to "Jesus" nor the ways of referring to him are distributed evenly in Romans. The absolute use of "Christ" begins at 5:6; prior to this, all references are to Jesus, Jesus Christ, Christ Jesus, or to God's Son. As a result the absolute use of "Christ" dominates chaps. 5–8. This is the sort of data used by Robin Scroggs to argue that Romans combines two homilies: chaps. 1–4; 9–11 and 5–8 ("Paul as Rhetorician: Two Homilies in Romans 1–11," in *Jews, Greeks and Christians: Religious Cultures in Late Antiquity* [ed. R. Hamerton-Kelly and R. Scroggs; Studies in Judaism in Late Antiquity 21; Festschrift for W. D. Davies; Leiden: Brill, 1976], 271–98).

[8] See also 1 Cor 8:11; 15:1; Gal 2:21.

[9] So, e.g., the commentaries by I. Howard Marshall and F. F. Bruce. In 2 Cor 4:10 Paul writes of τὴν νέκρωσιν and ἡ ζωὴ τοῦ Ἰησοῦ.

[10] Even an incomplete overview shows the wide range of Paul's usage apart from Romans (and apart from nonchristological uses of *kyrios* in Rom 14:4; 1 Cor 7:10; Gal 4:1). (a) *Kyrios* can be used of both biological and religious relationships ("brothers of the Lord" [1 Cor 9:5; Gal 1:19] and "brother in the Lord" [Phil 1:14]). (b) "The Lord" can refer both to the person who once lived and now lives a resurrected life, as is clear from the eucharistic passages: not only did Paul receive a tradition "from the Lord" (1 Cor 11:23), but he writes of the cup and the table of the Lord (1 Cor 10:21) and of the "body and blood of the Lord" which the Corinthians can now profane (1 Cor 11:27). So too, where we might refer to Jesus, Paul can refer to "the Lord": the rulers crucified "the Lord of glory" (1 Cor 2:8); Christians at the table proclaim "the Lord's death" (1 Cor 11:26); God "raised the Lord" (1 Cor 6:14). (c) The Parousia will be the coming of the Lord (1 Cor 4:5 [1 Thess 4:16]). (d) "The Lord" is the subject of verbs referring to present activity: he says (1 Cor 7:12), gives (1 Cor 7:17), commands (1 Cor 7:25; 9:14), judges (1 Cor 11:32). (e) "The Lord" can also be the object of verbs of human action: test (1 Cor 10:22), be persuaded (Gal 5:10; Phil 2:24), rejoice (Phil 3:1; 4:4, 10), think (Phil 4:2), stand steadfast (Phil 4:1; 1 Thess 3:8), extend hospitality (Phil 1:29). (g) Paul can speak "according to the Lord" (2 Cor 11:17) as well as "in the Lord's word" (1 Thess 4:15).

markedly,[11] and all uses of Κύριος which refer unambiguously to "Jesus" are found in chapters 14–16. Κύριος alone does, to be sure, appear in chapters 1–13, but always it either refers clearly to God or can be taken to refer to God as easily as to "Jesus."[12] Perhaps the massive use of Scripture has suppressed Paul's own usage except in phrases which mention "Jesus," like "Jesus Christ our Lord." If this inference is valid, one may conclude that whereas Paul assumes that the Roman readers too use Χριστός as a personal name, he does not assume that his customary use of Κύριος alone for "Jesus" is as common among them as in his own churches. (The Romans would not have known this, of course.) If this conclusion too be plausible, then he sensed that his absolute use of "Jesus" might imply that he blurs the distinction between "Jesus" and God; he would then have diminished his own usage lest he be accused of compromising monotheism. No comparable inhibition manifests itself, however, with regard to "Son" (Rom 1:3, 4, 9; 5:10; 8:3, 14, 19, 29, 32)—suggesting that this usage was well established also in Rome.

Two prepositions allow Paul to express the significance of "Jesus" in a remarkably wide range of ways, namely, ἐν and διά. Many of these references to "Jesus" have a formulaic quality. Frequently they appear at the beginning or at the end of a paragraph, and in those parts of the letter which follow epistolary conventions.[13] Such formulaic passages are to be distinguished from those in which the ἐν or διά expressions are essential to the argument, as we shall see.

Apart from three occurrences of ἐν Κυρίῳ Ἰησοῦ (Rom 14:14; Phil 2:9; 1 Thess 4:1), Paul consistently uses either ἐν Χριστῷ Ἰησοῦ or ἐν Χριστῷ, apparently interchangeably.[14] Never does he write ἐν Ἰησοῦ, indicating that

---

[11] "In the Lord" characterizes persons (Rom 16:8, 11, 12, 13) and their labor (16:12), as in n. 10. Also "we are the Lord's" (14:8) paraphrases 1 Cor 6:13. Unique to Romans, however, is the idea that certain activities are done "to the Lord" (14:6, 8).

[12] In Rom 4:6-8; 9:28; 10:16; 11:3, 34; 12:9; 14:11, it refers to God because the LXX is being cited. In 10:12-13 and 12:11, however, the referent is ambiguous; in the former because v. 13 quotes the LXX, in the latter because v. 9 refers to God.

[13] The beginning: e.g., 1:8—thank . . . God through (διά) our Lord Jesus Christ; 5:1—peace . . . through our Lord Jesus Christ; 8:1—no condemnation . . . in (ἐν) Christ Jesus; 15:30—I exhort . . . through ̎διά) our Lord Jesus Christ. The end: e.g., 5:11—boast . . . through (διά) our Lord Jesus Christ; 5:21—grace reigns . . . through (διά) Christ our Lord; 6:23—eternal life in (ἐν) Christ Jesus our Lord; 7:25—Thanks . . . through Jesus Christ our Lord; 8:39—love of God in (ἐν) Christ Jesus our Lord. Epistolary conventions: Rom 1:7 (grace wish); 16:3-16 (greetings).

[14] So also Fritz Neugebauer, *In Christus* (Göttingen: Vandenhoeck & Ruprecht, 1961), 51. Still worth reading is Friedrich Büchsel, " 'In Christus' bei Paulus," *ZNW* 42 (1949): 141–52, written to correct the excesses of Adolf Deissmann's views.

for him Χριστός and Ἰησοῦς are not simply interchangeable. Paul's customary ἐν Χριστῷ is used in three distinguishable senses. (1) The ecclesial sense is found in Romans 16, beginning with verse 3, where Prisca and Aquila are called his coworkers "in Christ Jesus."[15] (2) It appears as a christological warrant for what Paul says in Romans 14:14 ("persuaded in the Lord Jesus Christ") and in 15:17 (he boasts "in Christ Jesus"). He does not, however, use the phrase to warrant his argument in chapters 1–11. This datum, coupled with the observation that most warranting uses are found outside Romans,[16] suggests two things: that Paul is aware that his Roman readers are not as familiar with this idiom as those in his own churches, and that it is in pastoral and paraenetic materials that he deems it appropriate to appeal to such a warrant. The argument in Romans 1–11, however, must stand on its own and not appeal to what Paul's relation to Christ authorizes him to say.

(3) In contrast with these somewhat formulaic uses of the ἐν-phrases, Paul can also make his argument turn on the expression, as he had done previously.[17] In Romans 6:3 Paul reminds the readers that their baptism into Christ was a baptism into his death; accordingly, they hope to share his resurrection also. Meanwhile they should consider themselves dead to sin/alive to God ἐν Χριστῷ Ἰησοῦ (v. 11), because they are able to live a new life (v. 4). God's gift of eternal life comes ἐν Χριστῷ Ἰησοῦ τῷ Κυρίῳ ἡμῶν (v. 23).

---

[15] See also 1 Cor 1:2; 16:24; Phil 1:2; 4:21; Phlm 23. Perhaps "the dead in Christ" (1 Cor 15:15, 18) and "those who hoped in Christ" (1 Cor 15:19) belong here, too.

[16] In 1 Cor 15:31 Paul's boast is "in Christ Jesus our Lord" (see also Phil 3:3). In 2 Cor 2:17; 12:19 he speaks "in Christ," and in 2 Cor 12:2 he refers to himself as "a man in Christ." First Corinthians 4:17 refers to the style of his ministry as "my ways in Christ Jesus." The Philippians are to set their minds on what they see (implied) "in Christ Jesus" (viz., on what is celebrated in the hymn which follows). The Thessalonians, whom Paul exhorts "in the Lord Jesus" (1 Thess 4:1), are to know that giving thanks in all circumstances is God's will "in Christ" (1 Thess 5:18).

[17] In Phil 3:9 Paul hopes to be found "in him" (viz., Christ), and v. 14 refers to the "upward call of God in Christ Jesus." He tells the Corinthians that they are sanctified "in Christ Jesus" (1 Cor 1:2), and that God's grace was given "in Christ Jesus" (1 Cor 1:30), though they are still babes "in Christ" (1 Cor 3:1). In 1 Cor 4:10-11 he taunts them for being "in Christ" and for having many tutors "in Christ," though Paul himself had "begotten" them "in Christ." In 2 Cor 2:14 he thanks God for leading "in Christ" a triumphal procession. According to 2 Cor 3:14 the veil over the Jewish mind is destroyed "in Christ Jesus." The most important passages are 2 Cor 5:17—if anyone is "in Christ" he/she is καινὴ κτίσις, and v. 18—"in Christ" God was reconciling the world. The whole point of Galatians 3 turns on being "in Christ Jesus," the one seed of Abraham through which God's blessing reaches the Gentiles (Gal 3:19). Therefore "in Christ Jesus" the Galatians are (already) sons of God, and one "in Christ" (Gal 3:26, 28). Accordingly, (only) "in Christ Jesus" neither circumcision nor uncircumcision matters (Gal 5:6).

According to 8:1 no condemnation awaits those ἐν Χριστῷ Ἰησοῦ because "the spirit of life ἐν Χριστῷ Ἰησοῦ" has liberated them from the law of sin and death. Nothing can separate one from God's love ἐν Χριστῷ Ἰησοῦ τῷ Κυρίῳ ἡμῶν (v. 39, a formulaic use). Whether these uses of ἐν Χριστῷ are instrumental or locative,[18] Paul relies on the expression to emphasize the redemptive role of "Jesus." Still, it is remarkable that the expression does not occur more often in Romans; it bears full weight only in chapter 6, on which the use in chapter 8 depends.

The phrase which Paul prefers in Romans is its near equivalent, διὰ Χριστοῦ[19] (12 out of 23 occurrences are in Romans). It can refer to what Paul does as well as to what God does.[20] God's action διὰ Χριστοῦ can refer to the past, the present, or the future.[21] Likewise the phrase can refer to what Christians enjoy in the present or their future.[22] "Jesus" is the instrument through which God has acted, is acting, and will act.

Three conclusions can be drawn from Paul's characteristic ways of referring to "Jesus." (1) Although Romans is a theocentric book, everything about Paul that matters and everything that Christians are and hope for pivot on this figure "in" whom and "through" whom God effects salvation. That is, Paul refers to him "adverbially"—to specify and qualify God's act. (2) Combining all the references produces only a skeleton outline for which all the connecting links must be supplied: God's preexistent Son became also a descendant of David who as a minister of Israel did not please himself but was obedient; his death (implicitly by crucifixion) was God's own ἱλαστήριον; and after he was raised from the realm of the dead he sat down at God's right

[18] Büchsel finds most uses are instrumental, and only occasionally "local" ("'In Christus,'" 149).

[19] See Wilhelm Thüsing, Per Christum in Deum (Münster: Aschendorff, 1965), chap. 5.

[20] Paul thanks God (1:8), boasts in God (5:2, 11 [bis]), exhorts (15:30). Comparable expressions occur elsewhere. In 2 Cor 1:20 he speaks the amen to God, and in 2 Cor 3:4 he has confidence toward God "through Christ." In 1 Cor 1:10 and 2 Cor 10:1 he uses an expanded form of the phrase as an equivalent of "in the Lord Jesus Christ" (1 Thess 4:1-2) in connection with exhortation. God is the unstated giver when Paul says he received his apostleship "through Christ" (Rom 1:5; see also Gal 1:1).

[21] The past: in Rom 8:37 "we triumph through him who loved us" might refer to Christ (see v. 35) rather than God; yet 5:8 shows that Paul does not separate them. The present: in Rom 3:22-24 it is rectification; see also Gal 3:16. The future: according to Rom 2:26 God will judge "through Jesus Christ."

[22] The present: in Rom 5:1 Christians "have peace with God through our Lord Jesus Christ" (assuming that the preferred reading is εχομεν and not εχωμεν). The future: according to Rom 5:19, many will be made righteous (δίκαιοι κατασταθήσονται) through Christ's obedience; if the future reference is implied also in v. 21, it is explicit in v. 17: βασιλεύσουσιν διὰ τοῦ ἑνὸς Ι. Χ.

hand, where he (as well as the Spirit) intercedes on behalf of the believers. This is all that Paul needs to mention in order to develop his case for the gospel; indeed, only rarely does Paul use the proper name alone which this figure was given by his parents, and which the Gospels use consistently.[23] (3) A discourse without a narrative profile of the "Jesus" on whom everything turns is effective, we may infer, only if the readers already know enough about "Jesus" that Paul can mention a single item, or, on occasion, several.

II

Can one infer what Paul assumed his Roman readers already knew about "Jesus"? In the opening sentence, Paul uses a tradition that expressed the significance of "Jesus" in a two-stage Christology; moreover, it is commonly held, probably rightly, that by incorporating it syntactically as a modifier of "Son," Paul subtly made it part of his own three-stage Christology, which begins with preexistence.[24] For Paul, the limitation of this tradition that had to be overcome was not its silence about everything between Christ's appearance and departure from earthly life but its starting point. Two implications are to be noted. First, Paul deviated from his customary greeting to include this tradition because he assumed that it was established in Rome; using it would demonstrate that his Christology was consonant with that of his readers. Second, he probably assumed that the Romans also had access to additional information about the Davidic descent and the resurrection. Such information probably had a narrative structure, for not only does the resurrection imply a prior death but one can scarcely imagine anyone confessing these things about a person's significance without some sort of narrative context.[25]

The dense paragraph about God's righteousness apart from law (3:21-26) has four references to "Jesus," two of which concern his πίστις (discussed later); the others mention "the redemption which is in Christ Jesus" (v. 24) and his death as ἱλαστήριον (v. 25). Here too it is generally agreed that Paul

[23] It is one thing to recognize that Paul sometimes finds it appropriate to refer to Christ by his proper name alone (as in Gal 6:17, "the stigmata of Jesus"), another for Walter Schmithals to claim that because of gnostic influence Paul uses it only to emphasize the earthly manifestation of the divine-human figure (*Gnosticism in Corinth* [Nashville: Abingdon, 1971], 130–32). Indeed, Rom 8:11 shows that Paul can use Christ and Jesus interchangeably.

[24] I am not persuaded by James D.G. Dunn's attempt to deny that preexistence was part of Paul's Christology (*Christology in the Making* [Philadelphia: Westminster, 1980]).

[25] The narrative structure of Paul's Christology has been shown by Richard B. Hays, *The Faith of Jesus Christ* (SBLDS 56; Chico, Calif.: Scholars Press, 1983).

uses a tradition,[26] though it has proved exceedingly difficult to recover it precisely from his cumbersome sentence. Four implications are to be seen. First, Paul assumes that the reader needs no explanation of "redemption" because syntactically it is the means (διά + genitive) by which justification occurs. Similarly, in 8:23 (the other occurrence of ἀπολύτρωσις in Romans[27]), "the redemption of our bodies" is in apposition to "adoption" (υἱοθεσία)— that is, the better known illumines the lesser known υἱοθεσία, which Paul is expounding in verses 14-25. Even if "the redemption of our bodies" would have been a phrase unfamiliar to the Romans, Paul assumes that "the redemption which is in Christ Jesus itself needs no explanation. Second, here too Paul assumes that the reader will recognize the concept and infer that he is interpreting shared material. Third, the ἱλαστήριον tradition construed the significance of Christ's death in sacrificial terms; moreover, the reference to the "blood" clearly implies a violent death. Since it is difficult to imagine such an interpretation for an accidental death (e.g., being crushed by a chariot) the sacrificial death implies execution—though it could have been by stoning as well as by crucifixion. Again, one can infer that Paul assumes that the reader has some narrative of this death as the appropriate referent of the formulation. Fourth, in using this tradition which says that God "put forth" (προέθετο) this person as ἱλαστήριον, Paul assumes that the reader too understands the death as God's act—a point he makes in his own words at 5:8. In short, while the tradition does not assume any particular narrative in order to be intelligible, it does imply a Passion Narrative of some sort.

Romans 6:1-11 shows that Paul assumes that the Romans also understand "Jesus" to be more than a historical phenomenon whose lineage and death can be narrated, because he reminds them ("do you not know?" v. 3) that baptism made them participants in Christ's death. Paul takes for granted that the readers too understand "Jesus" to be a reality into which one can be "inserted" (as in Rom 13:4), and which therefore qualifies one's existence definitively. Such an understanding requires no particular narrative about "Jesus."

The difficult passage in Romans 10:5-9 concentrates on the arrival and departure of "Jesus," as does 1:3-4. Paul interprets Deuteronomy 30:12-13,

---

[26] On the other hand, Charles H. Talbert has argued that the text contains an interpolation ("A Non-Pauline Fragment at Romans 3:24-26?" *JBL* 85 [1966]: 287–96).

[27] Apart from these two occurrences, Paul mentions "redemption" only in 1 Cor 1:30, in conjunction with "our righteousness and sanctification." The word is used four times by the deuteropaulines (Eph 1:7, 14; 4:30; Col 1:14).

which refers to the law, as referring to the Christ-event which has happened. Christ already has descended from heaven, and already he has been brought up from hades—the former referring to the incarnation, the latter to the resurrection. Paul assumes that his readers will grasp the allusion to the incarnation even though previously he had not written of Christ's descent from heaven. Furthermore, since this construal of Deuteronomy follows the assertion that "Christ is the τέλος of the law" (10:4), he assumes that it is this event as a whole that establishes it as the law's τέλος, not anything that Jesus had said about the law or had done with regard to it.

In 15:3 Paul supports his exhortation (that each Roman believer should edify his neighbor) by appealing to "Jesus," who did not please himself either—a claim said to accord with an allusion to the passion which he finds in Psalm 69:9. In this context, Christ's not pleasing himself means that he accepted the passion willingly and neither insisted on his own innocence nor sought to avoid death. Although later readers who also know the Gospels might associate Paul's statements with the Gethsemane tradition, there is no reason to infer that either Paul or the Romans would have done so. What interests Paul is the paraenetic function of Christ's demeanor: the strong in Rome are to forgo self-assertion and self-vindication for the sake of the weak as Christ, for the good of sinners, had not asserted himself. By saying that Psalm 69:9 was written "for our instruction," Paul either shows that he does not assume that this christological reading of Scripture is taken for granted in Rome or states the tacitly shared way of reading the text.

In 15:7-9 Paul sums up his exhortation by appealing to the readers' own experience of "Jesus": "as Christ welcomed you." Here he obviously assumes that they understand the one who welcomed them to be a figure who transcends the time and place of Jesus. His solemn declaration ("for I say to you") "that Christ became a servant/slave of the circumcised[28] in order to confirm the promises given to the patriarchs" not only states a basic theme in Romans but reminds the readers of his initial statement about "Jesus" in 1:3-4.

To summarize: (a) Paul assumes that his Roman readers already know certain things about "Jesus," partly narrative-type material which the christological traditions interpreted in specific ways, and partly a view of "Jesus" as a figure whose identity exceeds his "lifetime": on the one hand, he came from heaven (implying the incarnation of a preexisting being); on the

---

[28] Modern translations frequently paraphrase Paul here. Thus RSV and NASB have "servant to the circumcised," and the NJB has "Christ's work was to serve the circumcised"; NEB and NIV, however, are more correct in translating Paul's as "servant of the Jewish people/Jews," respectively.

other hand, he is now a reality into which the baptized are inserted. Paul also assumes that they could say something about the (messianic) lineage, and narrate the execution, resurrection, and session at God's right hand (assuming that 8:34 uses a tradition); he also assumes that they understand "Jesus" to be God's Son, through whom God wrought redemption. (b) The evidence adduced thus far does not indicate whether Paul assumed that the Romans also knew Jesus' teachings and deeds. There is no way of knowing, of course, whether his assumptions were right. What is clear is that Paul presents himself not as bearer of new information about "Jesus" but as the interpreter of the figure the readers already know about. Nor does Paul present himself as the recipient of information from or about "Jesus"; there are no christological warrants that go beyond the assumed "common knowledge" about "Jesus." (c) It is remarkable that Paul assumes so much continuity between what the Romans already know about "Jesus" and his own Christology. What is distinctive about "Jesus" in Romans, therefore, is the way Paul nuances and deepens this shared understanding.

III

There are three passages in which Paul reveals his own distinctive thought: 3:21-26, which twice mentions the πίστις Ἰησοῦ; 5:12-21, which emphasizes Christ's obedience; and 5:8, which identifies Christ's act and God's deed.

*Romans 3:21-26*

Several considerations can orient the discussion of Romans 3:21-26. To begin with, the two occurrences of πίστις Ἰησοῦ Χριστοῦ[29] stand in Paul's interpretive framework for the tradition. Second, like δικαιοσύνη/δικαιοῦν, the vocabulary which binds the paragraph together, the repetition of this phrase shows that it is especially important for Paul's argument. Third, although the Romans could scarcely have known that Paul had used the expression five times before, these prior uses should be examined before turning to Romans 3:21-26. Finally, customarily the genitive has been regarded as an objective genitive—as specifying the object toward which πίστις is directed ("faith in Jesus Christ"); but if it is a subjective genitive instead ("Jesus' own πίστις"), the consequences would be far-reaching indeed.

---

[29] From 3:22 B and Marcion omit Ιησου, thereby reading δια ποστεως χριστου. At 3:26 a number of manuscripts read τον εκ πιστεως Ιησου Χριστου; the majority ready simply Ιησου but FG omits all mention of Christ, reading simply τον εκ πιστεως. A few manuscripts (33 614, etc.) have τον εκ πιστεως Ιησουν—so that God justifies Jesus on the basis of faith! There is no significant difference between the πίστος Ἰησοῦ Χριστοῦ and the πίστος Ἰησοῦ.

The phrase has been regarded, with growing persistence, as a subjective genitive;[30] still, it remains the view of a minority, albeit a growing one.[31] Construing the genitive as objective is so widespread[32] that it is usually assumed that the burden of proof falls on the advocates of the subjective genitive. Actually, it should fall on the defenders of the traditional view. Not only does Liddell-Scott-Jones cite no objective genitive in connection with πίστος,[33] but, according to Howard, the subjective genitive is supported consistently by Hellenistic Jewish literature and by the Latin, Syriac, and Sahidic versions as well.[34] If the ancients understood the phrase as a subjective genitive, Paul would have departed from customary usage in writing not only to his own churches (where he might assume that his peculiar usage is known) but also to readers in Rome, who were unfamiliar with his idiosyncratic way of referring to the believers' relation to Christ.[35]

---

[30] "The faith of Christ" as the right rendering was first proposed in 1806 by J. MacKnight; so George Howard, "The 'Faith of Christ,'" *ExpTim* 85 (1973–1974): 212. J. Haussleiter made the same proposal near the end of the last century ("Der Glaube Jesu Christi und der christliche Glaube: Ein Beitrag zur Erklärung des Römerbriefes," *NKZ* [1891]: 109–45, 205–30); subsequently he claimed it is a genitive *auctoris* (so Karl Kertelge, *"Rechtfertigung" bei Paulus* [Münster: Aschendorff, 1972], 164). Gerhard Kittel agreed with Haussleiter's original view (*"Pistis Iesou Christou* bei Paulus," *TSK* 79 [1906]: 419–36). Apparently it was Gabriel Hebert who began the more recent discussion with " 'Faithfulness' and 'Faith,' " *Theology* 58 (1955): 373–79. For a useful brief history of the discussion, see Hays, *The Faith of Jesus Christ*, 158–62.

[31] E.g., Henrik Ljungmann, *Pistis* (Lund: Gleerup, 1964), 38–47 (who appears to affirm both!); George Howard, "On the 'Faith of Jesus Christ,'" *HTR* 60 (1967): 459–65; E. R. Goodenough and A. T. Kraabel, "Paul and the Hellenization of Christianity," in *Religions in Antiquity: Essays in Memory of Erwin Ramsdell Goodenough* (ed. J. Neusner; SHR 14; Leiden: Brill, 1968), 44–45; Markus Barth, " 'The Faith of the Messiah,' " *HeyJ* 10 (1969): 363–70; D. W. F. Robinson, " 'Faith of Jesus Christ'—A New Testament Debate," *Reformed Theological Review* 29 (1970): 71–81; George Howard, "Romans 3:21-31 and the Inclusion of the Gentiles," *HTR* 63 (1970): 223–33; idem, "The 'Faith of Christ,' " 212–15; Sam K. Williams, "The 'Righteousness of God' in Romans," *JBL* 99 (1980): 241–90, esp. 272–76; Luke T. Johnson, "Romans 3:21-26 and the Faith of Jesus," *CBQ* 44 (1982): 77–90; Hays, *The Faith of Jesus Christ*, 157–73; Sam K. Williams, "Again *Pistis Christou*," *CBQ* 49 (1987): 431–47.

[32] See C. E. B. Cranfield (*A Critical and Exegetical Commentary on the Epistle to the Romans* [2 vols.; ICC; Edinburgh: T&T Clark, 1983–1985]), who mentions only Haussleiter; U. Wilckens (*Der Brief an die Römer* [EKKNT 6; Zürich: Benziger Verlag, 1978]), who simply refers to Käsemann, who merely calls Haussleiter's view mistaken; O. Michel (*Der Brief an die Römer* [Göttingen: Vandenhoeck & Ruprecht, 1978]), who acknowledges the alternative; Heinrich Schlier (*Der Römerbrief* [HTKNT; Freiburg: Herder, 1977]), who ignores the question; and Hans Dieter Betz (*Galatians: A Commentary on Paul's Letter to the Churches in Galatia* [Hermeneia; Philadelphia: Fortress, 1979]).

[33] Noted by Robinson, " 'Faith of Jesus Christ'—A New Testament Debate," 71–72.

[34] Howard, " 'Faith of Christ,' " 212–13.

[35] A. J. Hultgren, without using Howard's evidence, defended the objective genitive by

Since the phrase πίστος Ἰησοῦ/Χριστοῦ discloses Paul's distinctive under-standing of "Jesus" in Romans, a brief review of his usage is in order. Because detailed evidence on behalf of the subjective genitive has been advanced (see nn. 30, 31), it suffices to note that in every case, construing πίστις Ἰησοῦ as the fidelity of Jesus not only removes unwarranted awkwardness from Paul's statements but clarifies the key point—the role of "Jesus" in salvation.

In Galatians 2:16 Paul uses the expression twice (changing from Ἰησοῦ to Χριστοῦ for stylistic reasons): "knowing that a person is not justified by works of the law but διὰ πίστεως Ἰησοῦ, we too have believed in Christ Jesus (εἰς Χριστὸν Ἰησοῦν ἐπιστεύσαμεν[36]) so that we might be justified ἐκ πίστεως Ἰησοῦ and not by works of law." Taking πίστις Ἰησοῦ as objective genitives creates two odd results. The one produces an un-Pauline, wooden redundancy: "knowing that a person is not justified by works of the law but through faith in Jesus Christ we too have believed in Christ Jesus in order to be justified by faith in Christ." The second separates Christ from justification, which now depends solely on human believing,[37] a separa-tion which conflicts with what verse 17 emphasizes—that justification is ἐν Χριστῷ. Actually, Paul deliberately distinguishes the believing in Christ from the πίστις of Christ, because this is the basis of justification which is contrasted with "works of law" (or simply "law," according to v. 21).[38] At stake here is emancipation from a subjectivist reading of justification, according to which its basis is either our "works" or our believing. However, the real alternative is our "works" or Christ's πίστις, not our deeds or our faith.[39] If

---

appealing to Paul's own usage: in referring to someone's Christian faith Paul regularly uses the article, as in ἡ πίστις ὑμῶν; accordingly, had he wanted to write of Christ's faith he would have written ἡ πίστις τοῦ Χριστοῦ. However, given the ἡ πίστις ὑμῶν as Paul's idiom for a per-son's faith, he could hardly have used ἡ πίστις [τοῦ] Ἰησοῦ to refer to Jesus' fidelity even if τὴν πίστιν τοῦ θεοῦ is formally similar. In other words, to accommodate πίστις = fidelity, Paul uses πίστις Ἰησοῦ/Χριστοῦ instead (Arland J. Hultgren, "The *Pistis Christou* Formulation in Paul," *NovT* 22 [1980]: 248–63). For a more detailed critique of Hultgren's argument from Paul's syn-tax, see Williams, "Again *Pistis Christou*," 431–35.

[36] Here Paul uses his customary verbal expression for the response to the gospel: πιστεύειν εἰς (or ἐπί or πρός). Never does he use its noun equivalent, πίστις εἰς; yet this is exactly what "through faith in Jesus" would imply: διὰ πίστεως εἰς Ἰησοῦν.

[37] Hays puts it well (with reference to Abraham): "If we are justified by believing in Jesus Christ, in what sense is Abraham's theocentric faith a precedent for ours, or in what sense is our Christocentric faith analogous to his? If Abraham could be justified by trusting God, why should we believe in *Christ* to be justified? Why not simply put our trust in God, as Abraham did?" (*Faith of Jesus Christ*, 165).

[38] So too Williams, "Again *Pistis Christou*," 444.

[39] Greer M. Taylor too sees the theological problem to which "faith in Christ" leads in

Christ's πίστις were not involved, why should one believe "in" him, and how would one be justified "in" him?[40]

When the RSV renders Galatians 2:20c as "the life I now live in the flesh I live by faith in the Son of God," it implies that Paul wrote ἐν πίστει ζῶ εἰς τὸν υἱὸν τοῦ θεοῦ instead of ἐν πίστει ζῶ τῇ[41] τοῦ υἱοῦ τοῦ θεοῦ plus a phrase characterizing God's Son: "who loved me and gave himself for me." If Paul writes of *his* "faith in the Son of God," then "who loved me" etc. is but a christological appendage, for which Paul could have substituted any other christological clause without affecting the logic of the sentence. But if Paul is writing about the *Son's* πίστις, then the christological clause exegetes this πίστις as Christ's self-giving, and the sentence is more cogent. Indeed, the whole passage is more coherent because now Paul writes of the Son's faithfulness: "I have been crucified with Christ; and the life I now live in the flesh I live by the faithfulness of God's Son, who loved me," etc.

In Galatians 3:22 Paul writes, "Scripture confined everything under sin so that the promise [to Abraham] ἐκ πίστεως Ἰησοῦ Χριστοῦ δοθῇ τοῖς πιστεύουσιν," which the RSV renders as "that what was promised to faith in Jesus Christ might be given to those who believe." The ἐκ πίστεως Ἰησοῦ Χριστοῦ surely modifies the verb δοθῇ, not the noun ἐπαγγελία. Here too Paul's point concerns the basis on which what was promised was given to those who believe, namely, the πίστις (fidelity) of Jesus Christ, the one seed of which the promise speaks (3:16): "that what was promised might be given, on the basis of the faithfulness of Jesus Christ, to those who believe."[42]

---

Galatia: "a system of justification simply by faith in Christ is ... objectionable, as assigning to man too much of a function and to Christ too little: it simply substitutes the mental act of having faith for the bodily one of being circumcised as the precondition for salvation, and (so far as the mechanism for justification is concerned) leaves Christ in the passive role of being the object of our justifying faith. The scheme of justification simply by our faith in Christ wholly fails to explain the significance of his death at the hands of the law ..." ("The Function of *Pistis Christou* in Galatians," *JBL* 85 [1966]: 75).

[40] Betz, who rejects the subjective genitive, ends up regarding this phrase as an ecclesiological abbreviation: "in Christ" means "in the body of Christ." Paul would be stunned to learn that he had advocated rectification through membership in the Christian community. Betz's whole discussion of Gal 2:16-17 shows the difficulties one generates by insisting that πίστις Ἰησοῦ Χριστοῦ is "an abbreviation" (for "faith in Jesus Christ"), whose pre-Pauline Jewish–Christian interpretation is then to be distinguished from Paul's own use (*Galatians*, 117–20).

[41] The customary translation ignores the τῇ; it clearly goes with the dative in ἐν πίστει, indicating that the whole phrase τῇ ... θεοῦ is in apposition to ἐν πίστει.

[42] The observations in this paragraph are stated even more forcefully in Richard B. Hays, "Christology and Ethics in Galatians: The Law of Christ," *CBQ* 49 (1987): 279. Taylor proposed

In Philippians 3:9 Paul writes that he hopes to be found in Christ, not having his righteousness based on law but "that which comes διὰ πίστεως Χριστοῦ, the righteousness from God which depends on faith" (τὴν ἐκ θεοῦ δικαιοσύνη ἐπὶ τῇ πίστει). By regarding διὰ πίστεως Χριστοῦ as an objective genitive, the RSV creates a curious redundancy: not having his own righteousness but one which comes through faith in Christ is repeated as "the righteousness from God that depends on faith." A subjective genitive, however, avoids this: "not having my own righteousness, based on the law, but that which comes through the faithfulness of Christ, that righteousness from God that depends on faith." This accords better with the scope of the paragraph, which emphasizes the desire to gain Christ, be found in him, share his sufferings, and be conformed to his death.

Many of the foregoing considerations apply also to Romans 3:21-26, where Paul specifies the righteousness of God which is now manifested as δικαιοσύνη δὲ θεοῦ πίστεως Ἰησοῦ Χριστοῦ εἰς . . . πιστεύοντας (v. 22). Here too construing πίστις Ἰησοῦ Χριστοῦ as "faith in Jesus Christ" makes the next phrase redundant. This awkwardness disappears if Paul is understood to write about Jesus Christ's πίστις. More important, it is by no means clear how *our* faith in Jesus manifests God's own rectitude;[43] this obscurity is removed if Paul asserts that God's righteousness is manifested through Christ's faithfulness, for this is just the sort of assertion that Paul makes in 5:8, as we shall see.

In verse 26 Paul says that the purpose of God's justifying work is to make it clear that God is righteous by rectifying τὸν ἐκ πίστεως Ἰησοῦ. If verse 22 refers to Christ's πίστις, it is likely that verse 26 does so as well, so that one should render it as "the one who lives by the faithfulness of Jesus." Moreover, this τὸν ἐκ πίστεως Ἰησοῦ has an exact parallel in 4:16, where Paul

---

that in Gal 3:22 ἐκ πίστεως renders a Latin legal instrument, the *fidei commissum*, by which something transferred to someone to hold in trust for subsequent distribution to others ("Function of *Pistis Christou* in Galatians"). This suggestion might illumine the use of the phrase in Galatians, but not in the other letters; hence, it is not necessary for understanding Galatians either.

[43] Cranfield either decided to ignore this consideration or else thought he dealt with it by writing that διὰ πίστεως, etc., "defines the righteousness in question as that which is received by means of faith in Christ" (*Romans*, 1:203). In other words, he must do away with the subjective genitive in δικαιοσύνη θεοῦ as well. Wilckens, on the other hand, rightly insists that δικαιοσύνη θεοῦ is a subjective genitive (*Der Brief an die Römer*, 1:187), but, because he regards διὰ πίστεως Ἰησοῦ Χριστοῦ as an objective genitive, he must follow Otto Kuss in regarding the phrase as referring to our "appropriation" and insist as well that here our faith is determined by its content (Christ). The effect of this insistence brings Wilckens much closer to the subjective genitive than he appears to realize.

argues that the promise comes τῷ ἐκ πίστεως Ἀβραάμ; does anyone think this means "to the person who has faith in Abraham?" If this cannot be the meaning here, then identically constructed phrases can scarcely mean different things simply because "Abraham" has been replaced by "Jesus."[44] Moreover in verses 17-21, it is precisely Abraham's πίστις nd that is explained.

If one takes 3:22, 26 to refer to the faithfulness of "Jesus," the paragraph has a consistent emphasis on the pivotal role of Christ. Indeed, even the vexing verse 25a is clarified. Here Paul interprets Christ as the one "whom God put forward as ἱλαστήριον διὰ πίστεως ἐν τῷ αἵματι αὐτοῦ." It has been claimed that Paul, ever the advocate of faith, inserted διὰ πίστεως into the tradition[45] in order to insist that God's act must be appropriated by faith in order to be salvific. However, no one appears to have been able to explain why he would have inserted the phrase precisely here,[46] or indeed, why he used διὰ πίστεως to make the point. However, if the phrase were part of the tradition itself, it might be construed as referring to God ("whom God through faithfulness put forward"[47]) or to "Jesus" ("whom God put forward as ἱλαστήριον, through [his] faithfulness [made concrete] in his blood").[48] The latter is preferable. Although no completely satisfactory explanation of διὰ πίστεως appears likely, this proposal strengthens the coherence of the paragraph: it is Christ's faithfulness that makes possible the redemption through which persons who believe the gospel are made right with God.

## Romans 5:12-21

Romans 5:12-21 compares Adam and Christ, concluding with a contrast between the disobedience of the former and the obedience of the latter (v. 19). Here Paul writes, "through the obedience of the one [man] many

[44] How important this phrase is for the entire discussion can be seen in Hultgren's effort so to construe it that it loses its force: it means "Abrahamic faith," "the faith of the people of God"—an interpretation buttressed by an appeal to the Hebrew construct state when used to express "the genitive of quality" ("The *Pistis Christou* Formulation in Paul," 256).

[45] E.g., E. Käsemann (following Bultmann); Kertlege, *"Rechtfertigung" bei Paulus,* 52–53; Wilckens, *Der Brief an die Römer;* Ben F. Meyer, "The Pre-Pauline Formula in Rom. 3:25-26a," *NTS* 29 (1983): 204; Michel leaves the question open. Because Cranfield does not discuss the possibility of a tradition, he has no need to consider a Pauline addition.

[46] See the perceptive discussion by Sam K. Williams, *Jesus' Death as Saving Event* (HDR 2; Missoula, Mont.: Scholars Press, 1975), 41–45.

[47] So Alphons Pluta, *Gottes Bundestreue—Ein Schlüsselbegriff in Rom 3, 25a* (SBS 34; Stuttgart: Katholisches Bibelwerk, 1969), 45–46.

[48] So Williams, *Jesus' Death as Saving Event,* 45–51 (where three interpretations are suggested); idem, " 'The Righteousness of God' in Romans," 277 n. 113; followed by Hays, *Faith of Jesus Christ,* 173; Johnson, "Romans 3:21-26 and the Faith of Jesus," 79–80.

will be made righteous" (διὰ τῆς ὑπακοῆς τοῦ ἑνὸς δίκαιοι κατασταθήσονται οὐ πολλοί). Käsemann is surely right in observing that this "obedience" is not limited to the cross but, like Philippians 2:8, alludes to the character of "Jesus'" life as a whole.[49] In Romans 5:19, however, this obedience has a specific role absent from Philippians 2:8[50] and different from that in Hebrews 5:8, which regards "learning obedience" as necessary for the salvific work. For Paul, this obedience is the means (διά + genitive) by which Christ accomplishes salvation. Since being justified/rectified (δικαιοῦν, 3:26) and being made righteous/put in the right (κατασταθήσονται, 5:19) are variant expressions for the same thing, the means is also the same: in 3:26 it is the πίστις of "Jesus," in 5:19 his ὑπακοή. In other words, Christ's "obedience" interprets his "faithfulness." As already noted, Paul paraphrases the same point in 15:3, where he writes of Christ not pleasing himself.

### Romans 5:8

The relation between the faithfulness of "Jesus" and his obedience illumines also Paul's remarkable statement in 5:8: "God shows his love for us because . . . Christ died on our behalf." Christ's dying can manifest God's love for us only if that dying expresses God's intent, if there is such congruence between them that the former discloses the latter.[51] This is why Paul emphasizes the faithfulness and the obedience of "Jesus." Moreover, the coinherence of God's act and Christ's demeanor is what Paul formulates in 2 Corinthians 5:19—"in Christ God was reconciling the world."

In this light, one should speak of the fidelity/obedience of "Jesus" rather than of his faith. To be sure, Johnson, whose discussion has informed this one, emphasized the obedience element in Paul's understanding of πίστις.[52] The problem, however, arises from modern associations with "faith" which readily insinuate themselves into our thinking about Paul. For him it is not Christ's believing—his psychological disposition or mental state, even less his response to the word—which is in view, but the consonance between his life and God's love and purpose for humanity. Talking about

---

[49] Ernst Käsemann, *Commentary on Romans* (trans. G. W. Bromiley; Grand Rapids: Eerdmans, 1980), 157.

[50] Rightly observed by T. Nagata, "A Neglected Feature of the Christ-hymn in Phil 2:6-11," *Annual of the Japanese Biblical Institute* 9 (1983): 28–39.

[51] Wilckens is right; Christ is not the representative of humanity before God (as is Adam) but God's representative to humanity, because he is the grace through whom sinners are made righteous (*Der Brief an die Römer*, 1:327).

[52] See n. 31 above.

the faith of "Jesus" too easily invites descriptions of it based on our own "dynamics of faith," thereby returning us to nineteenth-century liberal Protestant theology. Generally speaking, forgetting that Jesus too had faith may indeed lead to docetism, as Johnson claims, but, given the tendency to convert theology to psychology, this does not appear to be the prime danger in interpreting Paul. In any case, for him it is not Christ's believing that is the ground of our emancipation from sin but the Godward shape of his life.

## IV

To what conclusions have these considerations pointed? First, Paul writes about "Jesus" exactly what he needs to advance his argument and pursue his agenda, and no more. Presumably, like the Roman readers, he could have amplified his references to "Jesus" with brief narratives, especially about the passion (including the Lord's Supper!), had he thought that doing so would have been germane. From his point of view, however, it sufficed to characterize "Jesus" as faithful and obedient to God because these traits support his assertion that "God shows his love for us in that while we were yet sinners Christ died for us" (5:8). Further, since Paul did not know whether his Jesus tradition was known also in Rome, quoting Jesus could easily have given the impression that he will come as the bearer of information about "Jesus" which they lacked and that he would supplement their knowledge. Instead, Paul presents himself as the interpreter of what he does assume is accepted in Rome, thereby tacitly appealing to warrants the readers already acknowledge. Besides, in Romans "Jesus" is not an authority whose words are to be cited but a figure who is God's means for rectifying the human condition in which both Jews and Gentiles, despite real differences, find themselves; at the same time this one gospel for everyone cannot cancel God's promise to Israel or suggest that God is inconsistent. Quoting Jesus or appealing to his precedent would not have strengthened Paul's argument, because for him the human dilemma could not be dealt with by appealing to the words and deeds of any teacher.

Second, Paul does not explain why he emphasizes the fidelity/obedience of "Jesus," nor can we retrace his reasoning. We can discern the rationale of the result by noting the consequences of deleting this element from it. On the one hand, had he been content to allude to the "Jesus" which he shared with the Romans, it would not be clear whether or how Christ would constitute the material basis, the substantive ground, for the salvation delineated in the letter, because then the Christ-event would have intersected the human condition salvifically only at the point of death.

Baptismal participation in/solidarity with Christ would deal with our mortality because "if we have been united with him in a death like his, we shall certainly be united with him in a resurrection like his" (Rom 6:5 RSV). However, the real problem is not mortality but sin; indeed, Romans 5:12 insists that mortality is not the cause of sin but the reverse: death is the result of sin (so also 6:23). A salvation that overcomes only death deals only with the result, not the cause—sin itself. The logic of Paul's thought about overcoming death implies that overcoming sin also requires a basis, an event, just as the overcoming of death has its ground in an event, the resurrection of "Jesus." To participate in a "Jesus" who "will never die again" because "death has no dominion over him" (6:9) is to overcome one's mortality, a feature of one's existence. But sin entails a different, though related, kind of bondage because sin is not honoring God as God (1:21), a rebellious relation to God. What, then, provides the basis for our emancipation from sin? The πίστις/ ὑπακοὴ of "Jesus"![53] This is why Romans 5:19 asserts that "by one man's obedience many will be made righteous." Because Christ's death was the capstone of sin-defeating fidelity/obedience, Paul can say that "the death he died he died to sin, ἐφάπαξ" (6:10). In other words, Paul accents the fidelity/ obedience of "Jesus" because without it there would be no inner, material grounding of freedom from sin in "Jesus," and the relation between "Jesus" and the self would be extrinsic and arbitrary. At stake is whether what was constitutive of "Jesus' " own right relation to God—his fidelity/obedience— is the ground of our rectification or whether it stands outside of it as something incidental.

On the other hand, without such a grounding the correlative consequence is also clear: salvation would be grounded in our own believing/ trusting, as already noted. But then Paul would have advocated faith in faith. Given the difference between sin and death, Paul does not say that we participate in Christ's sin-breaking obedience; nor does he urge us to imitate Christ's obedience, for that would make it a requirement, a law.

Third, a major aim in this study of Paul's Christology is to bring into focus its internal soteriological rationale.[54] Understanding and interpreting Romans requires one to grasp the rationale of Paul's construal of the "Jesus"- event as God's act in which God's righteousness, God's love, and God's triumph over sin and death are manifest as effective for redemption from

---

[53] See also Hays, *Faith of Jesus Christ*, 250–51.

[54] The importance of this correlation for Christology has been summarized in chap. 1, "The Renewal of New Testament Christology."

the human condition as delineated in the letter. Comparable analysis can be made of "Jesus" in other Pauline letters. In any case, the discrete topic of "Jesus" in Romans opens out on much broader questions which must be considered if the theme of Paul and Jesus (i.e., Paul's "Jesus" and our Jesus) is to be pursued fruitfully.

# 9

# The New Testament and Nicea

Those who formulated this topic clearly have been blessed generously with imagination and verve. It is designed to overcome the oft-lamented silence between biblical exegetes and theologians as well as between *Neutestamentler* and *Patristiker*. More important, this topic tacitly doubts the accepted wisdom that Christology must begin "from below." Did ever a christological statement begin more aggressively "from above" than the Nicene Creed? Be that as it may, a topic as open-ended as this one not only promises to evoke discussion on many levels but invites one to post a caveat at the doorway: across the threshold lie not seasoned conclusions to vexing questions but "mostly preliminary remarks" designed to lure fruitful questions to the surface so that the promised discussion among readers can occur.

I

*The Formulation and Its Ambiguities*

The phrasing of the topic should not be taken for granted because none of the items in it, not even the "and," is ambiguity-free.

1. This "and" asks for some kind of comparison; indeed it implies an invitation to specify what sort of comparison is to be made. The topic is not "the New Testament *in* the Nicene Creed" nor "the New Testament *at* Nicea." What is sought is not historical information about the role of the older material in the younger but a comparison whose focus has yet to be determined.

Moreover, this "and" assumes that each item has its own integrity, and that juxtaposing them might assist our understanding each of them.

This "and" does not necessarily mean that there is an intrinsic relationship between the two entities. Thus the "and" in "Moses and Aaron" is not the same as the "and" in "Paul and Plato." The former are so intrinsically linked that one could treat the two figures as a single entity, like "bread and butter." One could discuss the latter, however, simply because it is possible, and illuminating, to juxtapose them. In the former case the "and" recognizes a historical relationship; in the latter, it establishes a heuristic one.

In our topic, the function of the "and" falls somewhere between these two possibilities, because it recognizes that there is a texture of historical relationships which connects them across the centuries. At the same time, this historical factor might be construed to mean "from . . . to," just as "Trent and Vatican II" could lead to a discussion of the historical factors that make the one different from the other. On such a construal, our topic would invite a discussion of the differences in first- and fourth-century polemics, use of Greek philosophy, and social context. Such a construal might also leave the shores of the topic sufficiently unattended that value judgments could be smuggled into the discussion: the "and" might imply development and maturation as in "the acorn and the oak," or it might imply decline as in the (Protestant) contrast between God's word and "man-made creeds." This discussion, in any case, assumes none of these uses of "and"; its agenda will be primarily comparative and analytical, though informed throughout by historical understanding.

2. Precisely from a historical point of view, both "the New Testament" and "Nicea" are ambiguous. To what does Nicea refer? To the council? To the creed? If the latter, what text is in view? What today is commonly confessed as "the Nicene Creed" or to what was agreed upon at the council, anathemas included? This paper regards Nicea as an abbreviation for the whole phenomenon of controversy, council and creed, as a pointer to the central issue—Christology.

From a historical angle, "the New Testament is even more ambiguous, but for a quite different set of reasons. To begin with, whereas Nicea can function as a convenient abbreviation for a clearly focused set of issues, the same cannot be said of "the New Testament"—a rather heterogeneous anthology. In other words, the relationship to a coherent subject matter which Nicea enjoys does not obtain in the case of "the New Testament."

In the next place, "the New Testament" we know did not yet exist at Nicea, even though everything now in it had been written long before, and despite the fact that its core collection had long established itself as Scripture, even if it was not yet a (closed) canon. "The New Testament" has both a content and a status which must not be read back into the Nicene era. Not until half a century after the Nicene Council did Athanasius' Easter letter provide the oldest extant list of NT books whose items coincide with the table of contents of our canon. Moreover, the shape of the NT differed from what we know because the sequence of books was not yet fixed. Consequently, were our comparison governed by consistent historical considerations, we would need to think our way back into the early fourth century when "the New Testament" was still a more malleable entity than it is for us.

Moreover, this "us" too is ambiguous because the NT that functions in the minds of its professional students is not the NT that the Christian community reads. We professionals may well teach the four Gospels back to back and before we come to Acts and Paul, but it is altogether likely that we think of John as "the Fourth Gospel" not only because of its place in the list but because we regard it as the fourth to have been written. Likewise, we separate in our minds the Apocalypse of John from the rest of the Johannine corpus, and Hebrews from the Pauline letters, creating for ourselves a context for reading which differs markedly from that of the Nicene fathers. In "our" minds, the NT has been disassembled and rearranged into a corpus of selected early Christian literature that begins with 1 Thessalonians and ends with 2 Peter. Consequently, it is altogether possible that for "us" the comparison will be between Nicea and literature *in* the NT.

3. Whereas the forementioned ambiguities need to be acknowledged, the key ambiguity—the focus of the comparison—can be minimized by agreeing that the exercise will concentrate on Christology. Indeed, the heart of the matter will reflect the central issue in the Nicene Creed—the significance of *homoousios* for Christology. If the topic is not without its ambiguities, the focus is not without its difficulties. These too deserve to be noted at the outset.

## Difficulties in Comparing the Christology of Nicea and the New Testament

Because my craft is NT study, the difficulties which are most apparent to me emerge from the nature of the NT and from the course which the critical study of it has taken.

1. Comparing the Christology of the NT and Nicea runs counter to the ethos of NT scholarship. It can hardly be stated too strongly that Nicea plays no role whatever in historical-critical NT study. That is to be expected because, from a historical perspective, bringing Nicea into the discussion would be as anachronistic as bringing Sacco-Vanzetti into a discussion of

the Mayflower Compact. In fact, to a considerable degree, often unacknowl-
edged, the engine of historical criticism was driven by a revolt against the
influence of Nicea (and Chalcedon) on the interpretation of the NT. That
is to say, historical criticism undertook to liberate the texts from the dogmatic reading of Scripture which Nicea represents.

The real tension between what Nicea represents and what NT criticism
undertakes has to do with the historical method as it was applied to the NT.
Two aspects of this are germane here. First, by insisting that each text (and
its antecedent components like Q or the signs source in John) be read in
light of its particular historical setting, NT criticism emphasized more and
more the diversity of early Christianity, precisely in its Christologies. The
more the particular profiles of these Christologies are reconstructed, the
more arbitrary it appears to allow Nicea into a discussion of them at all—
save by contrast. Indeed, it is a commonplace even among "conservative"
scholars to point out that there is no such thing as "the New Testament"
view in Christology, or in most areas for that matter. By specifying who
Jesus Christ is and thereby determining how the NT is to be understood,
Nicea threatens to obscure, if not obliterate, precisely what historical criticism has sought to achieve. This is why the *Neutestamentler* may be willing
to compare Nicene Christology with parts of the NT but not with "the New
Testament."

2. The second difficulty is of a somewhat different sort: historical criticism's bondage to the genetic fallacy. It has concentrated almost exclusively
on the immediate context in which and for which the text was produced,
and on the antecedents of that context and of the text. It is assumed, almost
universally, that what will best explain and illumine a text or a context is
what lies behind it. Why else would one hunt down, like an avid genealo-
gist, the ancestry of the Son of Man theology in ancient Iranian or Indo-
European *Urmensch* mythology? No one would dispute that antecedents
are essential, explaining the causal connections which led up to an event or
a text. The point, rather, is that this preoccupation with etymological concerns is only half historical. The other half is no less important for understanding, if it is true that to the text (or event) belongs its future as well.
On this basis for understanding Paul it is as important to see how he generates the deuteropauline letters as it is to probe his background. Because
NT scholarship has not, thus far at least, been willing to understand its
texts by seeing what they permit, inhibit, or set in motion, it has not found
much reason to converse with patristics or the history of doctrine. Indeed,
NT scholarship has preferred to look outside the Christian community for
parallels in order to explain and understand the text, rather than looking

forward within the same community in order to see what would become of the text or what it would generate. Our topic therefore might presage an advance, but pursuing it must deal with the difficulty which customary criticism has created for itself.

3. If the second difficulty exposes the limits of prevailing historical-critical NT study (sometimes turned into Christian origins), the third concerns its success precisely with regard to Christology—namely, the conversion of NT Christology into the antecedent history of christological motifs and titles. The consequences for the study of NT theology are serious enough to require correction,[1] but the point of noting them here is that they make fruitful conversation with historical and systematic theology more difficult.

This conversion of NT Christology into the history of ideas has several aspects. (a) Apart from the Bultmannians, the study of NT theology, and hence of Christology as well, has heeded William Wrede's demand that this discipline become purely descriptive, "totally indifferent to all dogmatic and systematic theology."[2] The real subject matter was to be a description of what early Christians believed, not what the texts say about doctrine.[3] "How the systematic theologian gets on with the results, and deals with them—that is his own affair."[4] What Wrede called for came to pass with Bousset's *Kyrios Christos*.[5] Reconstructing the history of early Christian Christology on the basis of all relevant data is surely as valid as it is important; however, the result is not a Christology of the NT.

(b) Impressive as Bousset's work was, and remains, in retrospect both his approach and many of his judgments now seem rather unsophisticated. In his time, reconstructing a Hellenistic Christianity prior to and apart from Paul promised to solve the vexing question of the transition from Jesus to Paul because Bousset saw the sequence as Jesus, Jerusalem, Hellenistic Gentile Christianity, Paul. Since then, students have sifted and graded the

---

[1] See chap. 1, "The Renewal of New Testament Christology."

[2] William Wrede, "The Task and Methods of 'New Testament Theology,'" in *The Nature of New Testament Theology* (trans. and ed. Robert Morgan; SBTH 2/25; Naperville, Ill.: Alex R. Allenson, 1973), 69. Morgan's extensive introduction deals also with Schlatter, whose essay on the same theme is included. The page numbers following the quotations refer to Morgan's volume.

[3] Wrede, "Task and Methods," 84–85.

[4] Wrede, "Task and Methods," 69.

[5] Wilhelm Bousset, *Kyrios Christos : A History of the Belief in Christ from the Beginnings of Christianity to Irenaeus* (Nashville: Abingdon, 1970; repr., Waco, Tex.: Baylor University Press, 2013; German original, 1913).

material ever more finely; for example, some scholars distinguish two or more stages, and hence christological accents as well, in the history of Q. Indeed, as texts (especially the Gospels) were scrutinized ever more closely and scholars distinguished sources and strata (each with a nuanced discrete Christology), the picture of early Christology which emerged was kaleidoscopic and rather chaotic.

(c) Since Bousset, and others, had not only located the use of "Lord" for Jesus in Hellenistic Gentile Christianity, while at the same time had called into question Jesus' own messianic self-understanding—thereby severing the link between early Christian Christologies and Jesus' self-interpretation, this conversion into history made it inevitable that the study of NT Christology would trace the history of these titles to Jesus and beyond, and sometimes forward, into the first century. Frequently, the governing issue was the origin of Christology. Indeed, the morphology of titles has come to dominate the field. An enormous amount of work was devoted to exploring and tracing the origin of myths (e.g., descending/ascending gods), motifs (e.g., wisdom), and concepts (e.g., preexistence). Larger movements in the history of ideas were also brought to bear, especially apocalypticism and Gnosticism.

The more successful such efforts were—and the gains were substantial—the greater became the difficulty of pursuing our topic because the history of christological materials and motifs is not yet Christology. Indeed, one scarcely asks, "What is the relation between philology and theology?"

II

NT study has identified christological formulae and creeds now embedded in the texts. It is useful to make some general comparisons, first with regard to form, then with respect to the focus of these creedal materials.

*The Form of New Testament Creeds and the Nicene Creed*

After Lohmeyer's pioneering analysis of Philippians 2:5-11 showed that Paul was quoting a Christ-hymn, students refined the procedures for identifying and reconstructing other liturgical pieces. As a result, one can assemble a rather extensive corpus of such materials of various lengths and degrees of complexity, ranging from the simplest (and perhaps earliest) "Jesus is Lord" (Rom 10:9; 1 Cor 12:3) to the extensive and complex "hymns" in John 1:1-14, Philippians 2:6-11, and Colossians 1:15-20. At the same time it has proven to be exceedingly difficult to reconstruct convincingly the structure of these larger pieces, partly because there is considerable uncertainty about what principles govern the poetic structure, and partly because the NT authors appear to have inserted their own comments into the tradition. For example, it is widely conceded that Paul inserted "even death on a cross" into the hymn of Philippians 2:6-11, and many believe that the Johannine prologue we know has undergone at least one expansion. So too, scholars are divided over whether Philippians 2:6-11 celebrates the Christ-event as a two-stage event (vv. 6-8, 9-11) or as the three-stage event (v. 6-7b, 7c-8, 9-11); according to the latter, the hymn would distinguish the career of the incarnate one from his preexistent and postexistent phases. Such matters cannot be explored here; it must suffice to note that a goodly degree of caution is in order, especially when drawing far-reaching inferences from this important material.

1. Given the complex history of "the Nicene Creed," it is useful to set out what was adopted at Nicea:

> We believe in one God
> > and in one Lord Jesus Christ
> > > the Son of God
> > > > begotten of the Father
> > > > unique [*monogenē*]
> > > > > that is, of the being [*ousia*] of the Father
> > > > > > God of God
> > > > > > Light of Light
> > > > > > true God of true God
> > > > > > begotten not made
> > > > > > of one being [*homoousios*] with the Father
> > > > through whom all things came to be
> > > > > all things in heaven and all things on the earth
> > > > who for the sake of us men
> > > > and for our salvation
> > > > > came down
> > > > and was made flesh
> > > > and became man
> > > > > suffered
> > > > and rose on the third day
> > > > > ascended into the heavens
> > > > and is coming to judge the living and the dead.
> > and in the Holy Spirit . . .

This was developed as follows:

- "unique" (*monogenē*) was shifted forward: "the unique Son of God"

- "begotten of the Father" was elaborated by adding "before all the ages"
- the exegetical "that is, of the being of the Father" was omitted
- "all things in heaven and all things on earth" was omitted
- "came down" was elaborated: "from the heavens"
- the incarnation was combined with the birth: "of the Holy Spirit and the Virgin Mary"
- "and was crucified for us under Pontius Pilate" was inserted before "suffered"
- "and was buried" was added
- "according to the Scriptures" was added to the reference to the resurrection
- "and sitteth on the right hand of the Father" was added
- "is coming" is elaborated to "is coming again"
- "of whose kingdom their shall be no end" adds a happy ending.

The overall structure is clear: first the relation of the preexistent one to God, then to the created order, then to human beings—the latter being an outline of the Christ-event from incarnation to Parousia.

2. In the NT, there are four hymnic/creedal passages which approach this structure: Philippians 2:6-11; Colossians 1:15-20; Hebrews 1:3; John 1:1-18, though none of them—or any other creedal piece—concludes with the Parousia. Nor do any of them begin with "I believe in . . ." because, apart from the openings of John and Hebrews, the NT texts cite the hymnic/creedal pieces as part of a long complex period. Consequently, they begin with "who . . ." (cf. Rom 1:3; Phil 2:6; Col 1:15; 1 Tim 3:16; Heb 1:3).

Philippians 2:6-11 lacks a reference to the relation between Christ and creation, and refers but briefly to his relation to God: "though being in the form of God [en morphē theou]. It alone refers to his "attitude" toward this status: "did not count equality with God a thing to be grasped." The vexing question whether ouk harpagmon should be construed as res rapta or as res rapienda is intertwined with the larger question whether the hymn celebrates an event that begins with the preexistent one (the majority view) or whether it views Christ's action as the antithesis to Adam.[6] If it alludes to

---

[6] Among those who see no preexistence here are the following: Charles H. Talbert, "The Problem of Pre-Existence in Philippians 2:6-11," *JBL* 86 (1967): 141–53; J. Murphey-O'Connor, "Christological Anthropology in Phil, II, 6-11," *RB* 83 (1976): 25–50; George Howard, "Phil 2:6-11 and the Human Christ," *CBQ* 40 (1978): 368–87; James D. G. Dunn, *Christology in the Making* (Philadelphia: Westminster, 1980): 114–21.

Adam, or to rebellious angels,[7] it must mean *res rapienda*—being equal to God was a status for which Christ declined to reach. If it refers to the pre-existent Christ, then it must mean *res rapta*—a status he declined to hang on to. Hoover's recent analysis shows that the line must be understood as a whole: "not something to use for his own advantage did he regard equality with God"—i.e., *res rapta*.[8] The relation of the preexistent one to God is mentioned not as a topic on its own right but as the foil for his movement into the human condition. The relation between Christ and creation does, on the other hand, figure much more prominently in the conclusion of the Philippians hymn than in the Nicene texts, where it is no more than implied in the reference to the ascension and the session *ad dexteram*. The hymn celebrates Christ's lordship which all cosmic powers acknowledge by making the same confession which believers make. The language of verses 9-11 (Isaiah 45:23 [LXX]) expresses the vindication of the humiliated one by exalting him from the nadir to the apex. Finally, there is nothing in the Nicene texts comparable to the turning point in the "plot" of the hymn, marked by "therefore"; in verses 6-8 it is the Son who acts, but in verses 9-11 the Son is "acted upon" by God. Thus the hymn has two stanzas, not three.

Hebrews 1:3 appears to be a hymnic piece now embedded in one sentence which begins in verse 1 and ends at verse 4. Verse 3 begins with "who"; and is complete in itself; it is the last phrase of verse 3 that really interests the author. Whether this unit consists of five lines or four depends on whether one thinks it is structured on the basis of sense lines and meter. On this basis it can be presented as follows:

> who being the radiation of glory and the stamp of his nature
>> bearing all things by the word of his power
>> having made purification of sins
>> sat down at the right hand of majesty in the heights.

The first line celebrates the Son's relation to God, the second his relation to the created order, the third his salvific significance for humanity, and the last his exaltation. Not mentioned at all, though assumed, are the incarnation and the resurrection—the points of entry and departure from the human condition. What governs the structure is the "shape" of the event: three stages—preexistence, existence, and postexistence. This "shape" governs the Christology of Hebrews as a whole. That this hymnic piece, despite

---

[7] J. A. Sanders, "Dissenting Deities and Philippians 2:1-11," *JBL* 88 (1969): 279–90.

[8] R. W. Hoover, "The Harpagmos Enigma: A Philological Solution," *HTR* 64 (1971): 95–119, esp. 118.

its brevity, has a structure similar to the Nicene texts (apart from the omission of the Parousia) is obvious.

Colossians 1:15-20 presents a set of far more complex problems.[9] Here too, the hymn is part of a single period which it begins at verse 9 and ends at verse 20. Moreover, it is introduced, so to speak, by verses 13-14 which make clear that the one celebrated in verses 15-20 is the Redeemer: "who rescued us from the authority of darkness and transferred us to the kingdom of his beloved Son, in whom we have the redemption, the forgiveness of sins." Then comes the hymn, also stitched into the sentence with "who." Remarkably, the two parts of the first stanza appear to be parallel; that is, instead of celebrating an event in stages, as in Philippians 2, they repeat the same themes. Attempts to reconstruct the hymn have led to diverse results, partly because it appears that the author of Colossians expanded the hymn in order to emphasize certain ideas, and partly because no one knows just how symmetrical the hymn was originally. Consequently, it is difficult to determine exactly what should be subtracted. Here, the words in brackets may well be additions.

> Who is the image of the invisible God
> > (the) firstborn of all creation
> > because in him were created all things in the heavens and on the
> > > earth
> > > things visible and things invisible
> > > [whether thrones, whether dominions, whether rulers, whether
> > > > authorities]
> > all things through him and for him were created.
> > and he is before all things
> > and all things in him cohere
> > and he is the head of the body [the church].
>
> Who is the beginning
> > (the) firstborn of the dead
> > so that in all things he might be preeminent
> > because in him the fullness was pleased to dwell
> > and through him to reconcile all things unto him
> > making peace [through the blood of his cross] through him
> > whether the things on the earth or the things in the heavens.

[9] For a good, succinct discussion, with bibliography, see Eduard Lohse and Helmut Koester, eds., *Colossians and Philemon* (trans. Robert J. Karris; Hermeneia; Minneapolis: Fortress, 1972).

If one deletes the reference to the church from the first stanza (no other NT hymn or creed mentions the church), then the first stanza celebrates the Son's relation to God and to creation; the second celebrates his role in redemption, that is, his role as the beginning (*arche*) of the new creation. The Nicene texts do not know such a structure at all; the affinity with Nicea lies in the vocabulary and in certain concepts.

The prologue of John (1:1-18)[10] is even more complex than Colossians 1:15-20, and the range of solutions to its problems on which a consensus has been reached is small: it does incorporate a hymnic piece, and the present prologue is the result of extensive, and probably repeated, expansion. Three types of expansion are readily identified: the references to John the Baptist (vv. 6-8, 15), the lines which introduce a confessional element by the use of "we" (vv. 14, 17), and the concluding verse which functions as a theological transition to the narrative that follows. Once these have been subtracted, there remain verses 1-5, 9-13. These too appear to have been expanded by explanatory comments, especially clear in verse 13, but probably including "to those who believe in his name" in verse 12 as well. With regard to verses 1-5, E. L. Miller's reconstruction (which regards 1c-2 as glosses) is attractive:[11]

> In the beginning was the Logos
> And the Logos was with God
>
> All things came into being through him
> And apart from him nothing came into being
>
> What appeared in him was Life
> And the Life was the Light of men
>
> And the Light shines in the darkness
> And the darkness has not put it out.

On this basis, the third couplet speaks of the incarnation, not the fourth as is often held. If this is correct, then the couplets celebrate the Logos' relation to God, to creation, to humanity, and to ongoing evil; they represent four "moments": preexistence, creation, incarnation, and the author's present (no futuristic eschatology, as represented by the references to the Parousia in the Nicene texts).

---

[10] The prologue as a whole has an integrity of its own which is intimately linked to its structure, which may well be chiastic, as Alan Culpepper has proposed, "The Pivot of John's Prologue," *NTS* 27 (1980): 1–31.

[11] E. L. Miller, "The Logic of the Logos Hymn: A New View," *NTS* 29 (1983): 552–61.

If one subtracts explanatory glosses from verses 9-12b, the result is a second stanza:

> He was the true Light
> Coming into the world
>
> He was in the world
> And the world did not know him
>
> He came to his own things
> And his own people did not receive him
>
> But whoever did receive him
> To them he gave authority to become children of God.

No reconstruction is problem-free, including this one. In any case, the "original" Logos-hymn is probably found in the opening five verses; the Christ-event which it celebrates has a distinct shape: it is governed by the soteriological significance of Christ, and grounds this in his identity which begins with preexistence, as did the other hymnic pieces.

Not all christological traditions used by NT writers have this shape. Two well-known instances make this clear.

Romans 1:3-4 contains a christological tradition which Paul has incorporated into his opening sentence (vv. 1-7),

> Who came to be of the seed of David according to the flesh
> Who was designated Son of God [in power] according to the
>     Spirit of holiness by (since?) (his) resurrection from the dead.

Critics are generally agreed that "in power" is Paul's own addition. Several things are to be noted: (a) This tradition operates with a two-stage Christology: a descendent of David is installed into the office of "Son of God" at the resurrection, as in Acts 13:33. (b) Since Paul works with a three-stage Christology which begins with preexistence, he "frames" this tradition by mentioning the Son at the outset ("concerning his son, who . . ."); and by adding "Jesus Christ our Lord" at the end. (c) By inserting "in power" he distinguished the earthly phase of the Christ-event (without power, consistent with the hymn in Philippians 2) from the postresurrection phase.

1 Timothy 3:16 represents a quite different structure:

> Who was manifested in the flesh
>     vindicated in the Spirit
>         seen by angels
>         preached among the nations

believed on in the world
taken up in glory.

Here the pattern is governed by the contrast between heaven and earth: earth-heaven, heaven-earth, earth-heaven. The three-stage shape of the event is simply presupposed.

3. What has this all too terse overview of these traditions shown us about their form in light of the Nicene Creed? (a) The latter elaborates the structural pattern found not only in the NT but *behind* it as well. (b) This elaborating process was capable of assimilating older, simpler patterns (e.g., Rom 1:3-4), so that it is not surprising that the churches which read all the NT texts (and others) could easily add details like the birth, ascension, session, and coming. (c) All the materials surveyed, like the creed, have a narrative structure. These materials and the creed share a way of answering the question, "Who is Jesus Christ?"—namely, by narrating, in whatever form, an event which, apart from the formulation used in Romans 1:3-4, begins "before Jesus" and which has not yet been brought to a conclusion.

The NT contains another way of answering the christological question, "Who is Jesus and what is his significance?" It does not begin "before Jesus" but either with Jesus' installation into the office of Son of God at baptism, or from the moment of conception. Consequently the content of "Son" differs as well: an obedient person through whom God acted. The Synoptics have a two-stage Christology, structurally the same as the tradition used in Romans 1:3-4. Since there is a correlation between soteriology/anthropology (the work of Christ) and the identity of Christ (his person), so that a shift in one entails a corresponding shift in the other, this difference in patterns implies a corresponding difference in anthropology and soteriology.

Some Christologies, including the Nicene, shift from statements of what God did through the Son to those which say that the Son of God is the actor. (There are interesting exceptions: in John 1:14 "the Word became flesh" [contrast the Nicene formulation in the passive: "was made flesh"]; Hebrews 1:3 also speaks only of who the Son is and what he did; however, 1 Timothy 3:16 celebrates the entire event with passive verbs, suggesting that God is the real actor. Thus in Philippians 2:6-11, the Son is the actor in the first part, and is acted upon in the second. Colossians 1:15-20, despite its remarkable "he is . . ." in verses 15, 17, and 18, nonetheless emphasizes God's action *through* him, first in creation (v. 16), and finally in cosmic reconciliation (vv. 19-20 use "through" him, first in creation [v. 16], and finally in cosmic reconciliation, verses 19-20 use "through" three times). That God is the real actor in the Christ-event is clear also in passages which speak of God's "sending" the preexistent Son into the human situation (e.g., Rom 8:3-4; John 3:17; 17:3, 8); with such passages belongs also 2 Corinthians 5:18-21 (God acted through Christ, reconciled in Christ, and made Christ "to be sin"). Although the Nicene language also can speak of God acting through Christ ("was made flesh"), it emphasizes what Christ did: came down, became man, suffered, rose, ascended, sits, comes. To conclude: the view that God acted through Jesus appears in Christologies that work with preexistence as well as in those that do not do so; further, christological statements can combine Jesus as agent with Jesus the actant. These data suggest that Nicea stabilizes the language and the ideas by emphasizing the action of the Son.

*The Shifting Focus*

It is regrettable that the distinction between functional Christology in the NT and metaphysical Christologies of the great creeds should have been allowed to affect the way we approach "the New Testament and Nicea." Not only does the Nicene Creed balance the "metaphysics of the Son" with a recital of his "functional" soteriological activity (introduced by "who for us men and for our salvation"!), but the NT is not wanting "metaphysical" concerns. Indeed, it is the purpose of this section to show a movement toward this focus, evident as a shift in focus toward the preexistence of the Son.

1. It is useful to begin with Paul, who, despite Dunn's denials, manifestly works with a preexistence Christology, for quite apart from the hymn quoted in Philippians 2:6-11, he assumes it in Romans 8:3-4; 2 Corinthians 8:9; Galatians 4:4-5. The question, "How important was preexistence for Paul's construal of the identity and significance of Jesus?" cannot be answered because Paul's Christology is known but partially, namely, only insofar as he expresses elements of it in order to get leverage on something else, on some issue at hand. What appears as an aside, a terse formulation, or an allusion may well have played a greater role in his teaching than it does in his Letters. Consequently, caution is in order: in tracing the shift toward more concern with the preexistence one should not assume that preexistence was as marginal for Paul as it is in his seven undisputed Letters.

Given the futurist orientation of 1 Thessalonians, it is natural that Paul speaks of the postexistent Lord, not the preexistent Son. No conclusion about preexistence can be drawn from that fact that 1 Thessalonians 1:10 mentions only waiting "for his Son from heaven, whom he raised from the dead, Jesus who delivers us from the wrath to come." There are passages in which he does mention preexistence. One of these is 1 Corinthians 10:1-4, where he appropriates the Jewish tradition of the rock which accompanied Israel's wandering and simply identifies it: "the rock was Christ." Since Hellenistic Judaism's wisdom theology regarded this rock as wisdom, and since Paul elsewhere shows signs of being influenced by wisdom theology, it may well be that here he "identifies Christ with this preexistent wisdom," as Hammerton-Kelly claims.[12] More important may be what Paul does *not* say: never does he regard Israel's history as the story of wisdom's work, as does Wisdom of Solomon. Paul's Letters find the gospel in the Old Testament, but apart from 1 Corinthians 10:4, not Christ. In 1 Corinthians 8:6, Paul mentions the role of the preexistent one in creation: for us Christians, he points out, there is

> One God, the Father
> > from whom are all things and for whom we exist, and
> One Lord, Jesus Christ
> > through whom are all things and through whom we exist.

The influence of Stoic language has been noted frequently, in the use of prepositions and in *ta panta* (all things). Here Paul fuses Hellenistic philosophy, Jewish monotheism, and Christian confession ("we"). Evidently Christ is regarded as the agent of both creation and the new creation. This is the only time Paul's Letters identify Christ with the preexistent Creator-Logos, and even this is implicit. The fact that he need not explain it implies that his Corinthian readers had already heard him speak in this vein. On the other hand, it is doubtful whether 1 Corinthians 1:18-25 has in mind the figure of preexistent Wisdom. Rather he speaks of the inner meaning or rationale of God's way of salvation; thus 1 Corinthians 1:30 says God made Christ "our wisdom, our righteousness, etc." Paul also refers to Christ as the "image" (*eikōn*) of God: Romans 8:29; 2 Corinthians 4:4; 1 Corinthians 15:49. Here too, Paul appears to have adopted language from Hellenized Judaism about *Sophia*. Paul uses *eikōn* language in a soteriological context; that is, its function is to ground salvation in the Christ, the image of God, not to explain who Christ is. Only in what he quotes, namely in Philippians 2:6-11, does Paul state the relation between the preexistent one and God: "being in the form [*morphē*] of God," having status "equal" to God (*isa*).

2. The growing interest in the preexistent one is palpable in the Colossian hymn, especially in its first stanza. While his relation to God is expressed in

---

[12] Robert Hammerton-Kelly, *Pre-Existence, Wisdom and the Son of Man* (SNTSMS 21; Cambridge: Cambridge University Press, 1973), 132.

a single line (the image [*eikōn*] of the invisible God), considerable attention is devoted to his relation to the created order: as God's means of creating, he is by nature the head, the sovereign of the creation, understood as "body." This sets the stage for the second stanza's concern for the cosmic reach of salvation: "that in all things [*ta panta*] he might be preeminent." Evidently something happened which is not mentioned but assumed: the headship was challenged, and so must be reestablished. This occurred by the incarnation, here expressed as the fullness (*to plērōma*) residing (*katoikēsai*) in Christ. The creator in the particular creature reconciles all things by making peace, by reintegrating the rebellious cosmos under the head. That is, what happened in this one creature affects the whole creation.

The author of Colossians was even more interested in the cosmological relation of the preexistent one—assuming that "whether thrones . . . authorities" was added, as well as "things visible and things invisible." Moreover, by adding "through the blood of his cross" the author anchored the saving event in the climax of the Jesus story, making it clear that it was not the incarnation alone that achieved the preeminence.

If we place this passage alongside the Nicene Creed, we are struck by the reversal of proportions: Colossians is concerned with the cosmological sweep of Christology but is content with one line to express the relation of the preexistent to God; the Creed expresses the cosmological sweep in one couplet, but concentrates attention on the relation of the preexistent to the Godhead. Clearly, the Arian controversy is responsible for the latter: it no longer sufficed to affirm that the preexistent one is the image of God.

3. Even clearer is the shift toward preexistence in the opening paragraph of Hebrews. The hymnic piece in verse 3 itself had devoted two of its four lines to preexistence, the first expressing the relation to the Godhead, the second to creation:

> Who is the radiation [*apaugasma*] of glory and the stamp
> [*charaktēr*] of his being [*hypostaseos*]
> bearing all things [*ta panta*] by the word of his power

But the author introduces this by saying that the Son was made the "heir of all things," through whom he [God] also created the aeons—a clear allusion first to the exaltation, then to the creation. Given the Christology of Christ's high priesthood in this book, the concern for the preexistent one is closer to Philippians 2 than to Colossians 1, because in Hebrews too, preexistence is emphasized as the starting point for the Christ-event. It attracts no real interest in its own right. In Hebrews, what qualifies the Son to be an

effective high priest is not his preexistence but his experience as an existent (see p. 151 below).

4. The Johannine prologue has the most fully developed interest in
the preexistence of the Son. In the "original" Logos-hymn (vv. 1-5), the first
half (two couplets) is concerned with the Logos' relation to God and to creation, as in Hebrews 1:3. The evangelist elaborated this by adding to the first
couplet "and the logos was God" (v. 1c), and "he was in the beginning with
God" to the second. So too, in the second stanza, to "He was the true light"
he added "he who enlightens every man" (assuming that the point is not
"who enlightens every man coming into the world," as some interpreters
punctuate and interpret here). The evangelist's interest is motivated by the
climax of the prologue: "No one has ever seen God; the only Son, who is in
the bosom of the father, he has made him known." These additions to the
"original" hymn underscore the relation between the preexistent one and
the Godhead (and in v. 9 to humanity) in order to make it clear why the
incarnate Son is the only one qualified to "exegete" the Father on earth.

What this terse overview suggests is that however different may be the
focus, and however diverse the detail, interest in Christ's preexistence is
motivated by soteriology, and cannot be demythologized to mean "preve-
nient grace" as Bultmann said. Exactly the same motor drives the Nicene
Creed, as we will see.

*Jesus as "God" in the New Testament*

Since the Nicene fathers insisted that the preexistent one is "God of God"
and "true God of true God," and so on, it is appropriate to ask whether, and
to what extent, the NT also shares this insistence, or at least implies it. The
question has been discussed frequently,[13] usually with meager and cau-
tiously expressed results. The reasons for this are not difficult to see: the
texts are not clear. Sometimes the manuscript evidence is uncertain about
the wording.[14] Sometimes the grammar or syntax is not clear.[15] In Romans

---

[13] See, e.g., Raymond E. Brown, "Does the New Testament Call Jesus God?" in *Jesus, God and Man* (Milwaukee: Bruce, 1967), chap. 1.

[14] Thus John 1:18 reads either *monogenēs theos* (only God) or *ho monogenēs theos* (the only God), or *ho monogenēs huios* (the only Son). Colossians 2:2 reads either "the knowledge and the mystery of God" or "of Christ" or "of God which is Christ" or "of God which is in Christ" or "of God the father of Christ" or "of the God and Father of Christ" or "of the God and Father and of Christ" or "of God, Christ."

[15] Thus 2 Pet 1:1 refers to the "righteousness of our God and Savior Jesus Christ" (*dikaiosynē tou theou hēmōn kai sōtēros I.X.*). Is the absence of an article before *sōtēros* merely stylistic? If so, should one supply it in order to render, "of our God and of our Savior Jesus Christ"? Or,

9:5 the matter turns on punctuation.[16] In Hebrews 1:8-9 the matter is exegetical, for the author cites Psalm 45, "thy throne, O God, is forever and ever," as referring to the Son. But where the author does not quote, he regards the Son as the radiation of God's glory (1:2)—less than a flat equation with "God."

The only text which unambiguously calls Jesus "God" is John 20:28—the confession of Thomas: "My lord and my God"—but this refers to the resurrected Jesus. Only John 1:1 unambiguously calls the preexistent Son "God"—but here scholars are divided over whether the absence of the article (*theos*, not *ho theos*) is significant. Even if one construes all these texts to mean that "God" is used of Jesus Christ, it is clear that this predication is not characteristic of the NT. Moreover, Titus 2:13; Hebrews 1:8-9 (and in a way John 20:28) all refer to the postexistent one, whereas in 1 John 5:20 and 2 Peter 1:1 the referent is not precise. In a word, the NT literature does not find it necessary to express the identity of Jesus Christ by directly calling him "God." Its soteriology "works" without this designation. This is clearly not the case for the Nicene fathers.

## III

We come at last to the heart of the issue—the Nicene insistence that the preexistent Son was not only "true God of true God" but *homoousios* with God. Neither the ante-Nicene history of the term nor its subsequent construal is of concern here. Rather, the focal point is the issue which is at stake in its adoption—and in its rejection. The discussion will move in three steps: first, a terse formal analysis of the nature of christological discourse;

---

is this construction like 1:11 (our Lord and Savior Jesus Christ), so that the title "God" does in fact refer to Jesus Christ? Titus 2:13 mentions the "appearing of the glory of the great God and our Savior Jesus Christ" (*theou kai sōtēros hēmōn*). Or should we regard "God and Savior" as a title, and translate "our God and Savior Jesus Christ"? In 1 John 5:20 the text says that the Son came to give us knowledge of the one who is true (God), and then goes on to say, "we are in the One who is true, in his Son Jesus Christ." Then it adds, "this is the true God and life eternal." To whom or to what does "this" refer? The closest antecedent is "Jesus Christ." Or does it actually refer to God?

[16] Here Paul lists the advantages of the Jew, concluding with "to whom belong the patriarchs of whom is the Christ according to the flesh," to which are added the following words, *ho ōn epi pantōn theos eulogētos.* . . . If one puts a period after "flesh," then the last clause means "He who is God over all be blessed," but without the period it means "the Christ according to the flesh, the God over all be blessed." Or should one put a period after "all" and a comma after "flesh" and translate, "the Christ according to the flesh, who is over all. God be blessed . . ." or should we put the period at the end and translate, "the Christ according to the flesh, who is over all, God blessed forever"?

then a look at Arius and Athanasius in this light; and finally the question of whether three NT Christologies are closer to Arius or to Athanasius.

## The Nature of Christological Discourse

Christology states the identity and (religious) significance of Jesus for the human condition; in traditional terms, it expresses the person and the work of Christ. Since neither identity nor significance are meaningful in isolation, the subject matter of Christology is really the syntax of relationships, the grammar of correlations. In developed Christology, the structure of signification has three interdependent correlations: the theological (Christ's relation to God), the cosmological (his relation to the created order), and the anthropological/soteriological (his relation to the human condition). Because each implies the others, from statements about God, or world, or humans one can infer appropriate statements about Christ.

The anthropological correlate invites three observations. First, there would be no Christology were there no soteriology, because it is what Christians claim about Jesus as the bringer or effecter of salvation (the work of Christ) that prompts questions about his identity (the person of Christ), since it is necessary to know whether he is able to do for humans what Christians claim he does. In a word, soteriology makes Christology necessary; Christology makes soteriology possible. At the same time, Christology is not simply soteriology because Christ is always more than Savior. (In this light, the currently popular substitution of "Creator, Redeemer, Sustainer" not only replaces a trinity of persons with a triad of functions, but constricts the function of the Son to redemption.)

Second, the formal grammar of Christology allows a great variety of material expressions of Jesus' identity and significance. Whether one says, "Jesus is God's Son who died for us" or "Jesus was a devout man who showed us how to live," the formal logic is the same. Moreover, each material content has its own rationale. Thus if the human condition is bondage, then Christ is the liberator and soteriology will be expressed as emancipation. If Christ is the teacher, then the human plight is construed as ignorance or illusion, and soteriology will be expressed in terms of education, coupled with the obligation to do what the teacher says or exemplifies. Elemental categories, moreover, undergo mutations, so that one can speak of ignorance as bondage. The point is that a changed Christology implies a changed anthropology; a different view of humanity entails a different Christology as well.

Third, christological correlations tend to obey the law of parsimony. That is, Christology and soteriology are not wasted on each other. What

Christians claim about Jesus' identity and significance usually does not exceed what is required to deal with the human dilemma. A superficial view of Jesus cannot deal with a profound view of sin. Thus if the human problem is guilt, saying that Jesus showed us how to live cannot deal with the problem but only exacerbate it.

In light of these tersely formulated considerations, it is immediately clear that whether we have in view the NT Christologies or that of the Nicene fathers, understanding requires us to see them whole.

## The Arian Controversy and the New Testament

Robert Gregg and Dennis Groh's analysis and interpretation of the controversy between the early Arians and Athanasius comports remarkably well with the foregoing understanding of the nature of Christology.[17] They demonstrate that the formulation is correct: soteriology makes Christology necessary, and Christology makes soteriology possible; they show that the christological correlates are driven by soteriological concerns, and that this is as true of the Arians as of the Athanasians.

Neither the preexistence of the Son nor the reality of the incarnation was at issue. What was at issue was the identity of the Son because on this depended the nature of the salvation which he can effect. If salvation is essentially a moral transaction, a matter of moral improvement in which the person becomes the son of God the way Jesus became a Son of God (as Arius insisted), then God relates to creatures on the basis of will. If it is a matter of imparting, of communicating God's own being (as Athanasius argued) then it must have a basis in being. If the former, then God relates to creatures on the basis of will, if the latter, on the basis of being; if the former, the Son takes us toward God, if the latter the Son imparts God to us. As Gregg and Groh put it,

> The character of the savior, the savior's relation to God and to creatures, the process and means by which salvation comes to believers, and . . . anthropology, the estimate of the limitations and capacities which belong to the human creature—these were the issues.[18]

The correlations of Christology could hardly be paraphrased better.

We begin with the anthropological correlate. Gregg and Groh rightly see that what divides Athanasian from Arian anthropology is the question

---

[17] Robert C. Gregg and Dennis E. Groh, *Early Arianism—A View of Salvation* (Philadelphia: Fortress, 1981). For convenience, quotations from the primary sources are cited from this work.

of "essentialism." Is the human dilemma to be understood in terms of nature, according to which the fall produced a corruption, a death, which is now a part of human nature (so Athanasius), or is it to be understood as a "situation" which can be left behind (so the Arians)? If the former, repentance and moral improvement are really inadequate, as Athanasius saw.[19] For the Arians, however, the dilemma is "situational" so that the believer could advance toward God by learning from the Son how to be obedient, and so be rewarded by salvation.[20] The goal was not to overcome a vulnerability in human nature but disobedience.

The Arian view of the self produced (and still does!) a Christology which emphasizes imitating Christ, who is both wise teacher and paradigm. Indeed, as Gregg and Groh put it, "what is predicated of the redeemer must be predicated of the redeemed" because Christ gains and holds his Sonship exactly the way believers acquire their sonship. "No one is son of God by nature," not even Christ.[21] In the jargon of the history of religion "school," Christ is the "redeemed Redeemer"; in the words of Gregg and Groh, Christ is the "representative creature."[22] In insisting that whatever can be true of themselves is true also of Christ, they were accused of demoting Christ to the rank of creature—that is, of promoting themselves. In other words, the Athanasian anthropology emphasized the difference between God's nature and human nature, and the Arian insisted on the similarity between human nature and Christ's nature. In a word, the divergence in anthropology required Athanasius to insist that the Savior was *homoousios* with God but different from humans, but required Arius to insist that the Savior was different from God but implicitly *homoousios* with the saved. (Basilidean gnostics, in fact, first used the word in exactly this sense.)

If the Savior and the saved both acquire their status by obedience, by learning, by faithfulness, then changeability is fundamental to both. Not surprisingly, this appeared blasphemous to the Athanasians, who would have sung lustily the lines from "Abide with Me," whose sensibility is thoroughly Greek:

> Change and decay all around I see,
> O Thou who changest not,
> Abide with me.

[18] Gregg and Groh, *Early Arianism*, 65.
[19] Gregg and Groh, *Early Arianism*, 177.
[20] Gregg and Groh, *Early Arianism*, 162–63.
[21] Gregg and Groh, *Early Arianism*, 50, 52.
[22] Gregg and Groh, *Early Arianism*, 30.

The Arians insisted that the Logos of God could change, "for being begotten and created, he has a changeable nature."[23] Given their emphasis on Christ's moral advancement, they held that he could have succumbed to temptation, but did not. What mattered of course, was that Christ was "improvable,"[24] a perfected creature who as the obedient and faithful one became "Son" (= *theos* = *theios*). The Arians took with utter seriousness the "therefore" which marks the turning-point in the hymn of Philippians 2,[25] because this showed that God rewarded him. According to the Arians, the NT calls the preexistent one "Son" because God gave him the title proleptically on the basis of divine foreknowledge of Jesus' future achievement.[26] Indeed, as the foremost creature, even the preexistent one learned; thus the Arians used NT language about the earthly Jesus' relation to God also of the preexistent one's relation to God.[27] In short, what the Athanasians dreaded—change, because it meant instability and decay—the Arians celebrated.[28] Gregg and Groh put it well: for the Athanasians,

> Christ has given to us a physical nature redeemed from corruption by making available to human nature a grace that is irreversible, . . . while God and his Word are unchangeable, creatures are not. . . . Adam's nature was changeable, and Christ came to overcome and eliminate precisely the changeability, thus giving the flesh freedom not to sin.[29]

This is why Athanasius, observing that people are now good, now not, says that "there was need of an unchangeable one, in order that men might have as an image and type for virtue that immutability of the righteousness of the Logos."[30]

The Arian cosmological correlate is now inevitable. Like all creatures, there was a time when the Son was not. The Son is the first of the originate beings, and as the shaper (*demiourgos*) of the cosmos he learned his task in imitation of the Father. As Asterius put it:

> He is a creature and belongs to the things made.
> But he has learned to frame (*demiourgein*) as

---

[23] Gregg and Groh, *Early Arianism*, 14.
[24] Gregg and Groh, *Early Arianism*, 18.
[25] Gregg and Groh, *Early Arianism*, 59.
[26] Gregg and Groh, *Early Arianism*, 96.
[27] Gregg and Groh, *Early Arianism*, 91, 115.
[28] Gregg and Groh, *Early Arianism*, 180.
[29] Gregg and Groh, *Early Arianism*, 179.
[30] Gregg and Groh, *Early Arianism*, 179.

if at the side of a teacher and artisan, and thus
he rendered service to the God who taught him.[31]

The theological correlate is also clear. For the Arians, God is utterly God, and this Godhood is in no way shared. Indeed, God relates to everything that is not God on the basis of will, not on the basis of nature. There is no "great chain of being." What separated the Arians from the Athanasians was a quite different understanding of "nature": for the former, "nature" implied necessity, and will implied freedom. So Arius wrote, "Unless he [the Son] has by will come to be, then God had a Son by necessity and against his good pleasure."[32] Consequently, for the Arians "Father" and "Son" cannot be coextensive, because God becomes "Father" only when there is "Son." In other words, "Father" is not an eternal attribute of God but a relationship that has a beginning. Inevitably, for the Arians the "begetting" of the Son implied that there was when he was not, and this meant that there could be no parity, no equality, no shared being between Father and Son. Again the summary provided by Gregg and Groh can be cited:

> The long string of "alones" applied adjectivally to God underscored the Arian sense of divine sovereignty and freedom. Nothing in creation was the result of an outworking of the necessities of divine nature. All . . . was the result of the divine will.[33]

There is no ontic continuity between God and anyone or anything. Athanasius characterizes the Arian view as follows:

> And Christ is not true God, but by participation even he was made God. The Son does not know the Father exactly, nor does the Logos see the Father perfectly, and neither does he perceive nor the Logos understand the Father exactly; for he is not the true and only Logos of the Father, but by a name alone he is called Logos and Sophia and by grace is called Son and Power.[34]

In this formulation, Athanasius implies what was at stake when he asserted the opposite, the ontic continuity between Father and Son: the assurance that the Son truly reveals because he is not inferior to God. Moreover, Athanasius will not have the Son's identity depend on being "named";

---

[31] Gregg and Groh, *Early Arianism*, 165.
[32] Gregg and Groh, *Early Arianism*, 92.
[33] Gregg and Groh, *Early Arianism*, 117.
[34] Gregg and Groh, *Early Arianism*, 9.

therefore he insists that essences are prior to terms.[35] For Athanasius, therefore, the Son must share God's being by nature, not because of an "event" like naming. Only so could the Son impart a salvation capable of redeeming our nature; only so could that redemption have its ultimate and permanent ground in God, for only the unoriginate can heal the originate.

How does this debate appear in light of the NT? Conversely, how do the Christologies in the NT look in light of the Nicene issues? At this point, it is useful to expand our consideration of NT material beyond the scope of the hymnic/creedal materials used in order to see the Christologies of texts, and in the case of Paul, a corpus of texts. We will look briefly at Paul's Letters, Hebrews, and John, because they, like Arius and Athanasius, work with a preexistence Christology.

Two general observations will orient us to the discussion as a whole. First, to return to the NT from the controversies of the fourth century is to be struck by the imprecision of the NT formulations. Presumably, this reflects not only the fact that considerable theological reflection and refinement has taken place between the first century and the fourth, but also the fundamentally different genres of the literature involved. Paul wrote letters and the fourth evangelist wrote a gospel, not treatises; even Hebrews, which appears to be a treatise with the trappings of a letter, can develop its argument without making the precise distinctions which are the watermark of fourth-century Christology. Second, we find the same rationale at work in the three preexistence Christologies as in the Nicene fathers.

We begin with Paul, noting first that the debate over which view of salvation is dominant, the forensic (justification) or the "mystical" (being in Christ), is misplaced because they represent diverse yet complementary expressions of the same underlying conceptuality. Indeed, Paul not only moves from one to the other (e.g., Phil 3:7-11), but in Romans deepens the former by developing the latter. While one should delineate Paul's theology systemically in order to see how his construal of Christ functions within it, doing so would take us too far afield. It must suffice to note that Paul's incarnational Christology comes to the surface more clearly when he speaks of salvation as redemption than it does when he speaks of it in relational terms, that is, as the rectification of the relation to God ("justification").

In Romans, the fullest christological statement appears in Romans 8:1-11, where Paul not only shifts from relational language ("no condemnation," v. 1) to the participatory language associated with redemption, but presents the Christ-event as the radical solution to the radical anthropology

---

[35] Gregg and Groh, *Early Arianism*, 25.

to which he penetrated in chapter 7. There he contended that the bondage to which the self is beholden is not merely "external" (sin and death as lords over the self) but "internal": sin is the resident, alien, malign power that thwarts even the good intent. Now he writes,

> For God has done what the law, weakened by flesh, could not do: sending his own Son in the likeness of sinful flesh and for sin, he condemned sin in the flesh in order that the just requirement of the law might be fulfilled in us, who walk not according to the flesh but according to the Spirit. (8:3-4)

He goes on to make it clear that the Spirit now resides in the self to displace sin, the squatter which had moved in before. The rationale of the christological statement is clear: God sent the Son to participate in the human condition so that the tyranny of sin could be broken precisely where it operates—in "sinful flesh" (lit. "flesh of sin," flesh qualified by sin). Earlier in the letter, when Paul emphasized the relational aspect of salvation, he was content to say that God "put forward' " Christ as an expiatory sacrifice; the tradition he uses need not have implied the sending of the preexistent one, but Paul himself did.

The soteriological connection between preexistence and redemption is clearer in Galatians. Just as in Romans 1–3 Paul had to show how both Gentile and Jew are accountable for their wrong relation to God, and thus are guilty in terms of law, and as in Romans 5 he placed them both under the tyranny of sin and death by appealing to the Adamic situation, so in Galatians 3:23–4:11 he places them both under the control of law, a stern *paidagōgos*, where they lack freedom. Here he writes,

> So with us: when we were children, we were slaves to the elemental spirits of the universe [the *stoicheia*]. But when the time had fully come, God sent forth his Son, born of woman, born under law, to redeem those who were under law. (4:3-4)

Here it is even clearer that redemption depends on the Son's entering into the human plight. Paul uses this language to complement the language of participation: "we are no longer *under* a custodian; for *in* Christ you are all sons of God, through faith. For as many of you as were baptized *into* Christ have *put on* Christ" (Gal 3:27)—like putting the hand into a glove. Whether it is redemption from the tyrannous structure of law, or redemption from the tyranny of sin and death which had corrupted the self, Paul refers to God's sending of the Son into the plight.

When we read Paul in light of the disagreement between the Arians and the Athanasians, we have conflicting impressions. When Paul emphasizes redemption from bondage he is closer to Athanasius, but when he accents rectification of the relation to God he seems closer to the Arian concern for will. We are also struck by Paul's ability to make his point without specifying precisely who the sent Son is, or in what sense he is "Son." We find similar lack of concern for specifying how the Son is related to the Father in 1 Corinthians 8:6:

> There is one God, the Father,
> from whom are all things and for whom we exist
> and one Lord, Jesus Christ,
> through whom are all things and through whom we exist.

So too, the "apostolic benediction" (2 Cor 13:13) leaves entirely open the relation between Christ, God, and the Holy Spirit.

Paul's understanding of the salvation effected by the Christ-event is influenced by his futuristic eschatology. Indeed, according to the logic of 1 Corinthians 15:23-28, the Christ-event is still going on: since Easter Christ is conquering the hostile powers, making (or God making) them subject to Christ (an interpretation of Ps 110:1). "When all things are subjected to him, then the Son himself will also be subjected to him who put all things under him, that God may be everything to everyone." An instrumental view of Christ could hardly be more apparent. Indeed, one is tempted to infer that Christ's postresurrection lordship is a "temporary" status necessary for the completion of his salvific task. On the surface, at least, ideas like this appear to put Paul closer to Arius than to Athanasius, who ought to have found it difficult to reconcile Paul's language here with the idea that the Son shares being with the Father.

On the other hand, one thread that runs through Paul's diverse ways of regarding the situation of the unredeemed, unrectified self is the self's inability to save itself. Moreover, even though Paul talks about death as an enemy (1 Cor 15:26), he also recognizes that it is inadequate to view it as a foreign tyrant over the self; it also qualifies one's "nature." This is why "flesh and blood cannot inherit the kingdom of God" (1 Cor 15:50). Consequently, transformation is required, when the mortal "puts on" the immortal. Athanasius too held a radical view of human nature and its salvation. And it was precisely this radical need that he sought to satisfy by insisting that the Savior was nothing less than *homoousios* with the Father. No one less, would do, could do, what needed to be done. Does the same logic lie latent in Paul's understanding? Or will Paul's Christology "work" just as well without it? Apparently, in his time it did. But once the question was asked, once the exact identity of the preexistent one was in dispute, once one had to decide whether it was God and God's being that redeems, or someone other and lesser, then the defeat of the Arian view was inevitable. Then, too, the law of parsimony was in effect: the incarnation of "true God of true God" was not needed if repentance and moral progress sufficed to deal with the human situation, but it was needed to redeem from corruption. In deepening the inherited theology of rectification to redemption, Paul, in his own way, seems to have sensed this.

The Epistle to the Hebrews is the nearest thing in the NT to a treatise on Christology; even so, its aim is pastoral: so to expound the identity and significance of Christ that the readers will not "drift away" (2:1) but have full confidence in their future salvation. Given this general similarity to Athanasius' concern, it is interesting to note that Hebrews—more than any other book in the NT—is interested in each of the three phases of the Christ-event: preexistence, existence, and postexistence. God has now spoken through the Son, who is superior to angels, to Moses, and to Aaron. More clearly than for Paul's Letters, the work of Christ depends on his person, because for Hebrews, what is mediated cannot be separated from the mediator. Moreover, no other NT author insisted that the incarnate one "learned obedience through what he suffered" (5:8), and was thereby perfected, qualified to be the definitive high priest who represents humanity before God. Given the Arian insistence on the changeability of the Son, on his "learning," it is no surprise that Hebrews played a major role in Arian Christology.

Before undertaking to show that the Son is superior to angels, the author, as we saw, introduces the Son with a piece of tradition, to which we now return:

> Who being the radiation [*apaugasma*] of [his] glory
> and the stamp [*charaktēr*] of his being [*hypostaseōs*]. (Heb 1:3)

The RSV turns the noun into a verb: "reflects"—suggesting a mirror. However, *apaugasma* should probably be rendered "radiation," which can be both a process and the thing radiated. *Wisdom* 7:26 uses it of *Sophia*, and in parallel with "a spotless mirror [*esoptron*] of the working [*energeia*] of God." A few lines earlier, she is called the "emanation [*porroia*] of the glory of the Almighty." The same usage appears in Philo (e.g., *Op. Mund.* 146). Herbert Braun's formulation is apt: What this term, with its synonyms, expresses is "innerste Wesens Verbundenheit und nicht eine dem Original gegenuber mindere Kopie" (innermost being's involvement, not a lesser copy of the original).[36] The image is of outstreaming light, like rays of the sun. "Stamp" refers to the die-stamp used to strike coins; the idea here being exact likeness. This likeness is of God's essence or being (*hypostasis*); this couplet affirms that the preexistent Son is the expression of God, comparable to the Stoic Logos *prophorikos* (the outward manifestation of the Logos in distinction from the inward being, the Logos *endiathetos*). This is as close to Athanasius as any NT text comes.

Hebrews 2:10-18 outlines the three-stage Christ-event twice, first by citing the Old Testament in such a way that each quotation refers to one of the phases, then by commenting on the soteriological import.

| preexistence: | I will proclaim thy name . . . |
| | . . . I will praise thy name |
| existence: | I will put my trust in him |
| postexistence: | Here am I and the children God has given me. |

This is the only place in the NT where the preexistent announces his impending work on earth. It is the functional equivalent of "did not consider equality with God a thing to be held onto for advantage." By inserting "and again" into Isaiah 8:17-18, the author apportions the first line to the existent one (now the "second" quotation) and the second (now the "third") to the arrival of the Son before God as the head of the saved community. In this soteriological context, "I will put my trust in him" expresses the incarnate one's fidelity to God while on earth. That is, the pioneer of salvation (v. 10) is perfected through suffering. What is being expressed here is the solidarity of the Savior and the saved: "for he who sanctifies and those who are sanctified are all of one" (RSV: have all one origin). The incarnate Son can therefore call them "brothers." The same point is made at the end of the quotations: he was a partaker in flesh and blood so that "through death he might destroy him who has the power of death, the devil, and deliver all those who through fear of death were subject to lifelong bondage." Apart from the reference to the devil, this is the same motif which we found in Paul. At the end of the discussion, the author uses the same solidarity theme to establish the qualifications of the postexistent high priest: "he had to be made like his brethren in every respect so that he might become a merciful and faithful high priest" (v. 17); that is, "because he himself has suffered and been tempted, he is able to help those who are tempted" (v. 18). The same theme is repeated in 5:7-10. If the opening paragraph puts Hebrews at the side of Athanasius, chapter 2 appears to align it with Arius.

[36] Herbert Braun, *An die Hebräer* (HNT; Tubingen: Mohr, 1984), 25.

This seems to be reinforced by other passages which concern the life of Christ on earth, and its soteriological significance. In 2:5-9 the author gives a christological interpretation of Psalm 8. Then he comments, "we do not yet see everything in subjection to him." That is, the postexistent phase (Christ's lordship) is invisible on earth. What we see, and all we see, is "Jesus, who for a little while was made lower than angels, crowned . . . because of the suffering of death, so that by the grace of God he might taste death for everyone." The last line is problematic, because although the majority of texts read *chariti theou* ("by the grace of God"), a minority read *chōris theou* ("apart from God"). The minority, more difficult, reading is to be preferred (though scholarship is divided here). If so, the utter lowliness of the incarnation is expressed not by mentioning the cross (Paul's addition to the hymn in Philippians 2) but by the experience of death—without God—for everyone. The paradox could hardly be more striking: he who is the expression of God dies apart from God. Hebrews 5:5-10 is even more difficult (the complex details which suggest, at least to some, that a tradition is embedded here must be bracketed out of this discussion; it is unlikely that the author alludes to Gethsemane). Here too Hebrews insists that "although he was Son, he learned obedience through what he suffered." What is controversial is the "he was heard [his praying 'with loud cries and tears'] for his godly fear" (*apo tēs eulabeias*). Is the RSV, cited here, correct, or should one give a "negative" construction, emphasizing *apo* = from, so that one renders "out of his anxious fear" or even "out of the fear of God-forsakenness," as has also been suggested? In any case, the depth of this experience qualified him to be the Melchizedekian high priest: one "who in every respect has been tempted as we are, yet without sinning" (4:15). Accordingly, Jesus is the forerunner and perfector of our faith (12:2).

The anthropos-myth may well provide the pattern for this Christology. At the same time, what sharply distinguishes it from many gnostic schemes is the fact that in Hebrews there is no ontic continuity between Savior and saved; the Son does not gather to himself the souls which are consubstantial with him. Rather the solidarity between them must be established; indeed, it is not established sufficiently by the incarnation alone, but must be established also morally—by the experience of suffering, yet without succumbing to temptation. Jesus is not the example persons are to emulate; he is the archetype who defines their destiny, having first identified himself with them. In contrast with Paul, there is no participation in Christ; rather, Christ participated "for a while" in us.

The Arians could indeed appropriate much of Hebrews, with its insistence that the incarnate one too had to learn obedience, be perfected, to be the pioneer of salvation. What finally makes their appropriation inappropriate, however, is that they evidently were unable to maintain the sharp paradox which is fundamental to Hebrews: the learning Son was the incarnate Son who was the *apaugasma* of God.

To open the Gospel of John is to enter another world, not simply because here Christ is always teacher and never learner, but because in contrast with the relentlessly futuristic salvation in Hebrews, John offers a predominantly present salvation. Yet in both cases, it is the preexistent one, here flatly called *theos*, who effects salvation. Moreover, whereas Hebrews develops the paradox of the incarnation in the direction of Jesus' utter vulnerability, John develops its rationale in such a way as to keep in focus Jesus' absolute authority to act as God. Indeed, John's Jesus does not *become qualified* to represent us to God; he *comes qualified* to represent God to us, for he alone, as the incarnate Logos, has the qualification to exegete the Father (1:18).

This discussion must set aside, admittedly at considerable risk of oversimplifying, all considerations of the sources of John, and their respective christological accents. Likewise, it must assume that whatever be the history of the prologue and of its relation to the gospel as we have it, the gospel now should be read through the lens of the prologue. Concretely, this means that we should read it as the story of how the Logos incarnate exegetes God.

In John, the incarnation is expressed in four ways: (1) the most formal and "metaphysical" is in 1:14—"the Word became flesh"; (2) somewhat less abstract is verse 4: "what came to pass in him was life"; (3) more "mythic" are the assertions of his descent to earth (6:51; 16:28); and finally, (4) John has Jesus speak of both the "sending" of the Son (e.g., 3:39) and of his having "come" (e.g., 7:28; 8:42).

Arius certainly had it wrong, at least for John, in contending that titles like Son or God were given proleptically by God who foresaw that Jesus would earn them. In John he is the Logos, who is with God, is God, the only Son in the Father's bosom before he became Jesus. Because Jesus is the Logos-Creator enfleshed, his lifetime is the pivotal event for the world which the Paraclete perpetuates. Although Jesus never claims to be the Logos (nor does he say, "I am the Son," but simply refers to himself as "the Son") he claims to do on earth what God does in heaven, so that there is a basis for the charge that he makes himself "equal with God" (5:18). At the same time, the Arians could point to the fact that Jesus insists he is not God's peer but agent who can do "only what he sees the Father doing" (5:19;

see also 5:20-23, 26, 30-32). Because he repeats God on earth, so to speak, he is obedient to the Father, glorifies the Father, and speaks as the Father "taught" him. Indeed, Jesus declares, "I always do what is pleasing to him" (8:29). In other words, just as the Arians found support in what Hebrews said about Jesus on earth, so they appealed to these elements in John. They did so because they refused to distinguish what was said of the incarnate one from what was, and is to be, said of the preexistent one.

This general observation having been made, it must be qualified, at least as far as John is concerned. That is, John too, in its own way, does not construe the incarnation in such a way as to distinguish sharply the preexistent from the existent Son, but it "blends" them—not "from below" as did the Arians, but "from above." That is, the enfleshed Logos-Creator did not undergo such a change that he ceased to be what he was before, nor did he ever fully identify himself with humans, even if he did weep over Lazareth and die. He remains the "stranger from heaven" (de Jonge's phrase), who is "in the world" but never "of it" (8:23; 17:14, 16). He does not stand in solidarity with humanity, but stands over against it, proclaiming himself to be the bread from heaven, the door, the sheep gate, the way, the truth, and the life. Thereby he presents himself as the life-giver, the one who is for the hearer what God is for them. To reject him, therefore, is to reject life and God; to accept him is to pass from death to life. No Last Judgment can bring consequences more devastating than rejecting Jesus now. This certainly comports more with Athanasius than with Arius.

If what separated the two fourth-century combatants was the issue of "essentialism" or "will," then one must ask whether in this regard John was not closer to Arius. That is, the salvation which Jesus brings in John is not "metaphysical" redemption from corruption but more "relational," more a matter of "will." This is why those who believe *have* eternal life now (e.g., 5:24), a quality of existence which does not preclude them from having to die and decay. This emerges clearly in the complex story of Lazarus and Martha. To her Jesus said, "I am the resurrection and the life; he who believes in me, though he die, yet shall he live; and whoever lives and believes in me shall never die." Then she makes the only unqualifiedly accepted confession in the entire book. After that Lazarus is resuscitated, as a sign of future resurrection (and as the event that triggers the Passion story). The point, however, is that it is Martha, not Lazarus, who receives eternal life. Both remain mortal. That the salvation Jesus brings is more relational than metaphysical or "essential" is clear also from the way John emphasizes "of." Jesus tells Nicodemus, "that which is born *of* the flesh is flesh, and that which is born *of* the Spirit is spirit" (3:6). To "the Jews" he said, "you are *of* your father, the devil" (8:44). The alternative is to be "of God," to have God as one's Father. In a word, everything turns on one's "of-ness," one's whence, and ground. In offering life, Jesus restores the "of-ness" to the Father. In the last analysis, here too the proximity to Arius is finally superficial because, at least from Athanasius' point of view, no creature, no matter how preeminent, can restore the "of-ness" to the Father, no matter how relational and "nonessential" it may be. Besides, one might not be able to avoid categorically the question whether even the relational "of-ness" has an ontic ground.

By no means has everything been said that should be said about our topic. I am tempted to quote Hebrews: "About this we have much to say which is hard to explain"—though the reason for the difficulty lies in the subject matter and in the limits of the writer, not, as in Hebrews which explains, "since you have become dull of hearing" (5:11). The topic is not only inherently difficult, subtle, and beguiling, but resistant precisely to conclusion.

# Works Cited

Allison Jr., Dale C. "The Pauline Epistles and the Synoptic Gospels: The Pattern of the Parallels." *New Testament Studies* 28 (1982): 1–32.

Ashton, John. *Understanding the Fourth Gospel.* Oxford: Oxford University Press, 1991. Reprint, 2007.

Barr, James. *The Semantics of Biblical Language.* Oxford: Oxford University Press, 1961.

Barrett, C. K. *The Gospel according to St. John: An Introduction with Commentary and Notes on the Greek Text.* 2nd ed. Philadelphia: Westminster, 1978.

Barth, Markus. " 'The Faith of the Messiah.' " *Heythrop Journal* 10 (1969): 363–70.

Beasley-Murray, George R. *John.* Word Biblical Commentary 36. Waco, Tex.: Word Books, 1987.

Betz, Hans Dieter. *Galatians: A Commentary on Paul's Letter to the Churches in Galatia.* Hermeneia. Philadelphia: Fortress, 1979.

Boers, Hendrikus. "Jesus and the Christian Faith: New Testament Christology since Bousset's *Kyrios Christos.*" *Journal of Biblical Literature* 89 (1970): 450–56.

Borg, Marcus. *Jesus: A New Vision—Spirit, Culture and the Life of Discipleship.* New York: HarperOne, 1987.

————. *Meeting Jesus again for the First Time: The Historical Jesus and the Heart of Contemporary Faith.* New York: HarperCollins, 1995.

Boring, M. Eugene. "The Christology of Mark: Hermeneutical Issues for Systematic Theology." *Semeia* 30 (1984): 125–53.

Bornkamm, Günther. *Jesus of Nazareth.* New York: Harper & Bros., 1960. German original, 1956.

————. *Jesus von Nazareth.* Urban Taschenbücher 19. 10th rev. ed. Stuttgart: Kohlhammer, 1975.

Bousset, Wilhelm. *Jesu Predigt in ihrem Gegensatz zum Judentum: Ein religionsgeschichtlicher Vergleich.* Göttingen: Vandenhoeck & Ruprecht, 1892.

————. *Kyrios Christos: A History of the Belief in Christ from the Beginnings of Christianity to Irenaeus.* Nashville: Abingdon, 1970. Reprint, Waco, Tex.: Baylor University Press, 2013; German original, 1913.

Braun, Herbert. *An die Hebräer.* Handbuch zum Neuen Testament. Tübingen: Mohr, 1984.

————. "The Meaning of New Testament Christology." *Journal for Theology and Church* 5 (1968): 89–127. German original, "Der Sinn der neutestamentlichen Christologie." *Zeitschrift für Theologie und Kirche* 54 (1957): 341–77.

Brown, Raymond E. *The Community of the Beloved Disciple.* New York: Paulist Press, 1979.

————. "Does the New Testament Call Jesus God?" Chapter 1 in *Jesus, God and Man: Modern Biblical Reflections.* Milwaukee: Bruce, 1967.

Büchsel, Friedrich. "'In Christus' bei Paulus." *Zeitschrift für die neutestamentliche Wissenschaft und die Kunde der älteren Kirche* 42 (1949): 141–52.

Bultmann, Rudolf. "Glossen im Römerbrief." Pages 278–84 in *Exegetica.* Edited by E. Dinkler, 278–84. Tübingen: J. C. B. Mohr, 1967. Originally published in *Theologische Literaturzeitung* 72 (1947): 197–202.

————. *History of Synoptic Tradition.* New York: Harper & Row, 1963.

Casey, Maurice. *From Jewish Prophet to Gentile God.* Louisville, Ky.: Westminster John Knox, 1991.

Charlesworth, James H. "How the Dead Sea Scrolls Have Revolutionized Our Understanding of the Gospel of John." *Bible Review* 9 (1993): 27–38.

Childs, Brevard S. *The New Testament as Canon: An Introduction.* Philadelphia: Fortress, 1984.

Cranfield, C. E. B. *A Critical and Exegetical Commentary on the Epistle to the Romans.* International Critical Commentary. 2 vols. Edinburgh: T&T Clark, 1975–1979.

Crossan, John Dominic. *The Historical Jesus: The Life of a Mediterranean Jewish Peasant.* New York: HarperOne, 1991.

————. *Jesus: A Revolutionary Biography.* New York: HarperCollins, 1995.

Cullmann, Oscar. *The Christology of the New Testament.* Translated by Shirley C. Guthrie and Charles A. M. Hall. Rev. ed. Philadelpha: Westminster, 1959.

Culpepper, Alan. "The Pivot of John's Prologue." *New Testament Studies* 27 (1980): 1–31.

Dabelstein, Rolf. *Die Beurteilung der "Heiden" bei Paulus.* Frankfurt: Peter Lang, 1981.

Dahl, Nils A. "The Messiahship of Jesus." Pages 37–47 in *The Crucified Messiah and Other Essays.* Minneapolis: Augsburg, 1974.

———. "The Neglected Factor in New Testament Theology." *Reflection* 73 (1975): 5–8.

de Jonge, Marinus. *Christology in Context: The Earliest Christian Response to Jesus.* Philadelphia: Westminster, 1988.

———. *Jesus, Stranger from Heaven and Son of God: Jesus Christ and the Christians in Johannine Perspective.* Society of Biblical Literature Sources for Biblical Study 11. Missoula, Mont.: Scholars Press, 1977.

DeBoer, M. C., ed. *From Jesus to John.* M. de Jong Festschrift. Sheffield: JSOT Press, 1993.

Dunn, James D. G. *Baptism in the Holy Spirit: A Re-Examination of the New Testament Teaching on the Gift of the Spirit in Relation to Pentecostalism Today.* Philadelphia: Westminster, 1970.

———. *Christology in the Making.* Philadelphia: Westminster, 1980.

Edward, Schillebeeckx. *Jesus.* New York: Seabury, 1979.

Förster, Werner. *Gnosis: A Selection of Gnostic Texts.* Vol. 1, *Patristic Evidence.* Oxford: Clarendon, 1972.

Fraser, J. W. *Jesus and Paul: Paul as an Interpreter of Jesus from Harnack to Kümmel.* Abingdon, U.K.: Marcham Press, 1974.

Frid, Bo. "Jesaja und Paulus in Röm 15, 12." *Biblische Zeitschrift* 27 (1983): 237–41.

Friedrich, Gerhard. "'Begriffsgeschichtliche' Untersuchungen im Theologisches Wörterbuch zum Neuen Testament." *Archiv für Begriffsgeschichte* 20 (1976): 151–77.

———. "Das bisher noch fehlende Begriffslexikon zum Neuen Testament." *New Testament Studies* 19 (1972/1973): 127–52.

Funk, Robert W., Roy W. Hoover, and the Jesus Seminar. *The Five Gospels: The Search for the Authentic Words of Jesus. New Translation and Commentary.* New York: Macmillan, 1993.

Furnish, Victor Paul. "The Jesus-Paul Debate: from Baur to Bultmann." *Bulletin of the John Rylands University Library of Manchester* 47 (1965): 342–81.

Goodenough, E. R., and A. T. Kraabel. "Paul and the Hellenization of Christianity." Pages 23–68 in *Religions in Antiquity: Essays in Memory of Erwin Ramsdell Goodenough.* Edited by J. Neusner. Studies in the History of Religions 14. Leiden: Brill, 1968.

Gregg, Robert C., and Dennis E. Groh. *Early Arianism—A View of Salvation.* Philadelphia: Fortress, 1981.

Gunton, Colin E. *Yesterday and Today: A Study of Continuities in Christology.* London: Darton, Longman & Todd, 1983.

Güttgemanns, Erhardt. *Der leidende Apostel und sein Herr.* Forschungen zur Religion und Literatur des Alten und Neuen Testaments 90. Göttingen: Vandenhoeck & Ruprecht, 1966.

Hahn, Ferdinand. *The Titles of Jesus in Christology.* Cleveland, Ohio: World Publishing, 1969. German original, 1963.

Hammerton-Kelly, Robert. *Pre-Existence, Wisdom and the Son of Man.* Society for New Testament Studies Monograph Series 21. Cambridge: Cambridge University Press, 1973.

Hanson, A. T. *Studies in Paul's Technique and Theology.* London: SPCK, 1974.

Harnack, Adolf von. *What Is Christianity?* Translated by Thomas Bailey Sanders. Philadelphia: Fortress, 1986.

Haussleiter, J. "Der Glaube Jesu Christi und der Christliche Glaube: Ein Beitrag zur Erklärung des Römerbriefes." *Neue kirchliche Zeitschrift* (1891): 109–45, 205–30.

Hays, Richard B. "Christology and Ethics in Galatians: The Law of Christ." *Catholic Biblical Quarterly* 49 (1987): 268–90.

———. *Echoes of Scripture in the Letters of Paul.* New Haven: Yale University Press, 1989.

———. *The Faith of Jesus Christ.* Society of Biblical Literature Dissertation Series 56. Chico, Calif.: Scholars Press, 1983.

———. "Psalm 143 and the Logic of Romans 3." *Journal of Biblical Literature* 99 (1980): 107–15.

Hebert, Gabriel. " 'Faithfulness' and 'Faith.' " *Theology* 58 (1955): 373–79.

Hengel, Martin. *Between Jesus and Paul.* Philadelphia: Fortress, 1983. Reprint, Waco, Tex.: Baylor University Press, 2013. German original, 1972.

Hoover, R. W. "The Harpagmos Enigma: A Philological Solution." *Harvard Theological Review* 64 (1971): 95–119.

Howard, George. "The 'Faith of Christ.' " *Expository Times* 85 (1974): 212–15.

———. "On the 'Faith of Jesus Christ.' " *Harvard Theological Review* 60 (1967): 459–65.

———. "Phil 2:6-11 and the Human Christ." *Catholic Biblical Quarterly* 40 (1978): 368–87.

———. "Romans 3:21-31 and the Inclusion of the Gentiles." *Harvard Theological Review* 63 (1970): 223–33.

Hultgren, Arland J. "The *Pistis Christou* Formulation in Paul." *Novum Testamentum* 22 (1980): 248–63.

Jeremias, Joachim. *New Testament Theology.* New York: Scribner, 1971.

Jewett, Robert. "'The Form and Function of the Homiletic Benediction." *Australasian Theological Review* 51 (1969): 18–34.

Johnson, Luke T. "Romans 3:21-26 and the Faith of Jesus." *Catholic Biblical Quarterly* 44 (1982): 77–90.

Käsemann, Ernst. *Commentary on Romans.* Trans. G. W. Bromiley. Grand Rapids: Eerdmans, 1980.

————. "The Problem of a New Testament Theology." *New Testament Studies* 19 (1973): 235–45.

Keck, Leander E. *The Bible in the Pulpit.* Nashville: Abingdon, 1978.

————. "Bornkamm's *Jesus of Nazareth* Revisited." *Journal of Religion* 49 (1969): 1–17.

————. "From Jewish Prophet to Gentile God: The Origins and Development of New Testament Christology." Review of Maurice Casey's *From Jewish Prophet to Gentile God.* In *Interpretation* 47 (1993): 413–14.

————. "The Function of Rom 3:10-18." Pages 141–57 in *God's Christ and His People.* Festschrift for Nils Dahl. Oslo: Universitets Forlaget, 1978.

————. *A Future for the Historical Jesus.* 2nd rev. ed. Philadelphia: Fortress, 1981.

————. "Is the New Testament a Field of Study? or, From Outler to Overbeck and Back." *Second Century* 1 (1981): 19–35.

————. "On the Ethos of the Early Christians." *Journal of the American Academy of Religion* 42 (1974): 435–52. Later published as "Das Ethos der frühen Christen." Pages 123–36 in *Zur Soziologie des Urchristentums.* Edited by Wayne A. Meeks. München: Chr. Kaiser, 1979.

———— "Paul and Apocalyptic Theology." *Interpretation* 38 (1984): 229–41. Reprinted in *Christ's First Theologian: The Shape of Paul's Thought.* Waco, Tex.: Baylor University Press, 2015, 75–87.

————. "Paul as Thinker." *Interpretation* 47 (1993): 27–38. Reprinted in *Christ's First Theologian: The Shape of Paul's Thought.* Waco, Tex.: Baylor University Press, 2015, 89–101.

————. "The Post-Pauline Interpretation of Jesus' Death in Rom 5, 6-7." Pages 237–48 in *Theologia Crucis—Signum Crucis.* Edited by C. Andresen and G. Klein. Festschrift for E. Dinkler. Tübingen: Mohr Siebeck, 1979. Reprinted in *Christ's First Theologian: The Shape of Paul's Thought.* Waco, Tex.: Baylor University Press, 2015, 233–44.

————. "Romans 15:4—An Interpolation?" Pages 125–36 in *Faith and History: Essays in Honor of Paul W. Meyer.* Edited by John T. Carroll,

Charles H. Cosgrove, and E. Elizabeth Johnson. Atlanta, Ga.: Scholars Press, 1991. Reprint, Eugene, Ore.: Wipf & Stock, 2004.

———. "Toward the Renewal of New Testament Christology." *New Testament Studies* 32 (1986): 362–77. Reprint, pages 321–40 in *From Jesus to John*. Edited by M. C. deBoer. Festschrift for M. de Jonge. Sheffield: JSOT Press, 1993.

———. "Will the Historical-Critical Method Survive? Some Observations." Pages 115–27 in *Orientation by Disorientation: Studies in Literary Criticism and Biblical Criticism*. Edited by R. A. Spencer. Theological Monograph Series 35. Festschrift for W. Beardslee. Pittsburgh: Pickwick, 1980.

Kertelge, Karl. *"Rechtfertigung" bei Paulus*. Münster: Aschendorff, 1972.

Kingsbury, Jack Dean. "The Composition and Christology of Mt 28:16-20." *Journal of Biblical Literature* 93 (1974): 573–84.

———. "The Developing Conflict between Jesus and the Jewish Leaders in Matthew's Gospel: A Literary-Critical Study." *Catholic Biblical Quarterly* 49 (1987): 57–73.

———. "The 'Divine Man' as the Key to Mark's Christology—The End of an Era?" *Interpretation* 35 (1981): 243–57.

———. *Matthew: Structure, Christology, Kingdom*. Philadelphia: Fortress, 1975.

Kittel, Gerhard. *"Pistis Iēsou Christou* bei Paulus." *Theologische Studien und Kritiken* 79 (1906): 419–36.

Klausner, Joseph. *Jesus of Nazareth: His Life, Times, and Teaching*. Translated by Herbert Danby. London: Allen & Unwin, 1925.

Knierim, Rolf. "The Task of an Old Testament Theology." *Horizons in Biblical Theology* 6 (1984): 25–57.

Knox, John. " 'The Prophet' in the New Testament Christology." Pages 22–34 in *Lux in Lumine*. Edited by R. A. Norris. Festschrift for Norman Pittenger. New York: Seabury, 1966.

Koch, Dietrich-Alex. "Beobachtungen zum christologischen Schriftgebrauch in den vorpaulinischen Gemeinden." *Zeitschrift für die neutestamentliche Wissenschaft und die Kunde der älteren Kirche* 71 (1980): 174–91.

———. *Die Schrift als Zeuge des Evangeliums. Untersuchungen zu Verwendung u.z. Verständnis der Schrift bei Paulus*. Beiträge zur historischen Theologie 69. Tübingen: Mohr Siebeck, 1986.

Kohler, Kaufmann. *Jewish Theology Systematically and Historically Considered*. New York: Macmillan, 1918.

Kuss, Otto. *Der Römerbrief übersetzt und erklärt*. 3 vols. Regensburg: Pustet, 1957–1978.

Lagrange, Marie-Joseph. *Saint Paul Épitre aux Romains: Etudes bibliques.* Paris: J. Gabalda, 1922.

Lapide, Pinchas. *Der Rabbi von Nazaret: Wandlungen des jüdischen Jesusbildes.* Trier: Spee-Verlag, 1974.

Lee, Dorothy A. *The Symbolic Narratives of the Fourth Gospel: The Interplay of Form and Meaning.* Journal for the Study of the New Testament: Supplement Series 95. Sheffield: JSOT Press, 1994.

Léon-Defour, Xavier. "Towards a Symbolic Reading of the Fourth Gospel." *New Testament Studies* 27 (1981): 439–56.

Lindars, Barnabas. *The Gospel of John.* New Century Bible. London: Oliphants, 1972.

———. "John and the Synoptic Gospels: A Test Case." *New Testament Studies* 27 (1981): 287–94.

———. *New Testament Apologetic: The Doctrinal Significance of the Old Testament Quotations.* Philadelphia: Westminster, 1961.

Ljungmann, Henrik. *Pistis.* Lund: Gleerup, 1964.

Lohse, Eduard, and Helmut Koester, eds. *Colossians and Philemon.* Translated by Robert J. Karris. Hermeneia. Minneapolis: Fortress, 1972.

Maccoby, Hyam. *The Myth-Maker: Paul and the Invention of Christianity.* San Francisco: Harper & Row, 1986.

Martyn, J. Louis. *History and Theology in the Fourth Gospel.* Nashville: Abingdon, 1968. 2nd ed., 1979.

———. *Theological Issues in the Letters of Paul.* Nashville: Abingdon, 1997.

McCown, Chester C. *The Search for the Real Jesus.* New York: Scribner's, 1940.

Meeks, Wayne A. "The Man from Heaven in Johannine Sectarianism." *Journal of Biblical Literature* 91 (1972): 44–72.

Meier, John P. "Salvation History in Matthew: In Search of a Starting Point." *Catholic Biblical Quarterly* 37 (1975): 203–15.

Menken, Maarten J. J. "The Christology of the Fourth Gospel: A Survey of Recent Research." Pages 292–320 in *From Jesus to Paul: Essays on Jesus and New Testament Christology in Honour of Marinus de Jonge.* Edited by Martinus C. de Boer. Journal for the Study of the New Testament: Supplement Series 84. Sheffield: JSOT Press, 1993.

Meyer, Ben F. "The Pre-Pauline Formula in Rom. 3:25-26a." *New Testament Studies* 29 (1983): 198–208.

Michel, O. *Der Brief an die Römer.* Kritisch-exegetischer Kommentar über das Neue Testament. 5th ed. Göttingen: Vandenhoeck & Ruprecht, 1978.

Milet, Jean. *God or Christ? The Excesses of Christo-centricity.* New York: Crossroad, 1981.

Miller, E. L. "The Logic of the Logos Hymn: A New View." *New Testament Studies* 29 (1983): 552–61.

Minear, Paul S. *The Obedience of Faith*. Studies in Biblical Theology 19. Second Series. Naperville, Ill.: Alec R. Allenson, 1971.

Morgan, Robert. *The Nature of New Testament Theology*. Studies in Biblical Theology 25. Second Series. Naperville, Ill.: Alec R. Allenson, 1973.

Moule, C. F. D. *The Origin of Christology*. Cambridge: Cambridge University Press, 1977.

Murphey-O'Connor, J. "Christological Anthropology in Phil, II, 6-11." *Revue biblique* 83 (1976): 25–50.

Murray, J. *Romans*. New International Commentary on the New Testament. 2 vols. Grand Rapids: Eerdmans, 1967.

Nagata, T. "A Neglected Feature of the Christ-hymn in Phil 2:6-11." *Annual of the Japanese Biblical Institute* 9 (1983): 28–39.

Neugebauer, Fritz. *In Christus*. Göttingen: Vandenhoeck & Ruprecht, 1961.

Neusner, Jacob. "The Use of the Later Rabbinic Evidence for the Study of First-Century Pharisaism." Pages 215–28 in *Approaches to Ancient Judaism: Theory and Practice*. Brown Judaic Studies 1. Missoula, Mont.: Scholars Press, 1978.

Neyrey, Jerome H. *An Ideology of Revolt: John's Christology in Social-Scientific Perspective*. Philadelphia: Fortress, 1988.

———. "John III. A Debate over Johannine Epistemology and Christology." *Novum Testamentum* 23 (1981): 115–27.

Nicholson, Godfrey C. *Death as Departure: The Johannine Descent-Ascent Schema*. Society of Biblical Literature Dissertation Series 63. Chico, Calif.: Scholars Press, 1983.

O'Neill, John C. *Paul's Letter to the Romans*. Harmondsworth: Penguin, 1975.

Overman, J. Andrew. *Matthew's Gospel and Formative Judaism: The Social World of the Matthean Community*. Minneapolis: Fortress, 1990.

Pallis, Alexander. *To the Romans*. Liverpool: Liverpool Booksellers, 1920.

Petersen, Norman R. *The Gospel of John and the Sociology of Light: Language and Characterization in the Fourth Gospel*. Valley Forge, Pa.: Trinity International, 1993.

Pluta, Alfons. *Gottes Bundestreue: Ein Schlüsselbegriff in Röm 3, 25a*. Stuttgarter Bibelstudien 34. Stuttgart: Katholisches Bibelwerk, 1969.

Powell, Mark Allan, and David R. Bauer, eds. *Who Do You Say That I Am? Essays on Christology*. Festschrift for Jack Dean Kingsbury. Louisville, Ky.: Westminster John Knox, 1999.

Räisänen, Heikki. *Paul and the Law*. Wissenschaftliche Untersuchungen zum Neuen Testament 29. Tübingen: Mohr Siebeck, 1983.

Regner, Friedmann. *"Paulus und Jesus" im 19. Jahrhundert: Beiträge zur Geschichte des Themas "Paulus und Jesus" in der neutestamentlichen Theologie.* Göttingen: Vandenhoeck & Ruprecht, 1977.

Renan,Ernest. *Life of Jesus.* Amherst, N.Y.: Prometheus Books, 1991.

Robinson, D. W. F. " 'Faith of Jesus Christ'—A New Testament Debate." *Reformed Theological Review* 29 (1970): 71–81.

Robinson, James M. *A New Quest of the Historical Jesus.* Studies in Biblical Theology 25. London: SCM Press, 1966.

Sanday, William, and Arthur C. Headlam. *A Critical and Exegetical Commentary on the Epistle to the Romans.* International Critical Commentary. Edinburgh: T&T Clark, 1895.

Sanders, E. P. "Patterns of Religion in Paul and Rabbinic Judaism: A Holistic Method of Comparison." *Harvard Theological Review* 66 (1973): 455–78.

————. *Paul and Palestinian Judaism.* London: SCM Press, 1977.

Sanders, J. A. "Dissenting Deities and Philippians 2:1-11." *Journal of Biblical Literature* 88 (1969): 279–90.

Sandmel, Samuel. *Anti-Semitism in the New Testament?* Philadelphia: Fortress, 1978.

Schillebeeckx, Edward. *Jesus.* New York: Seabury, 1979.

Schlatter, Adolf. *Gottes Gerechtigkeit.* 2nd ed. Stuttgart: Calwer Verlag, 1952.

————. "The Theology of the New Testament and Dogmatics." Pages 117–66 in *The Nature of New Testament Theology.* Naperville, Ill.: Alec R. Allenson, 1973.

Schleiermacher, Friedrich. *The Life of Jesus.* Edited by Jack C. Verheyden. Philadelphia: Fortress, 1975.

Schlier, Heinrich. *Der Römerbrief.* Herders theologischer Kommentar zum Neuen Testament. Freiburg: Herder, 1977.

Schmidt, H. W. *Der Brief des Paulus an die Römer.* Berlin: Evangelische Verlagsanstalt, 1966.

Schmithals, Walter. *Der Römerbrief als historisches Problem.* Gütersloh: Gerd Mohn, 1975.

————. *Gnosticism in Corinth.* Nashville: Abingdon, 1971.

Schnelle, Udo. *Antidocetic Christology in the Gospel of John.* Minneapolis: Fortress, 1992.

Schottroff, Luise. *Der Glaubende und die feindliche Welt: Beobachtungen zum gnostischen Dualismus und seiner Bedeutung für Paulus und das Johannesevangelium.* Wissenschaftliche Monographien zum Alten und Neuen Testament 37. Neukirchen: Neukirchener Verlag, 1970.

————. "Heil als innerweltliche Entweltlichung." *Novum Testamentum* 11 (1969): 294–317.

Schumacher, Rudolf. *Die beiden letzten Kapitel des Römerbriefes: Ein Beitrag zu ihrer Geschichte u. Erklärung.* Münster: Aschendorff, 1929.

Scroggs, Robin. "Paul as Rhetorician: Two Homilies in Romans 1–11." Pages 271–98 in *Jews, Greeks and Christians: Studies in Judaism in Late Antiquity.* Festschrift for W. D. Davies. Edited by R. Hamerton-Kelly and R. Scroggs. Leiden: Brill, 1976.

Smith, D. Moody. *Johannine Christianity.* Columbia: University of South Carolina Press, 1984.

Strauss, David F. *The Christ of Faith and the Jesus of History: A Critique of Schliermacher's* The Life of Jesus. Translated and edited by Leander E. Keck. Philadelphia: Fortress, 1977.

Stuhlmacher, Peter. *Jesus of Nazareth, Christ of Faith.* Translated by Siegfried Schatzmann. Peabody, Mass.: Hendrickson, 1993.

———. "Jesustradition im Römerbrief?" *Theologische Beiträge* 14 (1983): 240–50.

Talbert, Charles H. "A Non-Pauline Fragment at Romans 3:24-26?" *Journal of Biblical Literature* 85 (1966): 287–96.

———. "The Problem of Pre-Existence in Philippians 2:6-11." *Journal of Biblical Literature* 86 (1967): 141–53.

———. *Reading John: A Literary and Theological Commentary on the Fourth Gospel and the Johannine Epistles.* New York: Crossroad, 1992.

Taylor, Greer M. "The Function of *Pistis Christou* in Galatians." *Journal of Biblical Literature* 85 (1966): 58–76.

Taylor, Vincent. *The Names of Jesus.* London: Macmillan, 1953.

Thüsing, Wilhelm. *Per Christum in Deum.* Münster: Aschendorff, 1965.

Trumbower, Jeffrey A. *Born from Above: The Anthropology of the Gospel of John.* Hermeneutische Untersuchungen zur Theologie 29. Tübingen: Mohr Siebeck, 1992.

Vermès, Géza. *Jesus the Jew: A Historian's Reading of the Gospels.* Minneapolis: Augsburg Fortress, 1973.

———. *Jesus and the World of Judaism.* Minneapolis: Augsburg Fortress, 1983.

———. *The Religion of Jesus the Jew.* Minneapolis: Augsburg Fortress, 1993.

Vielhauer, Philipp. "Ein Weg zur neutestamentliche Christologie?" *Evangelische Theologie* 25 (1965): 24–72.

———. "Zur Frage der christologischen Hoheitstitel." *Theologische Literaturzeitung* 90 (1965): 569–88.

Walter, Nikolaus. "Paulus und die urchristliche Jesustradition." *New Testament Studies* 31 (1985): 498–522.

Weiss, Bernhard. *Der Brief an die Römer.* Göttingen: Vandenhoeck & Ruprecht, 1899.

Wilckens, Ulrich. *Der Brief an die Römer.* Evangelisch-katholischer Kommentar zum Neuen Testament 6. 2 vols. Zürich: Benziger Verlag, 1978.

Williams, Sam K. "Again *Pistis Christou.*" *Catholic Biblical Quarterly* 49 (1987): 431–47.

———. *Jesus' Death as Saving Event.* Harvard Dissertations in Religion 2. Missoula, Mont.: Scholars Press, 1975.

———. "The 'Righteousness of God' in Romans." *Journal of Biblical Literature* 99 (1980): 241–90.

Winters, Joseph. *On the Trial of Jesus.* Studia Judaica. Berlin: de Gruyter, 1961.

Witherington III, Ben. *The Christology of Jesus.* Minneapolis: Fortress, 1990.

Wrede, William. *The Messianic Secret.* London: James Clarke, 1971.

———. *Paulus.* Tübingen: J. C. B. Mohr, 1904. ET: *Paul.* Boston: American Unitarian Association, 1907.

———. "The Task and Methods of New Testament Theology." Pages 68–116 in *The Nature of New Testament Theology: The Contribution of William Wrede and Adolf Schlatter.* Translated and edited by Robert Morgan. Studies in Biblical Theology 25. Second Series. Naperville, Ill.: Alec R. Allenson, 1973.

Wright, N. T. *Jesus and the Victory of God.* Minneapolis: Fortress, 1996.

Zahn, Theodor. *Der Brief des Paulus an die Römer.* Leipzig: Deichert, 1910.

Zeller, Dieter. *Juden und Heiden in der Mission des Paulus: Studien zum Römerbrief.* Stuttgart: Katholisches Bibelwerk, 1973.

# Details of Previous Publications

"The Renewal of New Testament Christology" was originally published in *New Testament Studies*, Vol. 32, Issue 3 (July 1986), 362–77. Copyright © Cambridge University Press, 1986. Reprinted with permission.

"What, Then, Is New Testament Christology?" was originally published in *Who Do You Say That I Am?: Essays on Christology*. Festschrift for Jack Dean Kingsbury, ed. Mark Allan Powell and David R. Bauer. Louisville, Ky.: Westminster John Knox Press (1999).

"The Second Coming of the Liberal Jesus?" Reprinted by permission from the August 24–31, 1994 issue of the *Christian Century*.

"Jesus the Jew" is a previously unpublished lecture to the Sunday Jewish Seminar at the College of Charleston, S.C., in March 1998.

"Jesus and Judaism in the New Testament" was published in *Earthing Christologies: From Jesus' Parables to Jesus the Parable*, ed. James H. Charlesworth and Walter P. Weaver. New York: Hart Publishing, 1995. Reprinted with permission by Bloomsbury Publishing Plc.

"Anthropology and Soteriology in Johannine Christology" was originally published as "Derivation as Destiny: 'Of-ness' in Johannine Christology, Anthropology, and Soteriology," in *Exploring the Gospel of John*. Festschrift for D. Moody Smith. Edited by R. Alan Culpepper and C. Clifton Black. Louisville, Ky.: Westminster John Knox (1996).

"Christology, Soteriology, and the Praise of God in Romans" was originally published in *The Conversation Continues: Studies in Paul and John.* Festschrift for J. Louis Martyn, ed. Robert T. Fortna and Beverly Roberts Gaventa. Abingdon, 1990. Used by permission.

" 'Jesus' in Romans" was originally published in *Journal of Biblical Literature* vol. 108, issue 3 (Fall 1989), 443–60.

"The New Testament and Nicea" is a previously unpublished paper prepared for the American Theological Society in 1986.

# Scripture Index